AF885319

I WROTE THIS BOOK FOR THE MERE FACT THAT I AM TIRED OF SEEING GOOD PEOPLE GET "TAKEN".

I DEDICATE THIS BOOK TO MY BROTHER TOM AND FRANK D. MORROW PHD.

I GIVE THANKS TO MY PARENTS, FAMILY & LOVING WIFE FOR BELIEVING IN ME.

I ALSO GIVE SPECIAL THANKS TO MY MOTHER-IN LAW FOR ALL THE COMPLAINING, TO PUSH ME ENOUGH, SO I COULD PROVE HER WRONG!!

ISBN 978-0-615-25965-9

52995

9 780615 259659

THE AUTOMOTIVE INDUSTRY IS ONE OF THE MOST CUT THROAT CONSUMER BUSINESSES THAT YOU CAN EVER ENCOUNTER, AND YOU MAY NEVER KNOW HOW BADLY THAT YOU HAVE BEEN TAKEN UNTIL IT'S ALL OVER.

IT IS MY MISSION TO HELP YOU SEE THROUGH ALL OF THE CLOAK AND DAGGER OF AUTOMOTIVE WORLD IN THE HOPES THAT YOU WILL HAVE A GOOD UNDERSTANDING OF WHAT IS REALLY GOING ON WITH THE AUTOMOTIVE INDUSTRY, YOUR CAR AND YOUR POCKETBOOK, IN THE HOPES THAT

YOU WILL NEVER BE TAKEN AGAIN!

SECTION 1

QUICK REVIEW

SECTION # 1 OVERVIEWS AUTOMOTIVE HISTORY, BASIC SYSTEMS MATERIALS, & COMMON KNOWLEDGE IN THE AUTOMOTIVE INDUSTRY.

INTRODUCTION

WHETHER IT IS MAINTENANCE OR REPAIR, WHEN YOU GO TO HAVE WORK DONE AT AN AUTOMOTIVE MAINTENANCE/REPAIR FACILITY, IT'S NOT LIKE ANY OTHER PURCHASE. WHEN YOU GO TO HAVE AUTOMOTIVE REPAIRS DONE, IT'S NOT LIKE BUYING A COUCH OR TV; YOU WANT TO BUY THAT COUCH. YOU WANT TO BUY THAT TV. BUT WHEN IT COMES TO AUTOMOTIVE REPAIR OR MAINTENANCE, IT'S LIKE PULLING TEETH. NO ONE WANTS TO SPEND THEIR GOOD MONEY ON THEIR CAR! YOU PUT YOUR KIDS IN IT AND DRIVE AROUND, YOU USE IT TO HAUL STUFF, TO MOVE, TO LOOK COOL IN, YOU DRIVE IT BACK AND FORTH TO WORK, YOU DEPEND ON IT TO GET YOU AROUND SAFELY AND START EVERY DAY!!

INSTEAD OF TAKING CARE OF THEIR CAR, MOST PEOPLE NEGLECT THEIR VEHICLE OR JUST DON'T WANT TO PUT ANY MONEY INTO IT.

I DON'T BLAME THESE PEOPLE! WHY? MOST PEOPLE FEEL LIKE THEY WILL GET ***RIPPED OFF*** *WHEN GOING INTO AN AUTOMOTIVE FACILITY, YOU CAN PUT THOUSANDS OF DOLLARS INTO YOUR VEHICLE AND YOU WILL STILL HAVE THE SAME CAR!! THIS CAN BE AN OVERWHELMING FEELING AT TIMES.*

SO OVER THE COURSE OF A FEW YEARS, EXACTLY HOW MUCH COULD YOU SPEND ON YOUR VEHICLE? THIS QUESTION CAN BE A HARD ONE TO ANSWER, BUT YOU CAN GET SOMEWHAT OF AN AVERAGE IF YOU DO THE MATH. IF YOU BUY A $20,000 CAR AND PLAN TO KEEP IT FOR OVER FIVE YEARS, YOU DIDN'T SPEND $20,000 ON THAT CAR, YOU SPENT CLOSE TO $50,000 AND DON'T FORGET ABOUT THE GAS!

LOOK AT THE ESTIMATED FIGURES ON THE FOLLOWING PAGES, THEY WILL SURPRISE YOU!

AVERAGE CONSUMER AUTOMOTIVE STATS

BASED ON A NEW AVERAGE AMERICAN MID-SIZED CAR

	CAR	$20,000
	50,000 MILE WARRANTY	$1,500
	LOAN INTEREST, TITLE, TAXES & TAGS OVER THE NEXT FIVE YEARS	$3,000

---

1 YEAR	OIL CHANGES & TIRE ROTATIONS $160	3160
20,000 MI	FULL COVERAGE INSURANCE $3,000	
2 YEAR	COOLANT FLUSH $70	
40,000MI	OIL CHANGES & TIRE ROTATIONS $160	
	MAY NEED BRAKES $250	3774
	FULL INSURANCE COVERAGE $3,000	
	TRANSMISSION FLUSH $109	
	FUEL FILTER DUE $100	
	AIR FILTER $15	
	DIFFERENTIAL FLUSH $70	
3 YEAR	OIL CHANGES & TIRE ROTATIONS $160	
60,000 MI	COOLANT FLUSH $70	
	BRAKES $450	
	TIRES $400	
	TRANSMISSION FLUSH $109	
	FUEL FILTER $100	
	FULL INSURANCE COVERAGE $3,000	
	ALIGNMENT $80	4154
	PLUGS $120 OR MORE	
	POWER STEERING FLUSH $70	
	AIR FILTER $15	

	IN CABIN AIR FILTER $30	
4 YEAR	OIL CHANGES & TIRE ROTATIONS $160	
80,000 MI	FULL INSURANCE COVERAGE $3,000	
	TIMING BELT $400	
	SENSORS $400	4850
	DIFFERENTIAL FLUSH $70	
	SHOCKS OR STRUTS $750	
	ALIGNMENT $70	
5 YEAR	OIL CHANGES & TIRE ROTATIONS $160	
100,000 MI	+MISC. REPAIRS $700	
	BRAKES $600	$4460
	FULL INSURANCE COVERAGE $3,000	
		$46,098.00

ABOUT $10,000 OR MORE IN MAINTENANCE AND OR REPAIR

*****NOT ALL STATEMENTS APPLY TO EVERY VEHICLE OR TO EVERY SITUATION*****

NOW YOU CAN SEE HOW QUICKLY THINGS ADD UP. THIS IS WHY STATISTICS SAY THE AUTOMOTIVE VEHICLE IS YOUR SECOND LARGEST PURCHASE NEXT TO YOUR HOUSE!!

CHAPTER 1

AUTOMOTIVE HISTORY

AUTOMOTIVE HISTORY

THE FIRST AUTOMOBILE

THE FIRST VEHICLE TO MOVE ON ITS OWN POWER WAS DESIGNED & BUILT BY TWO GUYS IN PARIS BY THE NAMES OF NICHOLAS J. CANNOT, AND M. BREZIN IN 1769. (A SCALE MODEL REPLICA OF THIS VEHICLE IS ON DISPLAY AT THE SMITHSONIAN MUSEUM IN WASHINGTON, D. C.) A SECOND UNIT WAS BUILT IN 1770 WHICH WEIGHED 8000 POUNDS!! IT HAD A TOP SPEED THAT WAS ABOUT 2 MILES PER HOUR; IT WAS A GOOD IDEA NOT TO GO ANY FASTER ON THE STONE STREETS OF PARIS. DURING THE VEHICLES FIRST RUN AROUND PARIS IT HIT AND KNOCKED DOWN A STONE WALL. IT ALSO HAD A TENDENCY TO TIP OVER FRONTWARDS UNLESS IT HAD SOME TYPE OF WEIGHT IN THE REAR OF THE VEHICLE TO KEEP IT STEADY. THE PURPOSE OF THE VEHICLE WAS TO DELIVER CANONS AROUND AREAS OF PARIS.

THE FIRST CAR MANUFACTURER

THE FIRST CAR MANUFACTURERS IN THE WORLD WERE THE FRENCH: PANHARD & LEVASSOR (1889) AND PEUGEOT (1891). BY CAR MANUFACTURER I MEAN BUILDERS OF THE ENTIRE VEHICLE!! (DAIMLER AND BENZ STARTED AS ENGINE INVENTORS BEFORE BECOMING FULL CAR MANUFACTURERS. THEY FIRST STARTED TO MAKE THEIR MONEY BY SELLING THEIR PATENTS AND ENGINES TO MANUFACTURERS.)

RENE PANHARD AND EMILE LEVASSOR WERE SELLING WOODWORKING MACHINERY BEFORE THEY WERE CAR MANUFACTURERS. THEIR FIRST CAR ROLLED OUT FULLY ASSEMBLED IN 1890 (BUT IT USED A DAIMLER ENGINE). EDOUARD SARAZIN HELD THE LICENSE RIGHTS TO THE DAIMLER PATENT. (WHEN YOU BUY RIGHTS TO A PATENT THIS MEANS THAT YOU HAVE THE RIGHT TO MANUFACTURE AND USE SOMEONE'S INVENTION FOR PROFIT. SARAZIN HAD THE RIGHT TO BUILD AND SELL DAIMLER ENGINES.) THESE TWO ALSO MADE MANY IMPROVEMENTS TO MANY ASPECTS OF THE WAY CARS WERE MANUFACTURED.

THE FIRST AUTOMOBILE MANUFACTURED IN THE U.S.A.

THE FIRST AUTOMOBILE TO BE MASS PRODUCED IN THE UNITED STATES WAS THE 1901, CURVED DASH OLDSMOBILE, BUILT BY THE AMERICAN CAR MANUFACTURER RANSOME ELI OLDS (1864-1950). OLDS INVENTED THE BASIC CONCEPT OF THE ASSEMBLY LINE AND STARTED THE DETROIT AREA AUTOMOBILE INDUSTRY. HE FIRST BEGAN MAKING STEAM AND GASOLINE ENGINES WITH HIS FATHER, PLINY FISK OLDS, IN LANSING, MICHIGAN IN 1885. OLDS DESIGNED HIS FIRST STEAM-POWERED CAR IN 1887. IN 1899, WITH A GROWING EXPERIENCE OF GASOLINE ENGINES, OLDS MOVED TO DETROIT TO START THE OLDS MOTOR WORKS, AND PRODUCE LOW-PRICED CARS. HE PRODUCED 425 "CURVED DASH OLDS" IN 1901, AND WAS AMERICA'S LEADING AUTO MANUFACTURER FROM 1901 TO 1904.

WHO MADE IT FAMOUS

HENRY FORD (1863-1947) INVENTED AN IMPROVED ASSEMBLY LINE AND INSTALLED THE FIRST CONVEYOR BELT-BASED ASSEMBLY LINE IN HIS CAR FACTORY IN FORD'S HIGHLAND PARK, MICHIGAN PLANT AROUND 1913-14. THE ASSEMBLY LINE REDUCED PRODUCTION COSTS FOR CARS BY REDUCING ASSEMBLY TIME. FORD'S FAMOUS MODEL T WAS ASSEMBLED IN NINETY-THREE MINUTES. (IT TOOK FORD MODELS A-S BEFORE COMING UP WITH A SUCCESSFUL ASSEMBLY LINE & THE MODEL "T"). FORD MADE HIS FIRST CAR, CALLED THE "QUADRICYCLE," IN JUNE, 1896. HOWEVER, SUCCESS CAME AFTER HE FORMED THE FORD MOTOR COMPANY IN 1903. THIS WAS THE THIRD CAR MANUFACTURING COMPANY FORMED TO PRODUCE THE CARS HE DESIGNED. HE INTRODUCED THE MODEL T IN 1908 AND IT WAS A SUCCESS. AFTER INSTALLING THE MOVING ASSEMBLY LINES IN HIS FACTORY IN 1913, FORD BECAME THE WORLD'S BIGGEST CAR MANUFACTURER. BY 1927, 15 MILLION MODEL T'S HAD BEEN MANUFACTURED.

ANOTHER VICTORY WON BY HENRY FORD WAS A PATENT BATTLE WITH GEORGE B. SELDEN. SELDEN, WHO HAD NEVER BUILT AN AUTOMOBILE, HELD A PATENT ON A "ROAD ENGINE", ON THAT BASIS SELDEN WAS PAID ROYALTIES BY ALL AMERICAN CAR MANUFACTURERS. FORD OVERTURNED SELDEN'S PATENT AND OPENED THE AMERICAN CAR MARKET FOR THE BUILDING OF INEXPENSIVE CARS.

LET'S MOVE TO THE 60'S

IN THE 60'S THE AUTOMOTIVE INDUSTRY REALLY STARTED TO BOOM, WHILE BRINGING OUT THE SPEED DEMON IN EVERYONE! THIS IS THE TIME WHEN THE CAR MANUFACTURER'S STARTED TO PRODUCE HIGH PERFORMANCE MUSCLE CARS AT AN ECONOMICAL COST. CAR RACING STARTED TO BECOME VERY POPULAR WITH THE GENERAL PUBLIC & CAR MANUFACTURES REALIZED THAT THE MORE RACES THEY WON, THE MORE CARS THEY SOLD. THE FIRST MUSCLE CAR WAS MADE BY A COMPANY THAT WAS BOUGHT OUT AND BECAME A SPAWN OF GENERAL MOTORS' RACING DIVISION, THE NAME WAS PONTIAC. THE PONTIAC G.T.O!! THIS WAS THE FIRST AMERICAN COMPACT CAR WITH A "BIG ENGINE" INSTALLED INTO A SMALL BODY, FROM THE FACTORY. THE 60'S ALSO BROUGHT OUT SOME OF AMERICAS WELL KNOWN MUSCLE CAR'S. THE MUSTANG, CAMARO, TRANS-AM, FIREBIRD, CHARGER, CHALLENGER, SUPERBEE, G.T.O. AND THE COBRA ARE JUST SOME OF THE MOST POPULAR.

THE 70'S & 80'S

DURING THE '70S AND EARLY 1980'S MANUFACTURERS STARTED USING ELECTRONIC COMPUTERS AS A MEANS TO CONTROL ENGINE FUNCTIONS, EFFICIENCY AND DIAGNOSE ENGINE PROBLEMS. THIS WAS PRIMARILY TO MEET EPA EMISSION STANDARDS DUE TO GAS EMISSIONS THAT AFFECTED THE EARTH'S OZONE. THE COMPUTER SYSTEMS WERE CALLED O.B.D. OR ON-BOARD DIAGNOSTICS. THROUGH THE YEARS, ON-BOARD DIAGNOSTIC SYSTEMS HAVE BECOME MORE COMPLEX AND SOPHISTICATED.

OBD WHAT?? IN THE 90'S

OBD-II, A NEW STANDARD INTRODUCED IN THE MID-'90S, PROVIDES ALMOST COMPLETE ENGINE CONTROL. IT ALSO MONITORS PARTS OF THE CHASSIS, BODY AND ACCESSORY DEVICES, AS WELL AS THE DIAGNOSTIC CONTROL NETWORK OF THE CAR. THE EPA ADAPTED MOST OF THEIR STANDARDS FROM THE SAE ON-BOARD DIAGNOSTIC PROGRAMS AND RECOMMENDATIONS. OBD-II IS AN EXPANDED SET OF STANDARDS AND PRACTICES DEVELOPED BY SAE AND ADOPTED BY THE EPA AND CARB (CALIFORNIA AIR RESOURCES BOARD) FOR IMPLEMENTATION BY JANUARY 1, 1996. BY LAW ALL CARS BUILT SINCE JANUARY 1, 1996 HAVE OBD-II SYSTEMS. MANUFACTURERS STARTED INCORPORATING OBD-II IN VARIOUS MODELS AS EARLY AS 1994. OBD –II GIVES AFTERMARKET FACILITIES A STANDARD PLUG PORT IN EVERY CAR TO BE ABLE TO INTERFACE WITH THE CAR'S COMPUTER.

2010 & BEYOND

I HAVE A FEELING 2010 & BEYOND WILL HOLD EXCITING NEW IDEAS AND TECHNOLOGIES FOR ALL OF US. WE CAN SEE THAT CAR MANUFACTURES HAVE TRIED TO MEET THE CONSUMER NEED OF A MORE ENVIRONMENTALLY AWARE SOCIETY. WE HAVE ALREADY SEEN THE INTRODUCTION OF HYBRID ENGINES, AND "FLEX-FUEL" VEHICLES. NEW FUELS ARE COMING OUR WAY, AND NEWER, STRONGER, SMALLER, FASTER COMPUTERS WILL BE SURE TO COME AS WELL. WE WILL ALSO BE SURE TO SEE NEW MAN-MADE MATERIALS THAT WILL CHANGE OUR LIVES IN SOME TYPE OF WAY. WHEN NEW IDEAS & TECHNOLOGIES BECOME AVAILABLE TO THE GENERAL PUBLIC, HAVE AN OPEN MIND. GENERALLY SPEAKING, TECHNOLOGY MAKES OUR LIVES EASY. NEW IDEAS & TECHNOLOGIES ARE OUR FRIENDS!!! EMBRACE NEW IDEAS; APPLAUD INNOVATION AND WHO KNOWS WHERE MANKIND MAY GO. IT'S EVEN POSSIBLE THAT AUTOMOTIVE COULD BECOME AIRMOTIVE!

CHAPTER 2

BREAKING DOWN THE SYSTEMS

BREAKING DOWN THE SYSTEMS

DUE TO THE COMPLEX NATURE OF TODAY'S MODERN MOTOR VEHICLES, WE WILL NOT GET INTO DEPTH ON HOW EVERYTHING WORKS. I WILL, HOWEVER, TRY TO GIVE YOU A BASIC UNDERSTANDING OF HOW MAJOR SYSTEM AND COMPONENTS WORK.

SEE, IF YOU GET THE WRONG INFORMATION FROM SOMEONE IT COULD COST YOU THOUSANDS OF DOLLARS! SO DON'T DEPEND ON ONE SOURCE FOR INFORMATION. IF YOU END UP WITH THE WRONG INFORMATION FROM ONE SOURCE **IT WILL BE JOB SECURITY FOR SOMEONE!!!** FOR MORE INFORMATION GO TO HTTP://WWW.HOWSTUFFWORKS.COM OR OTHER SITES OF THE SAME NATURE.

CARS AND THEIR SYSTEMS

MOST PEOPLE DO NOT:

1. REALIZE THAT THEIR VEHICLE IS MADE UP OF MANY SYSTEMS.
2. UNDERSTAND THAT THESE SYSTEMS WORK TOGETHER
3. UNDERSTAND THAT ONE SYSTEM CAN HAVE A MAJOR EFFECT ON THE OTHER SYSTEMS.
4. UNDERSTAND THAT MOST OF THE PARTS, ON THEIR CAR, WILL WEAR OUT.
5. UNDERSTAND THE DIFFERENCE BETWEEN MAINTENANCE & REPAIR.

NOW THAT WE KNOW THAT THERE ARE MAJOR SYSTEMS, THEY ALL WORK TOGETHER, ONE WILL AFFECT THE OTHER, AND THAT MOST PARTS WEAR OUT, WE CAN MOVE ON.

THE ONLY WAY TO GET A GOOD UNDERSTANDING OF WHY "STUFF" BREAKS ON YOUR VEHICLE, WE WILL NEED TO GET A SMALL GRASP OF HOW IT ALL WORKS.

QUICK TIP BEFORE WE START

NOTE: WHEN A CAR/TRUCK IS IN THE AIR, WITH THE WHEELS OFF THE GROUND, (WHILE THE CAR IS ON AND IN GEAR) IF THE ONLY TIRES IN THE FRONT SPIN IT IS CONSIDERED A "FRONT WHEEL DRIVE". IF ONLY THE REAR WHEELS SPIN, IT IS A "REAR WHEEL DRIVE", AND IF ALL FOUR ARE SPINNING (OR HAS THE CAPABILITY OF), IT IS A "FOUR WHEEL DRIVE". THESE ARE THE WHEELS THAT PROPEL THE CAR FORWARD & BACKWARDS.

PARTS AND "STUFF"

LET'S START AT WHAT YOUR VEHICLE IS MADE WITH: PLASTIC, ALUMINUM, NYLON, IRON, STEEL, RUBBER, CLOTH, GLASS, SOMETIMES WOOD, AND A HOST OF OTHER MATERIALS. THE OLDEST CARS WERE MADE WITH A LOT OF STEEL AND CAST IRON. IT GAVE THE CAR A HEAVY RIGID-FEEL. AS TIMES WENT ON, CARS GOT MORE AND MORE ADVANCED, THE STEEL GOT THINNER AND STRONGER. CAST IRON WAS REPLACED WITH STRONG, LIGHTER ALUMINUM. MODERN DAY PLASTICS HAVE NOT ONLY REPLACED A LOT OF INTERIOR PARTS BUT FILLS THE ENGINE COMPARTMENT WITH AN ARRAY OF COMPONENTS.

YOUR VEHICLE IS PROTECTED, LUBRICATED, AND OPERATES WITH: OILS, COOLANT, WAXES, GREASE, AND SYNTHETICS. JUST LIKE EVERYTHING ELSE ON YOUR MODERN DAY VEHICLE, ALL OF THESE PROTECTANTS HAVE ADVANCED OVER THE YEARS. THE OILS HAVE BECOME LIGHTER AND MORE DURABLE AT A HIGHER HEAT RANGE. THE COOLANT HAS BECOME MORE ENVIRONMENTALLY FRIENDLY, ALMOST NO ACIDITY OR PH LEVELS AND THE WAXES COAT THE PAINT TO HOLD THAT GREAT SHINE AND REACT WITH THE ENVIRONMENT BETTER THAN EVER BEFORE.

SYNTHETICS! SYNTHETICS! YOU COULD ALMOST WRITE A BOOK ON THE OUTSTANDING PROPERTIES OF SYNTHETICS! SYNTHETIC OILS DELIVER EXTRAORDINARY LUBRICATION IN DIESEL, GASOLINE ENGINES AND TRANSMISSION FOUND IN COMMERCIAL, FLEET, PERSONAL VEHICLES, AND ALMOST ALL OTHER ASPECTS OF THE SYSTEMS IN YOUR VEHICLE. IT WITHSTANDS THE STRESS OF HIGHER HEAT, HIGHER ACID LEVELS, EXCESSIVE SOOT, AND CARBON FOUND IN EGR EQUIPPED ENGINES. SYNTHETIC OILS CONSISTENTLY OUTPERFORM CONVENTIONAL OILS AND ARE EXCELLENT FOR LONG-LASTING PERFORMANCE AND PROTECTION.

YOUR CAR IS POWER CONTROLLED AND MONITORED BY: ELECTRIC, HYDROCARBON (GAS), NATURAL GAS, AND DIESEL FUEL, WHICH ARE THE MOST COMMON. -WHAT CAN I SAY; THIS IS THE AREA THAT I THINK HAS MADE THE MOST ADVANCEMENT. - THE EARLIER VEHICLE, HAD ALMOST ALL MECHANICAL/ELECTRICAL CONNECTIONS, AND NOW EVERYTHING IS ELECTRICAL! BECAUSE OF NEWER TECHNOLOGIES SCIENTISTS HAVE BEEN ABLE TO DO CONTROLLED STUDIES OF THE REACTION OF FUEL TO GIVE US BETTER FUEL ECONOMY. DUE TO THE VAST ADVANCEMENT AND THE CHEAP COST OF COMPUTERS, THE CAR MANUFACTURERS HAVE BEEN ABLE TO INTEGRATE THEM INTO OUR CARS TO GIVE US A SAFE, CONSISTENT, RELIABLE, SMART, ECONOMICAL VEHICLE.

ALL OF THESE MATERIALS ARE PREDESIGNED, COMPUTER TESTED, MELTED, MOLTED, STRETCHED, BUILT INTO PARTS, COMPONENTS, MATCHED AND TESTED BEFORE THEY ARE MADE INTO SYSTEMS. THESE SYSTEMS ARE WHAT MAKE UP YOUR MODERN DAY VEHICLE.

SECTION 2

HOW IT WORKS

SECTION # 2 OVERVIEWS BASIC SYSTEMS, EASY EXPLANATIONS OF OPERATIONS & INSIDE TIPS OF WHY COMPONENTS BREAK. *(IF YOU FEEL THAT YOU HAVE ENOUGH BASIC KNOWLEDGE ABOUT YOUR MODERN DAY MOTOR VEHICLE OR YOU JUST DON'T CARE, FEEL MORE THAN WELCOMED TO MOVE ON TO SECTION #3 & USE THIS PART OF THE BOOK AS A REFERENCE. I KNOW THIS IS THE BORING PART!)*

CHAPTER 3

EXPLANATION OF AN ENGINE

EXPLANATION OF AN ENGINE

Pistons? valves! internal combustion? What are they talking about? It is like that vocabulary is Greek. What is the real deal?

The engine is the heart of the automobile. It converts fuel into the energy that powers the automobile. To operate, it requires clean air for the fuel, water for cooling, electricity (which it generates) for igniting the fuel, and oil for lubrication. A battery and electric starter get it going.

The internal combustion engine burns fuel within the cylinders and converts the expanding force of the combustion or "explosion" into rotary force used to propel the vehicle. There are several types of internal combustion engines: two and four cycle reciprocating piston engines, gas turbines, free piston, and rotary combustion engines. The four-cylinder reciprocating engine has been refined to such a degree that it has almost complete dominance in the automotive industry

Most types of "Internal Combustion Engines" have at least one "cylinder". Per each cylinder is how the engine is known. Some good examples would be 4, 6, and 8 cylinder engines are known as a "In-Line Four Cylinder", "In-line six","V6", or a "V8". Each "cylinder" of the typical automobile engine has a "piston" and "valves" that moves back and forth within the cylinder (this is called "reciprocating"). Each piston is connected to a rotary "crankshaft" by means of a link known as a "connecting rod". These components help to transmit power to the wheels.

BASIC UNDERSTANDING

We will start with the basic understanding of the bottom the engine. The crankshaft or the crank!

In the "old days" when people needed water from a water well, they wouldn't throw in a bucket on a rope, down a well and try to pull up water. That would be too hard! If they would tie the rope to a stick and try to turn the stick to pull the bucket up, it would still be too hard. People would need something called <u>leverage</u>. If you offset a leverage point from that stick and attach the rope to the stick, it makes it easy to pull the bucket up when spinning the stick at that leverage point. This would be called a "crank" or crankshaft.

EXAMPLE OF A MODERN DAY AUTOMOTIVE CRANKSHAFT

EXAMPLE OF A "WATER WELL CRANK"

PISTONS

NEXT WOULD BE A PISTONS, CYLINDERS AND COMBUSTION CHAMBER. (NOW DON'T MAKE THIS HARDER THAN WHAT IT IS, THIS IS EASY!) IMAGINE A FIRE CRACKER GOING OFF:

NOW IMAGINE IF YOU PUT A CAN OVER THAT FIRE CRACKER. WHAT HAPPENS TO THE CAN? THE CAN DOESN'T BLOW UP!! WHEN THE FIRE CRACKER EXPLODES, THE CAN GOES IN THE AIR!

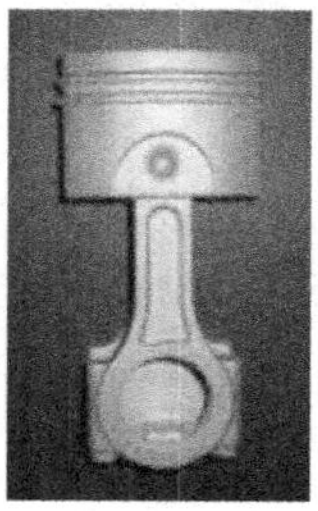

EXAMPLE OF A MODERN DAY PISTONS

NOW IMAGINE IF YOU PUT A TUBE AROUND THE CAN AND LIGHT THE FIRE CRACKER!! WHAT HAPPENS?? THIS HAPPENS!!!!

(O.K. SO I AM EXAGGERATING A LITTLE! BUT, YOU GET THE IDEA) THE CAN GOES STRAIGHT UP THROUGH THE TUBE AND IS GOING SUPER FAST BECAUSE ALL THAT ENERGY PUSHES THE CAN UPWARD. THE "CAN" REPRESENTS A PISTON, THE "TUBE" REPRESENTS A CYLINDER, AND THE "FIRECRACKER" REPRESENTS GAS EXPLODING. NOW, TIE IT ALL TOGETHER:

SIDE VIEW

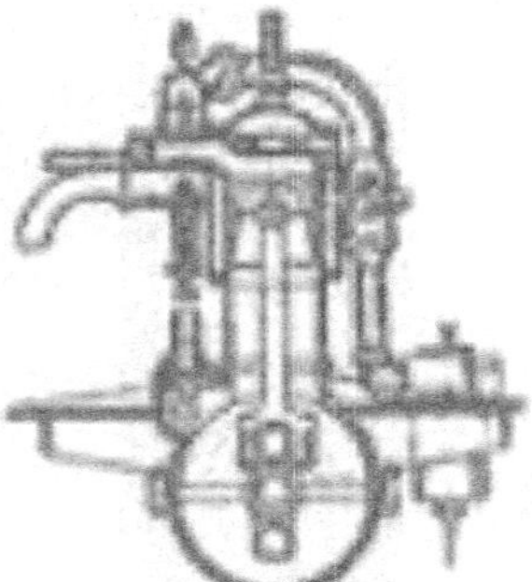

FRONT VIEW

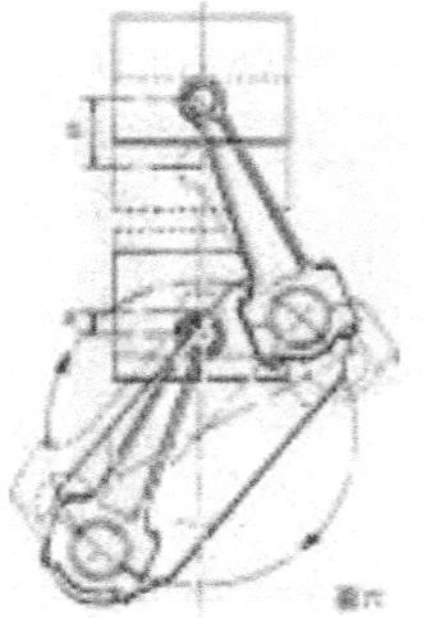

MOVING FRONT VIEW

As the explosion goes off, it pushes the "can" or piston down and causes the crankshaft to turn. If you do this many, many times in a row, the shaft will spin. These pictures are a good example of a basic internal engine layout.

**NOTE: An "in-line four or six" cylinder would have four (4) or six (6) cylinders in a row. A V6 would have the cylinders in a "V" pattern. A V8 would be the same way as a V6, but with two (2) more cylinders.*

IN-LINE 4 CYLINDER

INTERNAL V8

FRONT VIEW V8

INTAKE, CAMS, VALVES AND EXHAUST

AN ENGINE'S INTAKE, VALVES AND EXHAUST MAKE UP THE "UPPER HALF" OF YOUR ENGINE. THESE COMPONENTS ALLOW AIR & FUEL TO PASS & EXIT THE LOWER PART OF YOUR ENGINE, OR THE CYLINDERS. DON'T MAKE THE INTAKE, VALVES AND EXHAUST SCARES YOU. THERE IS NOT TOO MUCH TO THESE COMPONENTS. THEY ARE MAINLY MADE UP OF A PASSAGEWAY THAT ALLOWS AIR TO ENTER AND EXIT THE SYSTEM. MODERN DAY COMPUTERS MAKE THIS PROCESS COMPLEX TO LOWER EMISSION LEVELS TO HELP SAVE OUR ENVIRONMENT.

THE INTAKE

THE INTAKE MANIFOLD IS A SYSTEM OF PASSAGES, WHICH CONDUCT THE FUEL MIXTURE TO THE INTAKE VALVES OF THE ENGINE. MANIFOLD DESIGN HAS MUCH TO DO WITH THE EFFICIENT OPERATION OF AN ENGINE. FOR SMOOTH AND EVEN OPERATION, THE FUEL CHARGE TAKEN INTO EACH CYLINDER SHOULD BE OF THE SAME STRENGTH AND QUALITY.

THEREFORE, DISTRIBUTION OF THE FUEL SHOULD BE AS EVEN AS POSSIBLE. THIS DEPENDS GREATLY UPON THE DESIGN OF THE INTAKE MANIFOLD. DRY FUEL VAPOR IS AN IDEAL FORM OF FUEL CHARGE, BUT PRESENT-DAY FUEL CHARGE IS HEATED TOO HIGHLY AND THE POWER OF THE ENGINE IS REDUCED BECAUSE THE HEAT EXPANDS THE FUEL CHARGE. THEREFORE, IT IS BETTER TO HAVE SOME OF THE FUEL DEPOSITED ON THE WALLS OF THE CYLINDERS AND MANIFOLD. MANIFOLDS IN MODERN ENGINES ARE DESIGNED SO THAT THE AMOUNT OF FUEL CONDENSING ON THE INTAKE MANIFOLD WALLS IS REDUCED TO A MINIMUM.

MANY CAR MANUFACTURE ARE NOW MAKING THEIR INTAKE MANIFOLDS OUT OF PLASTICS. NOT ONLY DOES THIS MAKE FOR A LOWER VEHICLE WEIGHT, IT ALSO GIVES MORE FLEXIBILITY WITH DESIGN, AND IN MOST CASES ADDS MORE EFFICIENCY TO ENGINE SYSTEMS OPERATION.

THE INTAKE VALVES

THE INTAKE VALVES ARE WHAT THEY SOUND LIKE! THIS IS WHERE GAS & AIR **INTAKE** INTO THE ENGINES CYLINDER. MAINLY, A FUEL AND AIR MIXTURE -WE DON'T WANT ANYTHING ELSE COMING IN-. VALVES CAN COME IN MANY SHAPES AND SIZES, BUT THE MAIN JOB OF A VALVE IS TO OPEN AND CLOSE, WHILE ALLOWING ELEMENTS (GAS AND AIR) TO PASS THROUGH ITS PORTS.

CAM SHAFT

A CAM SHAFT LOOKS LIKE A LONG METAL ROD WITH EGG SHAPED LOBES CUT INTO IT. THE CAM SHAFT WILL SPIN IN PROPORTION WITH THE BOTTOM HALF OF THE ENGINE'S CRANKSHAFT. AS THE CAM SHAFT SPINS THE "EGG SHAPED" LOBES WILL SPIN CAUSING THE INTAKE & EXHAUST VALVES TO OPEN & CLOSE.

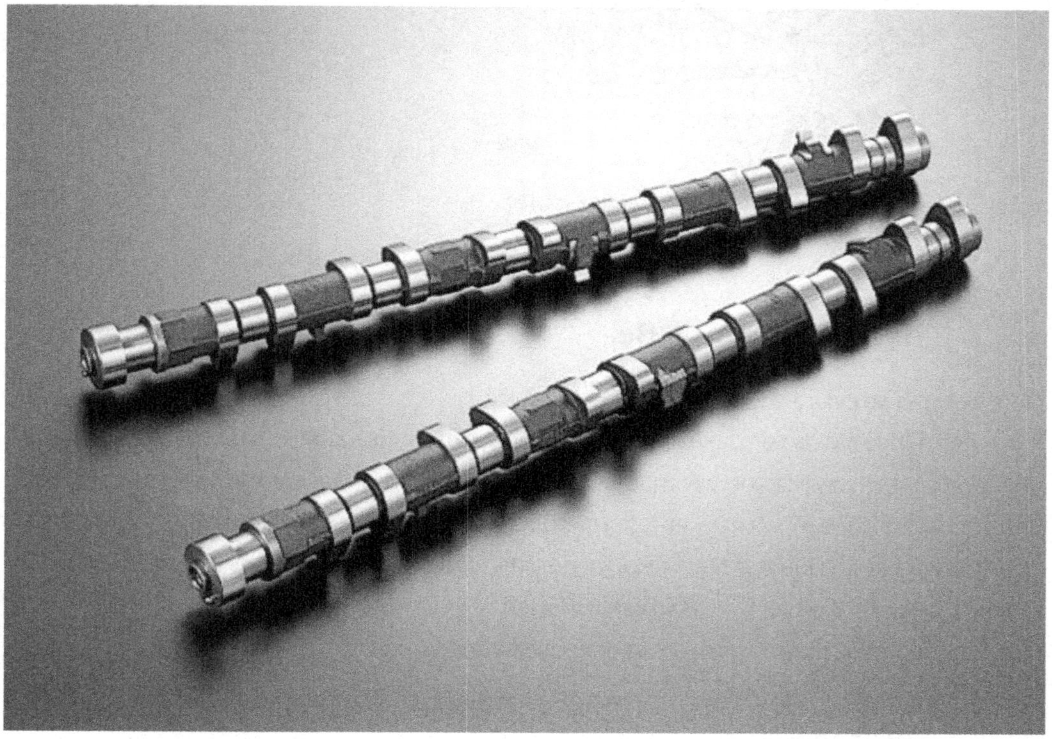

EXAMPLE OF TWO CAMS

TIMING BELT/ CHAIN

THE TIMING BELT/ CHAIN "TIES" THE UPPER HALF OF THE ENGINE (CAM SHAFT) TO THE LOWER HALF (CRANK SHAFT) AND KEEPS BOTH COMPONENTS IN ROTATIONAL PROPORTIONS TO ONE ANOTHER. THUS THE TERM "KEPT IN TIME" OR "TIMING" BELT/ CHAIN.

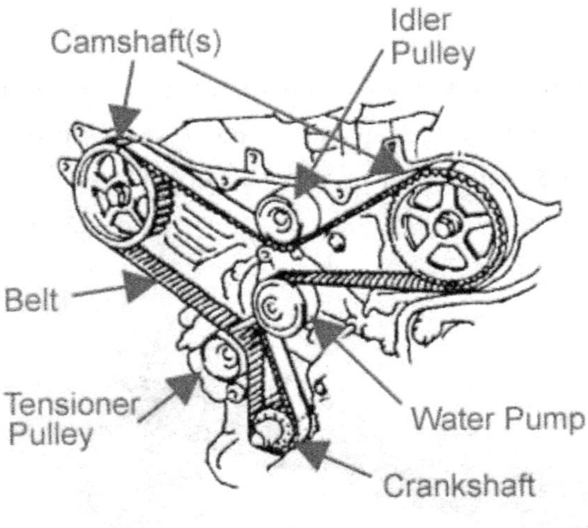

Typical V6 Timing Belt

THE EXHAUST VALVES & SYSTEM

LAST, BUT NOT LEAST, IS YOUR EXHAUST. THIS IS WHERE "STUFF" OR EXHAUST GAS (CO2, H2, ETC) EXITS THE SYSTEM. THIS COMPILES OF A SYSTEM OF VALVES "TUBES", CATALYTIC CONVERTERS, MUFFLERS AND TAIL PIPES. THE EXHAUST VALVES ARE JUST LIKE THE INTAKE VALVES. THESE VALVES ALLOW EXHAUST TO EXIT THE ENGINES CYLINDERS. THE "TUBES" DIRECT THE EXHAUST GAS FLOW AWAY FROM THE ENGINE, CABIN OF THE CAR, THE GAS TANK, AND CAR ITSELF. THE CATALYTIC CONVERTER IGNITES THE REST OF THE UNUSED FUEL, AND THE MUFFLERS ARE TO QUIET THE SYSTEM.

BLOCK AND HEADS

THE CYLINDER BLOCK AND ENGINE HEADS ARE THE "OUTER HOUSINGS" THAT HOLDS THE UPPER AND LOWER COMPONENTS INTO PLACE. THE BLOCK IS THE LOWER HOUSING AND THE HEADS ARE THE UPPER.

WORKING TOGETHER

SO NOW WE KNOW MOST OF THE ENGINE COMPONENTS. HOW DO THEY WORK TOGETHER? IT IS LIKE THIS. AS YOUR PISTONS MOVES DOWN, YOUR INTAKE VALVE WILL OPEN ALLOWING AIR AND GAS TO ENTER (15 PARTS AIR AND 1 PART FUEL IS THE IDEAL MIXTURE!) INTO THE CYLINDER. AS THE PISTON GOES UP, ALL THE VALVES CLOSE CAUSING PRESSURE IN THE CYLINDER. (WHEN AN EXPLOSION IS UNDER PRESSURE, THE EXPLOSION IS MUCH, MUCH GREATER, DUE TO THE "BURNING" OF MOST OF THE FUEL.) YOUR SPARK PLUG WILL IGNITE THE MIXTURE, CAUSE AN EXPLOSION AND CAUSE THE CYLINDER TO GO DOWN. AS THE CAN/PISTON COMES BACK UP IN THE CYLINDER, THE EXHAUST VALVE OPENS AND THE BURN WILL EXIT THE SYSTEM.

**NOTE: THE "BURN" WILL LEAVE CARBON IN THE INTAKE VALVE AND CYLINDER, CAUSING CARBON ISSUES.*

THE RECOMMENDATION, DO A FUEL SYSTEM CLEANING EVERY 20 TO 30,000 MILES.

OILS

OILS/FLUIDS

ALL OF THIS CRAZY STUFF THAT HAPPENS INSIDE THE ENGINE IS TO MAKE THE CRANK SHAFT SPIN AS FAST AS POSSIBLE, THUS MAKING YOUR WHEELS SPIN AND PROPELLING THE CAR FORWARD. SINCE THE ENGINE SPINS 2,000 TO 10,000 TIME A MINUTE, IT IS EASY TO SEE THAT LUBRICATION IS VERY IMPORTANT TO THE ENGINE. SOME CLEARANCE IN YOUR ENGINE ARE ONLY AS THICK AS THIS LINE (----------), MORE OR LESS. THE MOST COMMON TYPE OF OIL USED FOR MODERN DAY CARS WOULD BE A **5W30OIL**; SOME ENGINES TAKE OTHER WEIGHTS OF OILS OR SYNTHETICS. PAY ATTENTION TO THE TYPES OF OILS YOUR VEHICLE TAKES. THERE IS A REASON THAT I SAY THIS.

YOUR ENGINE BEARINGS DO NOT RIDE ON ANYTHING BUT A BEAD OF OIL!!

EXAMPLE:

5W30 OIL MOLECULES ARE, LET'S SAY THIS BIG: **O**

AND THEN WE WILL SAY THAT 5W20 OIL MOLECULES ARE ONLY THAT BIG: o

IF YOUR ENGINE HAS A 5W20 OILING SYSTEM AND YOU PUT 5W30 OIL IN IT, THE 5W30 OIL WILL WORK, BUT NOT AS WELL AS THE 5W20. THE MOLECULES ARE TOO BIG TO BE ABLE TO PROPERLY LUBRICATE THE ENGINE.

EXAMPLE: THIS IS A GOOD EXAMPLE OF AN ENGINE BEARING CAP. IF YOU LOOK CLOSE (BOTTOM / MIDDLE) YOU WILL SEE THE GAP OR SPACE (CLOSE TO 12-2 NUMBERS) WHERE THE OIL WOULD RIDE IN-BETWEEN THE CAP AND THE CRANK.

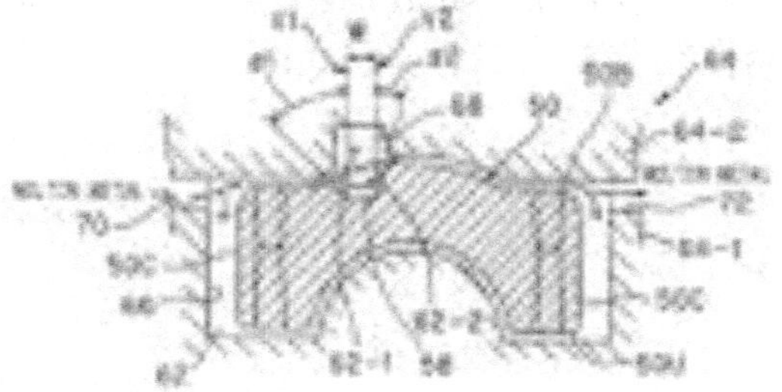

THE OIL PUMP WILL HAVE TROUBLE PICKING THE OIL UP TO THE TOP OF THE ENGINE AS WELL, BECAUSE THE OIL IS JUST TOO HEAVY. THIS COULD CAUSE SERIOUS ENGINE DAMAGE OVER THE COURSE OF TIME.

SOME CUSTOMERS WILL SAY "I USE 5W30, 5W20, 10W30 SYNTHETICS, WHAT'S THE BIG DEAL? THEY ALL WORK!"

DON'T USE THE WRONG OIL IN YOUR CAR FOR THE 50,000 MILES OF THE CARS LIFE AND GET MAD AT IT BECAUSE THE ENGINE HAS ISSUES. IT'S NOT A BAD CAR, THAT'S JUST A BAD OWNER.

GASKETS & SEALS

HEAD GASKET

THE MOST IMPORTANT GASKET THAT YOU HAVE IN THE ENGINE IS THE HEAD GASKET. THE HEAD GASKET SEPARATES THE UPPER HALF OF THE ENGINE FROM THE LOWER. IF THIS GASKET DETERIORATES, IT IS POSSIBLE THAT COOLANT COULD ENTER INTO THE OILING SYSTEM AND DESTROY THE ENGINE. KEEP ON TOP OF YOUR OIL CHANGES AND COOLANT FLUSHES AND YOU SHOULD NOT HAVE ANY PROBLEMS WITH THIS **COSTLY LABOR REPAIR!!!**

OIL GASKETS

MOST ENGINES HAVE TWO OTHER MAJOR OILING GASKETS, OTHER THAN THE HEAD GASKET. THE UPPER GASKET WOULD BE YOUR VALVE COVER GASKET AND THE LOWER WOULD BE YOUR OIL PAN GASKET. OIL GASKETS KEEP THE OIL IN AND KEEP ANYTHING THAT IS NOT OIL OUT OF THE SYSTEM. MOST OF THESE GASKETS ARE MADE OF A TYPE OF RUBBER OR SILICONE.

DEPENDING ON LOCATION, THESE GASKETS COULD BE A COSTLY LABOR REPAIR.

OIL SEALS

MOST ENGINES WILL HAVE TWO SEALS. THE FRONT AND REAR CRANK SEALS. THE OILING SEALS HAVE THE SAME JOB AS THE GASKET, KEEP THE OIL IN AND EVERYTHING ELSE OUT.

NOTE: OVER THE COURSE OF TIME, OIL GASKETS AND SEALS WILL DETERIORATE, WEAKEN, AND BECOME BRITTLE. WHEN THESE PARTS START TO LEAK, IT COULD CAUSE SIGNIFICANT DAMAGES TO THE ENGINE. YOU CAN HELP TO PREVENT FAILURES OF THESE SEALS AND GASKETS BY JUST KEEPING UP ON YOUR OIL CHANGES.

CHAPTER 4

IGNITIONS

IGNITIONS

AN AUTOMOTIVE VEHICLE IGNITION SYSTEMS SEEM TO BE COMPLEX TO MANY PEOPLE. THESE PEOPLE FEEL CONFUSED ABOUT THE OPERATIONS OF THEIR CAR'S IGNITION SYSTEMS JUST FOR THE MERE FACT THAT IGNITIONS ARE ELECTRICAL! WELL, THESE PEOPLE HAVE EVERY RIGHT TO FEEL CONFUSED! AUTOMOTIVE IGNITION SYSTEMS ARE COMPLEX AND HAVE MANY, MANY VARIABLES. THEREFORE, DUE TO THE COMPLEX NATURE OF TODAY'S MODERN IGNITION SYSTEMS, WE WILL NOT GET INTO DEPTH ON HOW EVERYTHING WORKS. BUT WE WILL GO OVER SOME OF THE MAJOR COMPONENTS!

MOST AUTOMOTIVE IGNITIONS WILL HAVE TWO INTEGRATED SYSTEMS. THESE SYSTEMS WOULD BE THE PRIMARY IGNITION, AND THE SECONDARY IGNITION SYSTEM.

PRIMARY IGNITION

THE PRIMARY IGNITION BASICALLY GETS THE ENGINE SPINNING AND POWERS THE REST OF THE ELECTRICAL SYSTEMS. THE PROCESS STARTS WITH THE DRIVER'S KEY. WHEN THE DRIVER OF THE VEHICLE PLACES THE IGNITION KEY INTO ITS SOCKET AND TURNS THE KEY TO THE "START POSITION", THE **IGNITION SWITCH** WILL SEND AN ELECTRICAL SIGNAL TO THE **STARTER SOLENOID**. THE STARTER SOLENOID WILL ALLOW ELECTRICITY TO FLOW FROM THE CAR'S **BATTERY** TO THE STARTER. THE **STARTER** FORCES THE ENGINE TO SPIN, WHICH ROTATES THE BELTS, THE BELTS MAKE THE ALTERNATOR SPIN, AS THE **ALTERNATOR** SPINS IT CREATES CONTINUOUS ENERGY THAT IS DISTRIBUTED BACK TO THE BATTERY, THE REST OF THE VEHICLE AND THE CAR'S SECONDARY IGNITION

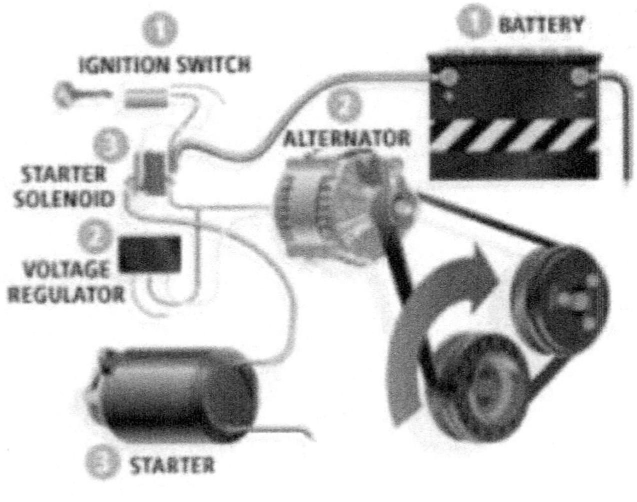

SECONDARY IGNITION

THE EXPLOSION THAT TAKES PLACE IN THE CYLINDER IS CREATED BY A FEW FACTORS. ONE FACTOR IS HOW MUCH COMBUSTION YOUR ENGINE CREATES, THE SECOND FACTOR IS YOUR GAS TO AIR RATIO, AND THE THIRD FACTOR THAT WE WILL FOCUS ON AT THIS POINT OF THE BOOK IS THE SPARK.

SPARK PLUG

A SPARK PLUG IS A DEVICE, INSERTED INTO THE COMBUSTION CHAMBER OF AN ENGINE, CONTAINING A SIDE ELECTRODE AND INSULATED CENTER ELECTRODE SPACED TO PROVIDE A GAP FOR FIRING AN ELECTRICAL SPARK TO IGNITE THROUGH AIR-FUEL MIXTURES.

THE HIGH-VOLTAGE BURST FROM THE COIL VIA THE DISTRIBUTOR OR COIL PACKS IS RECEIVED AT THE SPARK PLUGS TERMINAL AND CONDUCTED DOWN A CENTER ELECTRODE PROTECTED BY A PORCELAIN INSULATOR. AT THE BOTTOM OF THE PLUG, (WHICH PROJECTS INTO THE CYLINDER) THE VOLTAGE MUST BE POWERFUL ENOUGH TO JUMP A GAP BETWEEN THE CENTER AND THE SIDE ELECTRODES THROUGH A THICK ATMOSPHERE OF AIR-FUEL MIXTURE. WHEN THE SPARK BRIDGES THE GAP, IT IGNITES THE FUEL IN THE CYLINDER.

NOTE: WHEN REPLACING THE SPARK PLUGS MAKE SURE YOU USE THE SAME SPARK PLUGS THAT CAME FROM THE MANUFACTURER ONLY!!! IF YOU DON'T, YOU WILL HAVE ODD ISSUES IN THE FUTURE. LET ME GIVE YOU A QUICK EXAMPLE OF WHY I SAY THIS.

THERE ARE THREE TYPES OF SPARK PLUGS THAT ARE STANDARD FOR THE INDUSTRY, A COPPER PLUG, A PLATINUM PLUG, AND A IRIDIUM PLUG. THE COPPER PLUG IS A STANDARD PLUG AND WILL WORK WELL ON <u>SOME CARS</u> FOR ABOUT 25,000 MILES. A PLATINUM PLUG HAS A BIT HIGHER HEAT RATING AND WILL LAST ABOUT 75,000 MILES. THE IRIDIUM PLUG IS A GREAT PLUG AND WILL LAST IABOUT 110,000 MILES. SOME CUSTOMERS WILL HAVE A CAR THAT CALLS FOR A IRIDIUM OR PLATINUM PLUG, SOME OF THESE CUSTOMERS WILL TRY TO SAVE A FEW DOLLORS BY REPLACING THE URIDIUM OR PLATINUM PLUG WITH A STANDARD PLUG.

MOST SHOPS WILL BE OK WITH THAT CHOICE AND WILL ADVISE YOU IN A ROUND ABOUT WAY (WITHOUT PUSHING THE SALE) TO USE THE CORRECT PLUG. THE REASON THAT THEY ARE OKAY WITH YOUR CHOICE IS BECAUSE A STANDARD PLUG WILL BURN OUT QUICKLY!!! WHEN YOU COME BACK TO THAT SAME SHOP WITH A PROBLEM, THEY WILL SAY "SIR/ MA'AM.WE TOLD YOU TO PUT IN A IRIDIUM PLUGS AND YOU DIDN'T DO IT! YOU WILL NOW HAVE TO DO THE JOB OVER AND PAY $$???" WHO KNOWS? MOST LIKLEY THE SAME PRICE THAT WAS QUOTED WHEN YOU HAD YOUR FIRST VISIT TO THAT SHOP.

SPARK PLUG WIRES

HIGH HEAT RATED WIRES THAT LEAD FROM THE DISTRIBUTOR CAP AND OR THE COIL PACK TO THE SPARK PLUG ITSELF. THIS ALLOWS LARGE AMOUNTS OF ENERGY TO FLOW FREELY TO THE SPARK PLUGS.

NOTE: MOST SPARK PLUG WIRES SHOULD BE REPLACED AROUND 70,000 MILES FOR MOST VEHICLES, IF THEY STILL LOOK GOOD, CHECK THEM AGAIN AT 90,000 MILES.

COIL PACKS / OR DISTRIBUTOR

A SYSTEM WITH NO DISTRIBUTOR WILL HAVE COIL PACKS THAT WILL HOLD MASSIVE AMOUNTS OF ENERGY UNTIL IT IS TIME FOR THE ENERGY TO BE RELEASED TO THE SPARK PLUGS.

A SYSTEM WITH A DISTRIBUTOR WILL HAVE A DISTRIBUTOR, A DISTRIBUTOR BUTTON/ROTOR AND A DISTRIBUTOR CAP.

NOTE: THE DISTRIBUTOR CAP&BUTTON/ ROTOR SHOULD BE REPLACED AT THE TIME OF THE PLUGS.

CHAPTER 5

EMISSIONS & COMPUTERS

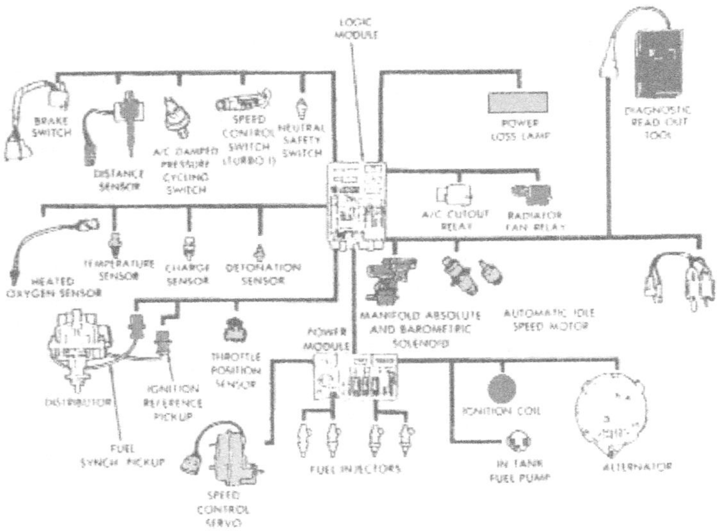

Emissions & computers

EMISSIONS

Fact: Emissions control systems have reduced carbon monoxide and hydrocarbon emissions by about ninety-six percent from pre-controlled vehicles.

Most emission systems consist of a PCV (Positive Crankcase Ventilation), EGR (Exhaust Gas Recirculation), Catalytic Converter (that have aluminum oxide, platinum and palladium in them to help re-ignite left over gases) and an Exhaust System.

Although emissions control systems vary between manufacturers and vehicles, they all have the same goal and use many of the same methods. The main purpose of the emission control system is just that; it controls the emissions and exhaust from your vehicle. The idea is to turn the harmful gases your car produces into harmless ones that don't ruin the environment, or us. Some of the problem gases are: hydrocarbons (unburned), carbon monoxide, carbon dioxide, nitrogen oxides, sulfur dioxide, phosphorus, lead and other metals.

To help control these substances, "Federal Regulations" have made changes in our gasoline to eliminate them and many states require emissions tests on vehicles. This means that you drive to a facility where "experts" will take a sample of your cars emissions and run it through some analysis. The results are printed, and your car passes or fails depending on the percentage of toxic emissions that turn up in your car's sample. One good thing to do is to save your printouts from the test from year to year. If you compare them, you will be able to monitor your car (if it's score is getting worse) and you can catch any problems before there is a major issue.

Federal regulations have caused development, (varying from state to state), to test emissions, that have caused automotive manufactures to develop better, safer emission systems. The addition of computers to ignition systems allows the engine to monitor and adjust itself continuously.

The only way to "study" or prepare for these tests is to take good care of your car, including its emission system. If you use preventative maintenance, and keep your car tuned properly, you should pass every time.

COMPUTERS (OBD) I / OBD II)

On-Board Diagnostic systems are in most cars and light trucks on the road today. During the '70s and early '80s manufacturers started using electronic means to control engine functions and diagnose engine problems. This was primarily to meet EPA emission standards. Through the years, on-board diagnostic systems have become more sophisticated. OBD-II, a new standard introduced in the mid-'90s, provides almost complete engine control and also monitors parts of the chassis, body and accessory devices, as well as the diagnostic control network of the car.

WHEN DID IT START?

To beat the smog issue in L.A., the State of California required "Emission control systems" on 1966 cars and above. The federal government adapted these controls nationwide in 1968.

Congress passed the Clean Air Act in 1970 and established the Environmental Protection Agency (EPA). This started a series of graduated emission standards and requirements for maintenance of vehicles for extended periods of time. To meet these standards, manufacturers turned to electronically controlled fuel feed and ignition systems. Sensors measured engine performance and adjusted the systems to provide minimum pollution. These sensors were also accessed to provide early diagnostic assistance.

At first there were few standards and each manufacturer had their own systems and signals. In 1988, the Society of Automotive Engineers (SAE) set out to find a standard connector plug and set of diagnostic test signals. The EPA adapted most of their standards from the SAE on-board diagnostic programs and recommendations. OBD-II is an expanded set of standards and practices developed by SAE and adopted by the EPA and CARB (California Air Resources Board) for implementation by January 1, 1996.

All cars built since January 1, 1996 have OBD-II systems. Manufacturers started incorporating OBD-II in various models as early as 1994. Some early OBD-II cars were not 100% compliant.

EACH YEAR, CARS SEEM TO GET MORE AND MORE COMPLICATED. CARS TODAY MIGHT HAVE AS MANY AS 50 MICROPROCESSORS ON THEM. ALTHOUGH THESE MICROPROCESSORS MAKE IT MORE DIFFICULT FOR YOU TO WORK ON YOUR OWN CAR, SOME OF THEM ACTUALLY MAKE YOUR CAR EASIER TO SERVICE.

SOME OF THE REASONS FOR THIS INCREASE IN THE NUMBER OF MICROPROCESSORS ARE:

- THE NEED FOR SOPHISTICATED ENGINE CONTROLS TO MEET EMISSIONS AND FUEL-ECONOMY STANDARDS
- ADVANCED DIAGNOSTICS
- SIMPLIFICATION OF THE MANUFACTURE AND DESIGN OF CARS
- REDUCTION OF THE AMOUNT OF WIRING IN CARS
- NEW SAFETY FEATURES
- NEW COMFORT AND CONVENIENCE FEATURES

BEFORE EMISSIONS LAWS WERE ENACTED, IT WAS POSSIBLE TO BUILD A CAR'S ENGINE WITHOUT MICROPROCESSORS. WITH THE ENACTMENT OF INCREASINGLY STRICTER EMISSIONS LAWS, SOPHISTICATED CONTROL SCHEMES WERE NEEDED TO REGULATE THE AIR/FUEL MIXTURE SO THAT THE CATALYTIC CONVERTER COULD REMOVE AS MUCH OF THE POLLUTION FROM THE EXHAUST AS POSSIBLE.

CONTROLLING THE ENGINE IS THE MOST PROCESSOR-INTENSIVE JOB ON YOUR CAR, AND THE ENGINE CONTROL UNIT (ECU) IS THE MOST POWERFUL COMPUTER ON MOST CARS. THE ECU USES CLOSED-LOOP CONTROL, A CONTROL SCHEME THAT MONITORS OUTPUTS OF A SYSTEM TO CONTROL THE INPUTS TO A SYSTEM, MANAGING THE EMISSIONS AND FUEL ECONOMY OF THE ENGINE (AS WELL AS A HOST OF OTHER PARAMETERS). GATHERING DATA FROM DOZENS OF DIFFERENT SENSORS, THE ECU KNOWS EVERYTHING FROM THE COOLANT TEMPERATURE TO THE AMOUNT OF OXYGEN IN THE EXHAUST. WITH THIS DATA, IT PERFORMS MILLIONS OF CALCULATIONS EACH SECOND, INCLUDING LOOKING UP VALUES IN TABLES, CALCULATING THE RESULTS OF LONG EQUATIONS TO DECIDE ON THE BEST TIMING AND DETERMINING HOW LONG THE FUEL INJECTOR IS OPEN. THE ECU DOES ALL OF THIS TO ENSURE THE LOWEST EMISSIONS AND BEST MILEAGE.

NOTE:* I DON'T KNOW OF ANY COMPUTER THAT "TIES" INTO THE CARS COMPUTER SYSTEM AND TELLS YOU WHAT IS WRONG!!! THE COMPUTERS THAT INTERFACE WITH YOUR CARS COMPUTER WILL HELP LEAD REPAIR SHOPS IN THE DIRECTION OF WHAT MIGHT BE WRONG! THAT IS WHY MOST SHOPS CHARGE A "DIAGNOSTIC FEE" DUE TO THE COMPLEXITY OF THE COMPUTER SYSTEM. I WILL TELL YOU HOW TO GET AROUND THIS "FEE" IN SECTION # 5.

CHAPTER 6

FUEL SYSTEMS

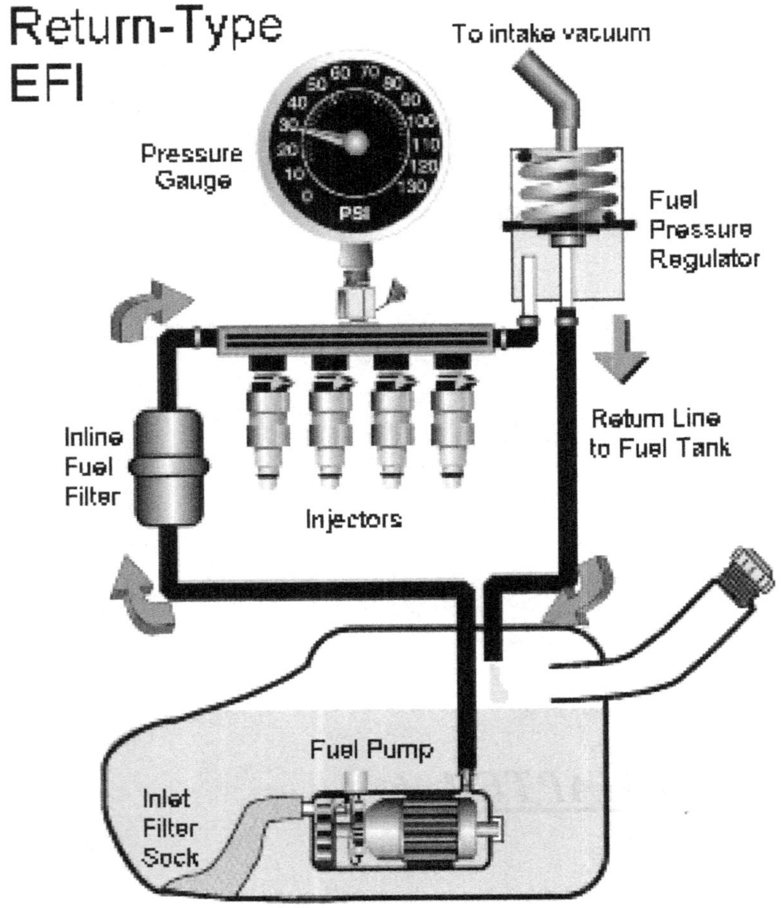

THE FUEL SYSTEM

THE PURPOSE OF THE FUEL SYSTEM IS TO PROVIDE A MIXTURE OF FUEL AND AIR TO THE ENGINE OF THE CAR. THE AIR-FUEL MIXTURE MUST BE IN PROPORTION TO THE SPEED AND LOAD PLACED ON THE ENGINE. MAJOR PARTS OF THE SYSTEM INCLUDE: FUEL CAP, EMISSION CONTROLS, FUEL LINE, FUEL PUMP, FUEL FILTER, CARBURETOR OR INJECTORS, INTAKE MANIFOLD AND FUEL GAUGE, WHICH INDICATES THE AMOUNT OF FUEL IN THE TANK.

ENGINE FUEL IS MAINLY MADE UP OF HYDROGEN AND CARBON, MIXED SO THAT IT WILL BURN WITH OXYGEN PRESENT, AND WILL FREE ITS HEAT ENERGY INTO MECHANICAL ENERGY. LIQUID FUELS ARE IDEAL FOR INTERNAL COMBUSTION ENGINES, BECAUSE THEY CAN BE ECONOMICALLY PRODUCED, HAVE A HIGH HEAT VALUE PER POUND, AN IDEAL RATE OF BURNING, AND CAN BE EASILY HANDLED AND STORED.

A GASOLINE'S ABILITY TO RESIST DETONATION IS CALLED ITS "OCTANE" OR ANTI-KNOCK RATING. GASOLINE FROM ASPHALTIC BASE CRUDE OIL PRODUCES LESS KNOCK THAN ONE FROM PARAFFINIC BASE CRUDE. CRACKED GAS HAS LESS TENDENCY TO KNOCK THAN STRAIGHT RUN GAS. ALL MARKETED

GASOLINES ARE A BLEND OF STRAIGHT RUN AND CRACKED GASOLINES, SO UNLESS THEIR BLENDING IS CONTROLLED, THE ANTI-KNOCK QUALITIES WILL VARY.

NOTE: THE CHEAP GAS AT YOUR GAS PUMPS WILL: USUALLY HAVE A "QUICK SPARK" AND "LOW ENERGY BURN" AS IT EXITS THE SYSTEM, IT WILL BE MORE PRONE TO RE-IGNITE. THE MOST EXPENSIVE GAS *USUALLY* ***TAKES A BIT MORE SPARK TO RELEASE THE HIGH ENERGY IT HOLDS SO IT CAN BE HARD ON IGNITION SYSTEMS. I RECOMMEND THAT YOU USE THE MID-RANGE GAS FOR AN AVERAGE VEHICLE DUE TO ITS AVERAGE IGNITION AND MID-RANGE ENERGY BURN. ALWAYS CHECK WITH YOUR MANUFACTURER'S RECOMMENDATIONS.***

FUEL DEPOSITS

THE FORMATION OF DEPOSITS IN A FUEL SYSTEM IS A NORMAL CONSEQUENCE OF ENGINE OPERATION.

WHERE DO THE DEPOSITS COME FROM? - MOSTLY FROM THE FUEL ITSELF- GASOLINE IS ALSO MIXED WITH OIL FINS, WHICH ARE HEAVY, WAXY COMPOUNDS. THE HEAVIER THE HYDROCARBON, THE MORE ENERGY IT YIELDS WHEN IT BURNS. WHEN THE ENGINE IS SHUT OFF, THE INJECTORS UNDERGO HEAT SOAK. FUEL RESIDUE IN THE INJECTOR NOZZLES EVAPORATES, LEAVING THE WAXY OIL FINS BEHIND. BECAUSE THE ENGINE IS OFF, THERE IS NO COOLING AIRFLOW THROUGH THE PORTS AND NO FUEL FLOW THROUGH THE INJECTORS TO WASH IT AWAY, SO HEAT BAKES THE OIL FINS INTO HARD VARNISH DEPOSITS. OVER TIME, THESE DEPOSITS CAN BUILD UP AND CLOG THE INJECTORS, SO DETERGENTS ARE ADDED TO GASOLINE THAT HELP KEEP THE INJECTORS CLEAN.

INJECTOR CLOGGING

ALL VEHICLES ARE VULNERABLE TO INJECTOR CLOGGING, BUT THE ONES THAT ARE MOST VULNERABLE, MOST LIKELY TO EXPERIENCE SUCH DRIVABILITY AND EMISSION PROBLEMS ARE VEHICLES THAT ARE USED PRIMARILY FOR SHORT-TRIP DRIVING, THE DEPOSITS BUILD UP FASTER THAN THE DETERGENTS CAN WASH AWAY.

ON FOUR-CYLINDER ENGINES, THE #2 AND #3 INJECTORS ARE IN THE HOTTEST LOCATION AND TEND TO CLOG UP FASTER THAN THE END INJECTORS ON CYLINDERS #1 AND #4. THE SAME APPLIES TO THE INJECTORS IN THE MIDDLE CYLINDERS IN SIX AND EIGHT CYLINDER ENGINES. THE HOTTER THE LOCATION, THE MORE VULNERABLE THE INJECTOR IS TO CLOGGING FROM HEAT SOAKS.

IF A VEHICLE IS EXPERIENCING ANY OF THE CLASSIC SYMPTOMS OF DIRTY INJECTORS, SUCH AS ROUGH IDLE, HESITATION, STUMBLING ON LIGHT ACCELERATION, A LOSS OF POWER, HIGHER CARBON MONOXIDE (CO) EMISSIONS, HIGHER HYDROCARBON (HC) EMISSIONS, AND LEAN MISFIRE, THE INJECTORS POSSIBLY JUST NEED TO BE CLEANED.

It doesn't take much of a restriction in an injector to lean out the fuel mixture. A restriction of only 8% to 10% in a single fuel injector can be enough to cause a misfire. When this occurs, unburned oxygen enters the exhaust and makes the O2 sensor read lean.

Lean misfire codes can also trigger and turn on the Check Engine light on vehicles with OBD systems. The code will often be a random misfire, or one individual cylinder misfire code, depending on which injectors are affected. The fuel feedback control systems will try to compensate for the leaning effect once it is in a closed loop, but it can't correct the underlying condition that is causing the problem.

As you can see clean fuel injectors are an essential for peak engine performance, fuel economy and emissions.

Recommendation: *Have your fuel system cleaned (intake, throttle port, filters & cylinders) every 20 to 30,000 miles.*

***CHAPTER* 7**

COOLANT

COOLANT

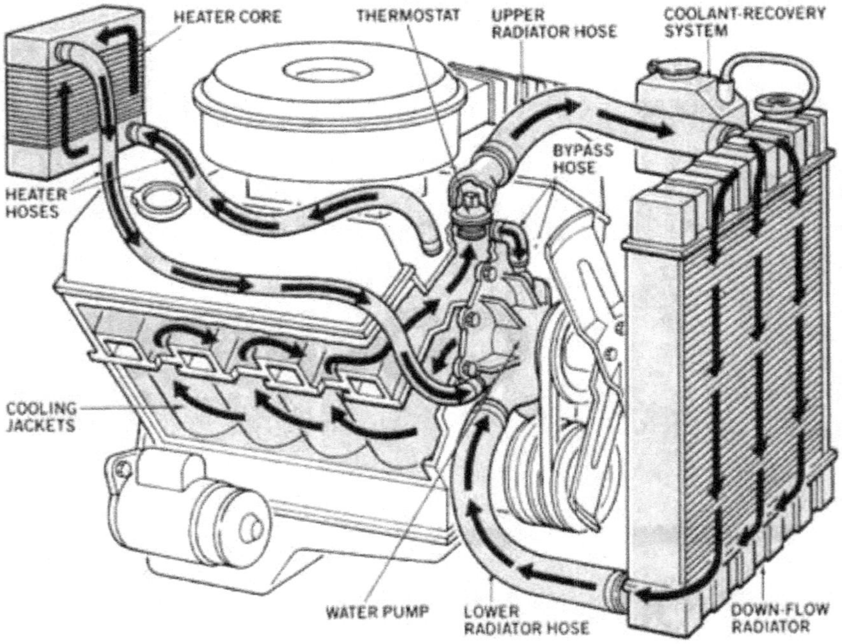

THE COOLING SYSTEM HAS A FEW FUNCTIONS, BUT ITS MAIN FUNCTION IS TO REMOVE EXCESS HEAT FROM YOUR ENGINE. AS YOUR ENGINE BURNS GASOLINE, LESS THAN A THIRD OF THE RELEASED ENERGY GOES INTO MECHANICAL ENERGY TO RUN YOUR CAR. THE REST IS CONVERTED TO HEAT. SOME OF THAT HEAT IS BLOWN OUT THE EXHAUST, WHILE THE REST OF THE HEAT STAYS IN THE ENGINE. WITHOUT A COOLING SYSTEM, THE ENGINE CAN BE DESTROYED BY HEAT WITHIN 30 MINUTES OF STARTUP.

THE COOLING SYSTEM WORKS BY MOVING COOLANT THROUGH THE ENGINE, AND MOVING THAT HEATED COOLANT THROUGH THE RADIATOR, WHERE COOLANT PASSES THROUGH VENTS IN THE RADIATOR. AS THE AIR PASSES BY THESE VENTS, IT COOLS THE COOLANT AND RE-ENTERS INTO THE ENGINE. THE COOLING SYSTEM MUST HAVE ENOUGH COOLING CAPACITY TO COOL A CAR ON A LONG, LONG TRIP.

THE ENTIRE SYSTEM IS SEALED WITH ONE EXCEPTION. THE RADIATOR CAP CONTAINS A SPRING WHICH MAINTAINS A CONSTANT PRESSURE BY VENTING COOLANT (TO THE RESERVOIR TANK) WHEN PRESSURE RISES ABOVE ITS SPECIFIED VALUE. IT'S NORMAL FOR SOME COOLANT TO VENT IN THIS WAY, WHICH IS WHY THE RESERVOIR IS MORE FULL WHEN THE CAR IS HOT THAN WHEN IT'S COLD. THE RADIATOR CAP ALSO ALLOWS THE VACUUM CREATED WHEN THE SYSTEM COOLS TO "SUCK BACK" COOLANT FROM THE RESERVOIR. BUT IN THE CASE OF AN EXTREME OVERHEAT, VENTED COOLANT OVERFLOWS THE RESERVOIR, THEREBY CREATING A LOW-COOLANT SITUATION AND MAKING THE OVERHEAT EVEN WORSE.

If the local shop doesn't understand the role of a broken head gasket as a cause of overheating, or the fact that such a broken head gasket might not exhibit the classic symptoms of white smoke billowing out of the exhaust or white/yellow foam/gunk on the oil cap, you probably want to look for a different shop. Also, the car owner needs to understand the cost of overheats (often exceeding $2000.00), and the fact that the single most important protection against overheating is regular coolant flushes (not a drain and fill)

THERMOSTAT

The thermostat is a heat sensitive valve that allows coolant to flow through the radiator at high temperatures, but cuts off that flow at low temperatures. The engine temperature must be regulated to the manufacturer's recommended operating temperature. The thermostat regulates this temperature.

RADIATOR

The radiator looks some-what like an old heating radiator in a house. The radiator basically has passageways inside of it that coolant and water can pass through. On the outside of these passageways there are fins. As air passes by these fins, heat is absorbed by the air and takes the heat away from the coolant

THE WATER PUMP

The water pump sucks cooled coolant from the radiator and pushes it into the engine. The coolant flows through the engine, absorbing the engine's heat. If the thermostat is open, that coolant then flows into the radiator for cooling.

COOLANT FANS

At low speeds air flow is maintained by the fan, and at high speeds it's maintained by the relative velocity of the vehicle in relation to the outside air.

AUTOMOTIVE ANTIFREEZE

Automotive Antifreeze has two jobs in helping the engine. To help keep the engine cool, and heat the inside of the passengers cab. Automotive Antifreeze is a conventional (green), ethylene glycol based antifreeze for use in automotive and light duty diesel applications. **Automotive Antifreeze** contains inhibitors that provide maximum protection from freezing to -84 F and boil-over to +276 F. Its formula protects all metals, including aluminum, against damaging rust and corrosion when used as recommended.

A NEW TYPE OF ANTIFREEZE

REFERRED TO AS EXTENDED LIFE OR LONG LIFE ANTIFREEZE, IS NOW AVAILABLE. THE CHEMISTRY USED IN THESE PRODUCTS ARE UNIQUE AND VERY DIFFERENT FROM THAT USED IN TRADITIONAL GREEN ANTIFREEZES. THESE ANTIFREEZES DOUBLE ALL EXISTING MANUFACTURER'S CURRENT RECOMMENDATIONS, SO SOME SPECIFIC MAINTENANCE PRACTICES MUST BE ADHERED TO IN ORDER TO REALIZE THE BENEFITS OF EXTENDED LIFE ANTIFREEZE. I HAVE SEEN SOME MANUFACTURER'S MAINTENANCE INTERVALS UP TO 100,000 MILES, OR FIVE (5) YEARS, WHICHEVER COMES FIRST.

NOTE: COOLANT SHOULD BE CHANGED EVERY 30,000 MILES IF THE COOLANT IS GREEN (I WOULD EVEN DO IT EARLY AT 25,000 MILES), IF THE COOLANT IS ANY OTHER COLOR, I WOULD CHANGE IT EVERY 60,000 MILES JUST TO BE ON THE SAFE SIDE...MAKE SURE WHATEVER FACILITY YOU HAVE THE COOLANT CHANGED AT USES THE MANUFACTURER'S RECOMMENDED COOLANT.

NOTE: WHEN THE MANUFACTURER'S MAINTENANCE GUIDE SAYS CHANGE THE COOLANT AT 100,000 MILES, IT WOULD BE A GOOD IDEA TO HAVE THAT SERVICE DONE JUST A LITTLE EARLIER. 75 TO 80,000 MILES WOULD BE MORE IDEAL.

EXTENDED LIFE ANTIFREEZES ARE AVAILABLE IN BOTH ETHYLENE AND PROPYLENE GLYCOL BASES. THESE CAN BE EITHER UNDILUTED OR PRE-MIXED 50/50 WITH WATER. THERE ARE SPECIFIC INTEREST IS THE CORROSION INHIBITOR ADDITIVE PACKAGE USED IN THE EXTENDED LIFE ANTIFREEZES. ITS MAJOR INGREDIENT IS AN ORGANIC ACID. BECAUSE OF THE ORGANIC ACID ADDITIVE PACKAGE AND SOME OTHER CHEMICAL CHARACTERISTICS OF EXTENDED LIFE ANTIFREEZE, THE DEPLETION OF THE CORROSION INHIBITORS IS VERY DIFFERENT THAN COOLANTS UTILIZING TRADITIONAL SUPPLEMENTAL COOLANT ADDITIVES (SCA'S).

WHILE SYSTEMS USING "GREEN" ANTIFREEZES REQUIRE THE PH & ACID LEVEL TO BE LOW AND MUST BE REPLENISHED ON A ROUTINE BASIS, COOLANTS USING EXTENDED LIFE ANTIFREEZE REQUIRE INHIBITOR PACKAGE REPLENISHMENT ONLY ONCE DURING ITS SERVICE LIFE. THE INHIBITOR ADDITIVE FOR EXTENDED LIFE ANTIFREEZE IS NOT AN SCA STYLE PACKAGE. ONLY A SPECIAL FORMULATION ADDITIVE PACKAGE IS TO BE USED WITH EXTENDED LIFE ANTIFREEZES. NEITHER THE CURRENT FORMULATION SCA PACKAGE NOR THE SPECIAL EXTENDED LIFE PACKAGES ARE TO BE SUBSTITUTED FOR EACH OTHER AT ANYTIME.

ALTHOUGH EXTENDED LIFE ANTIFREEZE IS CHEMICALLY COMPATIBLE WITH TRADITIONAL FORMULATION ANTIFREEZES, IT IS THE RECOMMENDATION OF ALL EXTENDED LIFE ANTIFREEZE MANUFACTURERS AND SUPPLIERS THAT THE TWO TYPES ARE NOT TO BE MIXED. MIXING THE TWO TYPES OF ANTIFREEZES COMPLETELY NEGATES ANY EXTENDED LIFE CHARACTERISTICS. FOR THIS REASON, EXTENDED LIFE ANTIFREEZES HAVE BEEN COLORED RED AND ORANGE DEPENDING ON THE SUPPLIER. OTHER COLORS MAY APPEAR IN THE FUTURE. TOP-OFF AND REFILL OF THESE SYSTEMS ARE TO BE DONE ONLY WITH THE APPROPRIATE PRODUCTS.

***CHAPTER* 8**

HEATING AND AIR CONDITIONING

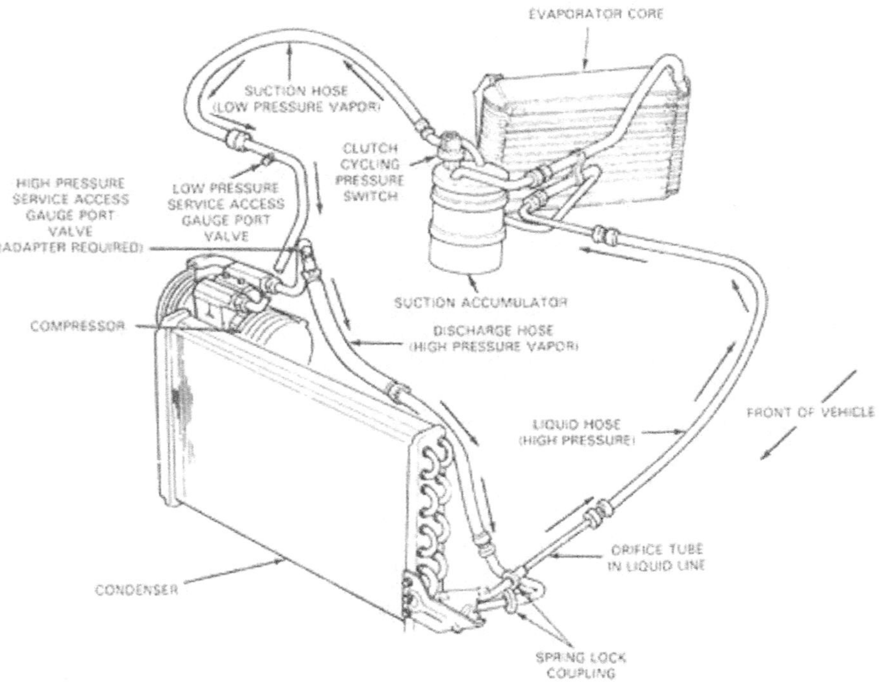

HEATING AND AIR

Heating and air conditioning systems seem to get mixed up with the vehicle's cooling system. Many people think that when you add coolant to the car, it keeps the air conditioning cold. This is so far from the truth, it is not even funny! Yet, it does hold a minute element of truth.

HEATING

Your vehicle's heating does tie into the cooling system of the vehicle. Basically, after the coolant has passed by the cylinder walls and absorbed the heat, the hot coolant will enter into the cabin of the vehicle via tubes that are connected to the heater core. The heater core sits behind the dash of the vehicle and looks like a small radiator.

As the hot coolant enters into the heater core, your vehicle's blower motor (the one that's controlled in the car) will blow air through the heater core, past the vents, causing the air to heat and exits directly into the cabin of the vehicle.

AIR CONDITIONING SYSTEM

Believe it or not, air conditioning systems and the way that they operate are still theory, not a scientific fact. I still don't understand why it is still a theory? Air conditioning systems seem to work just fine to me.

Air conditioning systems, once they are charged and operating properly, should have no leaks whatsoever. They are a sealed system. They can be complex in their nature due to

AMBIENT TEMPERATURES AND MOISTURE VARIATIONS. TRYING TO GET THE A/C SYSTEM TO PRODUCE A COMFORTABLE TEMPERATURE CAN SOMETIMES BE A CHALLENGE FOR ENGINEERS. THEY ARE REALLY NOT THAT COMPLICATED.

YOU BASICALLY HAVE FOUR (4) MAJOR ITEMS IN AN AIR CONDITIONING SYSTEM THAT HAVE ABSOLUTELY NOTHING TO DO WITH HEATING, ONLY AIR CONDITIONING. THE FOUR MAJOR COMPONENTS OF THE SYSTEM ARE THE COMPRESSOR, THE CONDENSER, THE EVAPORATOR, AND THE EXPANSION VALVE OR ORIFICE TUBE. THE REST OF THE SYSTEM IS BASICALLY A FEW EXPENSIVE HOSES, SENSORS, AND FANS.

AIR COMPRESSOR

THE AIR COMPRESSOR IS EXACTLY THAT. IT COMPRESSES THE GASES THAT WILL LEAD TO THE EXPANSION VALVE AND/OR ORIFICE TUBE.

ORIFICE TUBE/EXPANSION VALVE

THE ORIFICE TUBES/EXPANSION VALVES MAY HAVE DIFFERENT NAMES BUT THEY BASICALLY HAVE THE SAME FUNCTION. AS COMPRESSED GASES EXIT THE COMPRESSOR, THEY LEAD TO THE EXPANSION VALVE OR THE ORIFICE TUBE. ONCE THEY ENTER THE TUBE OR VALVE, THESE GASES ATOMIZE, CAUSING A COOLING EFFECT IN THE CARS EVAPORATOR.

EVAPORATOR

THE VEHICLE'S EVAPORATOR IS LOCATED BEHIND THE DASH IN THE CAB, NEXT TO THE COOLING SYSTEMS HEATER CORE. AS GASES PASS THROUGH THE EVAPORATOR, THEY WILL EXIT AND DIRECT BACK TO THE AIR CONDITIONING'S CONDENSER TO START THE PROCESS ALL OVER AGAIN.

THE CONDENSOR

THE CONDENSER BASICALLY LOOKS LIKE A RADIATOR AND SITS IN FRONT OF THE COOLING SYSTEM RADIATOR. BASICALLY AS GASES PASS THROUGH THE TUBES LOCATED INSIDE THE CONDENSER, THE OUTSIDE AIR PASSES BY THESE TUBES AND VENTS TO COOL THE GAS.

CHAPTER 9

TRANSMISSIONS

TRANSMISSIONS

TRANSMISSIONS ARE ALMOST WHAT THEY SOUND LIKE. THEY TRANSMIT THE POWER FROM YOUR CAR'S ENGINE TO OTHER COMPONENTS, TO TRANSFER THAT POWER TO THE GROUND. HOWEVER, TRANSMISSIONS DO MUCH, MUCH MORE THAN TRANSMIT POWER. THEREFORE, I WILL NOT GIVE A COMPLETE BREAKDOWN OF TRANSMISSIONS. WE WILL OVERVIEW THE MAJOR COMPONENTS TO A TRANSMISSION. IF YOU ARE SEEKING MORE INFORMATION I ADVISE GO TO HTTP://WWW.HOWSTUFFWORKS.COM OR OTHER SITES OF THE SAME NATURE.

MANUAL TRANS

MANUAL TRANSMISSIONS ARE A LITTLE LESS COMPLEX THAN AN AUTOMATIC TRANSMISSION. THE BIG DIFFERENCE THAT THE DRIVER CAN TELL BETWEEN THE TWO TYPES OF TRANSMISSIONS, IS THAT THE DRIVER NEEDS TO BE ABLE USE A "CLUTCH" AND "SHIFT-GEARS" WITH A CAR THAT HAS A MANUAL TRANSMISSION. ALTHOUGH A MANUAL TRANSMISSION AND AN AUTOMATIC TRANSMISSION SERVE THE SAME FUNCTION, INTERNALLY THEY ARE TOTALLY DIFFERENT.

THE KEY DIFFERENCE BETWEEN A MANUAL TRANSMISSION AND AN AUTOMATIC TRANSMISSION IS THAT THE MANUAL TRANSMISSION LOCKS AND UNLOCKS DIFFERENT SETS OF GEARS TO THE OUTPUT SHAFT TO ACHIEVE THE VARIOUS GEAR RATIOS AND SPEEDS. IN AN AUTOMATIC TRANSMISSION; THE SAME SET OF GEARS ARE USED TO PRODUCE ALL OF THE DIFFERENT GEAR RATIOS.

THE MANUAL TRANSMISSION WILL USE STEEL GEARS FOR OUTPUT GEAR RATIOS AS WHERE AN AUTOMATIC TRANSMISSION, USES CLUTCH PACKS FOR ITS GEAR RATIOS. WHEN OPERATING A VEHICLE WITH A MANUAL TRANSMISSION THE DRIVER WILL USE A SHAFT (AKA THE STICK) TO DETERMINE WHAT GEAR RATIO. IN AN AUTOMATIC TRANSMISSION, THE GEAR RATIO IS ALMOST SELECTED FOR THE DRIVER.

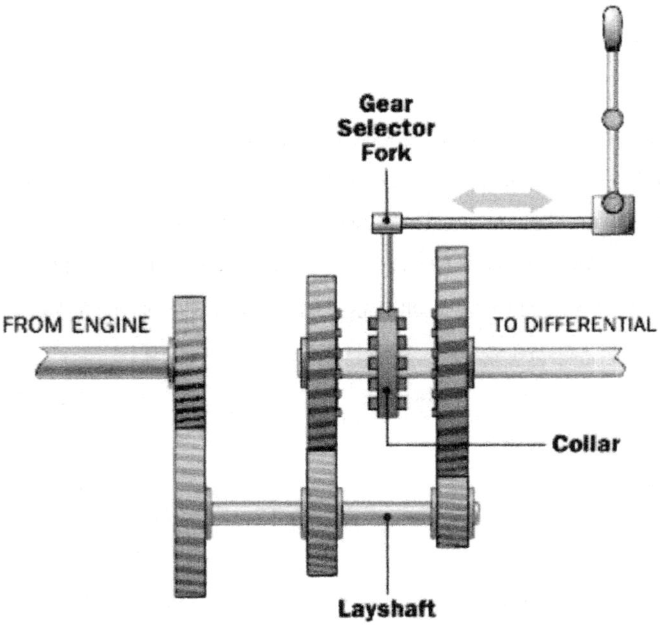

FROM THE CRANK SHAFT OF AN ENGINE TO A MANUAL TRANSMISSION YOU HAVE A FEW COMPONENTS. THESE COMPONENTS ARE A FLY WHEEL, PRESSURE PLATE, THROUGHOUT BEARING, AND ONE CLUTCH THAT PROVIDES SPRING AND FRICTION BETWEEN THE FLY WHEEL, AND THE PRESSURE PLATE. WITH A MANUAL TRANSMISSION, A "CLUTCH KIT" WILL INCLUDE MANY OF THESE COMPONENTS.

NOTE: *IN A MANUAL TRANSMISSION, THE "CLUTCH KIT" WILL BE THE ONE COMPONENT THAT WILL NEED TO BE REPLACED EVERY SO OFTEN DUE TO WEAR.*

AUTO TRANS

THE AUTOMATIC TRANSMISSION IS A SYSTEM OF LEVERAGES, HYDRAULIC TRANSFERS, AND GEAR TRANSFERS. AS YOU KNOW, ALL THE ENGINE DOES IS GET YOUR CRANKSHAFT TO SPIN. BUT THE ENGINES CRANKSHAFT WILL ONLY SPIN SO FAST. AS YOUR CAR GETS UP TO SPEED, THE TRANSMISSION VALVE BODY WILL "SHIFT GEARS" TO MAKE THE WHEELS SPIN FASTER AS YOUR ENGINE WILL SPIN SLOWER. AS THE VEHICLE PICKS UP MORE SPEED, THE TRANSMISSION WILL GO THROUGH A SIMILAR PROCESS TO "SHIFT GEARS" AGAIN, THUS MAKING THE CAR GO FASTER AND FASTER. THE MAJOR TRANSMISSION COMPONENTS ARE: VALVE BODY, CLUTCH PACKS, BANDS, AND TRANSFER GEARS. THESE COMPONENTS ALONE CAN BE VERY COMPLEX. HOW COMPLEX THEY CAN BE? THE NEXT PAGE IS A PARTIAL EXPLODED VIEW OF AN AUTOMATIC TRANSMISSION.

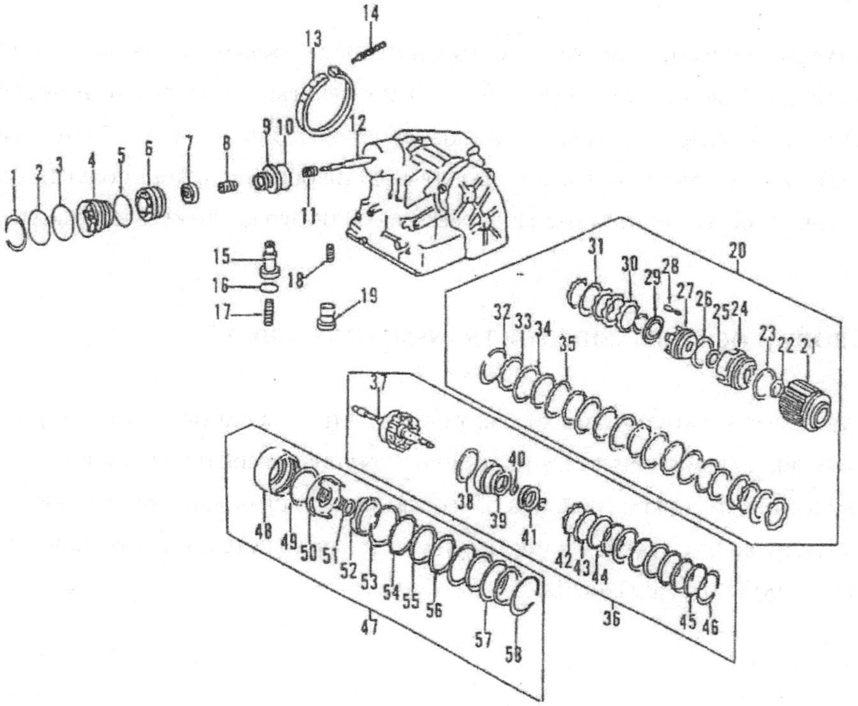

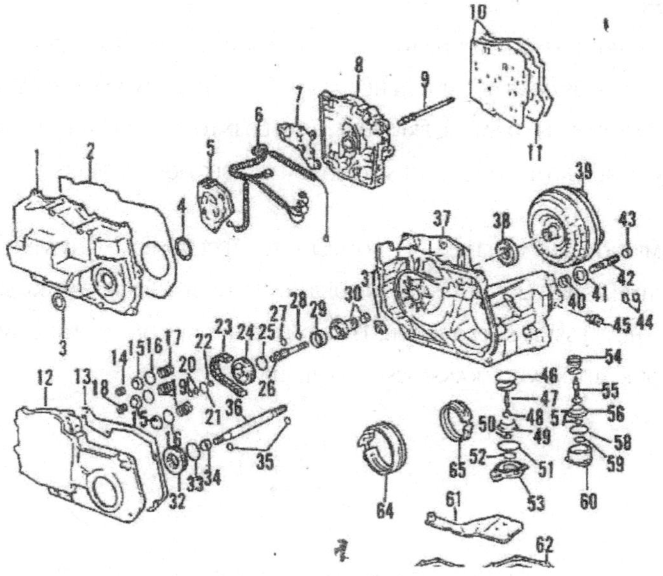

TORQUE CONVERTER

THIS IS A TYPE OF **FLUID COUPLING**, WHICH ALLOWS THE ENGINE TO SPIN SOMEWHAT INDEPENDENTLY OF THE TRANSMISSION. THE TORQUE CONVERTER IS ONE OF THE FIRST PARTS ATTACHED TO YOUR ENGINES END AND THE FIRST COMPONENT IN YOUR AUTOMATIC TRANSMISSION. IF THE ENGINE IS AT A LOW IDLING OR TURNING SLOWLY, THE AMOUNT OF ENERGY THAT IS PASSED THROUGH THE TORQUE CONVERTER IS MINIMAL. THIS MEANS YOU ONLY NEED A LIGHT PRESSURE ON THE BRAKES TO KEEP THE CAR AT A STOP.

VALVE BODY (LOCATED INSIDE THE TRANSMISSION BODY)

THE VALVE BODY IS A PLATE THAT HAS AN ARRAY OF VALVES (ELECTRICAL OR MECHANICAL) THAT DISTRIBUTES THE TRANSMISSIONS FLUIDS TO PRESET DESTINATIONS INSIDE THE TRANSMISSION TO ALLOW THE TRANSMISSIONS TO "SHIFT GEARS". THIS COMPONENT HELPS EXCHANGE THE TRANSMISSIONS FLUID INTO A LUBE STATE, HYDRAULIC STATE, OR A FRICTION STATE. IT BASICALLY UNLOCKS THE UNIQUE PROPERTIES OF THE FLUID THAT IT ALREADY INHIBITS.

CLUTCH PACKS & BANDS

THE BANDS IN A TRANSMISSION ARE, LITERALLY, STEEL BANDS THAT WRAP AROUND SECTIONS OF THE GEARS AND CONNECT TO THE TRANSMISSIONS HOUSING. THEY ARE ACTUATED BY HYDRAULIC CYLINDERS INSIDE THE CASE OF THE TRANSMISSION. HYDRAULIC PRESSURE, ROUTED INTO THE CYLINDER BY THE VALVE BODY, CAUSES THE PISTONS TO PUSH ON THE BANDS, THUS LOCKING THAT SECTION OF GEARS.

THE CLUTCHES IN THE TRANSMISSION ARE A LITTLE MORE COMPLEX. EACH CLUTCH IS ACTIVATED BY PRESSURIZED HYDRAULIC FLUID THAT ENTERS A PASSAGE INSIDE THE CLUTCHES. SPRINGS MAKE SURE THAT THE CLUTCH RELEASES WHEN THE PRESSURES IS LOWERED. THESE CLUTCHES ARE ONE OF THE COMPONENTS THAT ARE REPLACED WHEN YOUR AUTOMATIC TRANSMISSION IS REBUILT.

TRANSFER GEARS

GEARS ARE USED IN AN ARRAY OF AUTOMOTIVE COMPONENTS (WINDOWS, STEERING, ETC). THEY DO MANY IMPORTANT JOBS IN YOUR VEHICLE. BUT THEIR REAL FUNCTION IS VERY IMPORTANT! THEY PROVIDE A GEAR REDUCTION IN EQUIPMENT. WHAT IS GEAR REDUCTION? TO ANSWER YOUR QUESTION, IMAGINE A SMALL MOTOR SPINNING VERY FAST. THE MOTOR CAN PROVIDE ENOUGH POWER FOR A DEVICE, BUT NOT ENOUGH SPIN. GEAR REDUCTION PROVIDES THAT SPIN! A GOOD EXAMPLE WOULD BE AN ELECTRIC SCREWDRIVER. THEY HAVE A VERY LARGE GEAR REDUCTION BECAUSE IT NEEDS LOTS OF SPIN TO TURN SCREWS, BUT THE

MOTOR ONLY PRODUCES A SMALL AMOUNT OF SPIN AT A HIGH SPEED. WITH GEAR REDUCTION, THE OUTPUT SPEED CAN BE REDUCED WHILE THE TORQUE IS INCREASED.

THE PLANETARY GEAR SET OR THE TRANSFER GEARS ARE THE DEVICES THAT MAKES THIS POSSIBLE IN AN AUTOMATIC TRANSMISSION. AN AUTOMATIC TRANSMISSION COULD CONTAIN TWO COMPLETE PLANETARY GEAR SETS FOLDED TOGETHER INTO ONE COMPONENT FOR MORE EFFICIENCY.

Planetary gears from an automatic transmission

WITHOUT TRANSMISSION GEARS, YOUR CAR WOULD BE LIMITED TO ONE GEAR RATIO, AND THAT RATIO WOULD HAVE TO BE SELECTED TO ALLOW THE CAR TO TRAVEL AT THE DESIRED TOP SPEED. IF YOU WANTED A TOP SPEED OF 90 MPH, THEN THE GEAR RATIO WOULD BE CLOSE TO FOURTH GEAR IN MOST MANUAL TRANSMISSION. IF YOU HAVE EVER DRIVEN A MANUAL TRANSMISSION, YOU KNOW YOU WILL HAVE SOME ISSUES STARTING THE CAR OFF IN THIRD OR FOURTH GEAR!!

TRANSMISSION FLUID

AUTOMATIC TRANSMISSION FLUID SERVES A MULTITUDE OF PURPOSES. AMONG OTHER THINGS, IT CLEANS, COOLS, LUBRICATES, TRANSMITS FORCE, TRANSMITS PRESSURE, INHIBITS VARNISH BUILD-UP, PROTECTS THE TRANSMISSION ON A DAY-TO-DAY BASIS AND CAN EXPAND TEN TIMES (10X) ITS MASS WHEN HOT. AUTOMATIC TRANSMISSION FLUID IS SPECIALLY FORMULATED OIL CONTAINING NUMEROUS ADDITIVES TO WITHSTAND GRUELING OPERATING CONDITIONS. THERE ARE SEVERAL DIFFERENT TYPES OF AUTOMATIC TRANSMISSION FLUIDS AND SHOULD BE USED ACCORDING TO THE RECOMMENDATION IN YOUR CAR'S OWNER'S MANUAL. SOME EXAMPLES INCLUDE:

- DEXRON® III/MERCON® - RECOMMENDED FOR ALL AUTOMATIC TRANSMISSIONS REQUIRING DEXRON® III, DEXRON® IIE, DEXRON® II, DEXRON® OR MERCON ® TRANSMISSION FLUIDS. IT CAN ALSO BE USED WHERE FLUIDS MEETING FORD ESP-M2C138CJ OR FORD M2C166-H SPECIFICATIONS ARE REQUIRED.
- ATF+3 FORMULATED EXCLUSIVELY FOR CHRYSLER CORP. AUTOMATIC TRANSMISSIONS/TRANSAXLES WHERE A CHRYSLER MS-7176, MOPAR® OR MOPAR ATF+3® IS SPECIFIED.
- TYPE F (FLM) IS A SPECIALLY COMPOUNDED FLUID MEETING THE LATEST FORD ESW-M2C33F AND IS COMPATIBLE WITH ALL M2C33 SERIES FORD SPECIFICATIONS. IN ALL 1983 AND LATER MODEL FORD AUTOMATIC TRANSMISSIONS USE DEXRON ® III/MERCON ® OR MERCON ® V AUTOMATIC TRANSMISSION FLUIDS.

MAINTENANCE TIPS/SUGGESTIONS: OWNER'S MANUAL RECOMMENDATIONS ON TRANSMISSION FLUID CHANGES VARY CONSIDERABLY AND MAY GO AS HIGH AS 100,000 MILES OR MORE. FOR BEST RESULTS, HAVE YOUR CAR'S TRANSMISSION FLUID CHANGED ABOUT 5 TO 10,000 MILES BEFORE THE MANUFACTURER RECOMMEND THE SERVICE. BY DOING THIS IT WILL HELP WITH THE LIFE SPAN OF THE TRANSMISSION. ALWAYS USE THE TYPE OF FLUID SPECIFIED BY YOUR CAR'S MANUFACTURER. THIS INFORMATION CAN BE FOUND IN THE OWNER'S MANUAL OR ON THE END OF THE TRANSMISSION DIPSTICK (IF YOU'RE CAR HAS ONE!!). THE MAJORITY OF TRANSMISSION FAILURES ARE HEAT-RELATED AND AUTOMATIC TRANSMISSION FLUID BREAKS DOWN RAPIDLY WHEN SUBJECTED TO HIGH TEMPERATURES. DRIVING CONDITIONS SUCH AS TOWING, QUICK STOPS AND STARTS, MOUNTAIN DRIVING, AND WHEEL-SPINNING IN SLIPPERY CONDITIONS ARE BUT A FEW SCENARIOS THAT CAN DEVASTATE THE LIFE OF THE TRANSMISSION.

TO AVOID MAJOR TRANSMISSION FAILURES,

I recommend: a transmission fluid flush (NOT A FILTER CHANGE & FLUID TOP OFF!!) a few thousand miles before the manufacturer's recommendation. This is the best way to take care of the system.

CHAPTER 10

BRAKING SYSTEMS

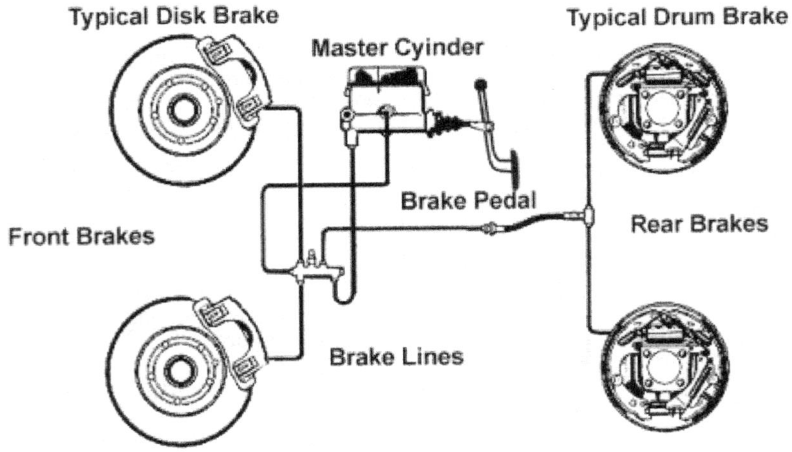

Typical Automotive Braking System

BRAKES

I always say that it's fine and great if a car starts and runs, but if a car doesn't stop, then there's a problem. To me brakes are the most important system on a vehicle. The brakes have over 2,000 working components, but don't make them out to be more complex than what they are. Actually, you have four (4) major working systems that make up your brakes. The first is the one that is most commonly heard of -the friction materials. The Friction materials would make up such parts as rotors, pads, shoes, etc. The second would be your hydraulics - Master cylinder, calipers, hoses, wheel cylinder, etc. The third would be your power assisted boost- brake booster, hydro boost, or a none assisted braking system. The last systems would be the car's ABS.

FRICTION MATERIALS

The pads, rotors or shoes, and the drums wear into each other. Imagine that the rotor is a record. As the record spins, if you put your fingers on that record, it will stop. It's the same concept with rotors and pads. As your rotors spin with the wheels, the pads go over both sides of the rotor, clasping on when you apply the brakes, thus stopping the car. Your shoes work in a similar way, but they push into the drums. All of those parts will wear out and will need to be replaced at some point in time.

HYDRAULICS

HYDRAULICS ARE ONE OF THE BEST WAYS TO PRODUCE MASSIVE AMOUNTS OF PRESSURE. HYDRAULICS CAN ALSO HELP MOVE OR STOP MASSIVE AMOUNTS OF WEIGHTS.

THE BASIC IDEA BEHIND ANY HYDRAULIC SYSTEM IS VERY SIMPLE. IT WORKS LIKE THIS: FORCE THAT IS APPLIED AT ONE POINT IS TRANSMITTED TO ANOTHER POINT USING AN INCOMPRESSIBLE FLUID. THE FLUID IS ALMOST ALWAYS AN OIL OF SOME SORT DUE TO ITS UNIQUE PROPERTIES. THE FORCE IS ALMOST ALWAYS MULTIPLIED IN THE PROCESS. THE PICTURE BELOW SHOWS A SIMPLE HYDRAULIC SYSTEM:

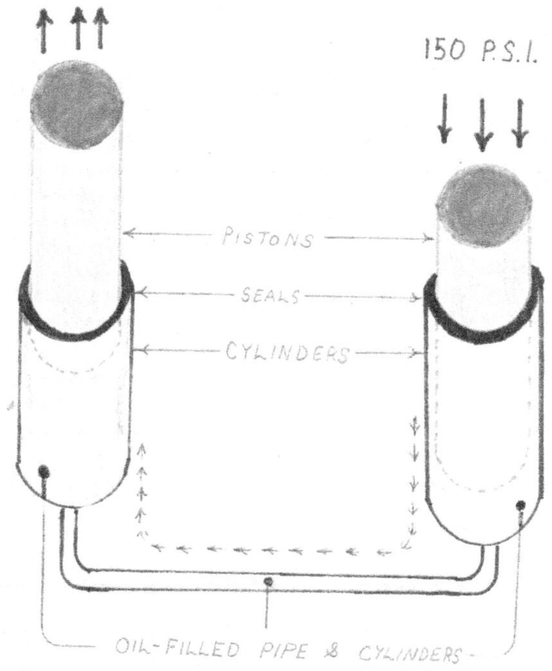

IN THIS DRAWING, TWO PISTONS FIT INTO TWO CYLINDERS. THESE CYLINDERS ARE FILLED WITH OIL AND CONNECTED TO ONE ANOTHER WITH AN OIL-FILLED PIPE. IF YOU APPLY A DOWNWARD FORCE TO ONE PISTON, (THE RIGHT ONE IN THIS DRAWING) THEN THE FORCE IS TRANSMITTED TO THE SECOND PISTON THROUGH THE OIL, IN THE OIL FILLED PIPE. SINCE OIL IS INCOMPRESSIBLE, ALMOST ALL OF THE APPLIED FORCE APPEARS AT THE SECOND PISTON. THE GREAT THING ABOUT HYDRAULIC SYSTEMS IS THAT THE PIPE CONNECTING THE TWO CYLINDERS CAN BE ANY LENGTH AND SHAPE, ALLOWING IT TO PASS THROUGH ALL SORTS OF VALVES AND PASSAGES SEPARATING THE TWO PISTONS. THE LINE CAN ALSO SPLIT, SO THAT ONE

"**MASTER CYLINDER**" CAN DRIVE MORE THAN ONE "**SLAVE CYLINDER**" IF DESIRED.

THE NEAT THING ABOUT HYDRAULIC SYSTEMS IS THAT IT IS VERY EASY TO ADD FORCE MULTIPLICATION (OR DIVISION) TO THE SYSTEM. **TRADING FORCE FOR DISTANCE** IS VERY COMMON IN MECHANICAL SYSTEMS. IN A HYDRAULIC SYSTEM, ALL YOU DO IS CHANGE THE SIZE OF ONE PISTON AND CYLINDER RELATIVE TO THE OTHER.

NOTE: IT IS IMPORTANT THAT A HYDRAULIC SYSTEM CONTAINS NO AIR BUBBLES. YOU MAY HAVE HEARD ABOUT THE NEED TO "BLEED THE BRAKES" ON YOUR CAR. IF THERE IS AN AIR BUBBLE IN THE SYSTEM, THEN THE FORCE APPLIED TO THE FIRST PISTON GETS USED COMPRESSING THE AIR IN THE BUBBLE RATHER THAN MOVING THE SECOND PISTON, WHICH HAS A BIG EFFECT ON THE EFFICIENCY OF THE SYSTEM.

YOU HAVE FIVE (5) MAJOR UNITS TO AN AUTOMOTIVE BRAKING HYDRAULIC SYSTEM: YOUR MASTER CYLINDER (THE HEART OF THE BRAKING SYSTEM), TWO (2) CALIPERS IN THE FRONT AND TWO (2) CYLINDERS (REAR DRUM) OR CALIPERS IN THE BACK (REAR DISK). AS YOU PUT YOUR FOOT ON THE BRAKE PEDAL, IT PUSHES A SHAFT INTO THE MASTER CYLINDER, CAUSING THE BRAKE FLUID TO PUSH THROUGH THE LINES, COLLAPSING AND EXPANDING THE CALIPER/WHEEL CYLINDERS, THUS CAUSING THE PADS/SHOES TO CLASP/EXPAND ONTO OR INTO THE ROTORS/DRUMS. TAKE A GOOD LOOK AT THE NEXT PAGE TO GET AN IDEA OF WHAT I AM TALKING ABOUT.

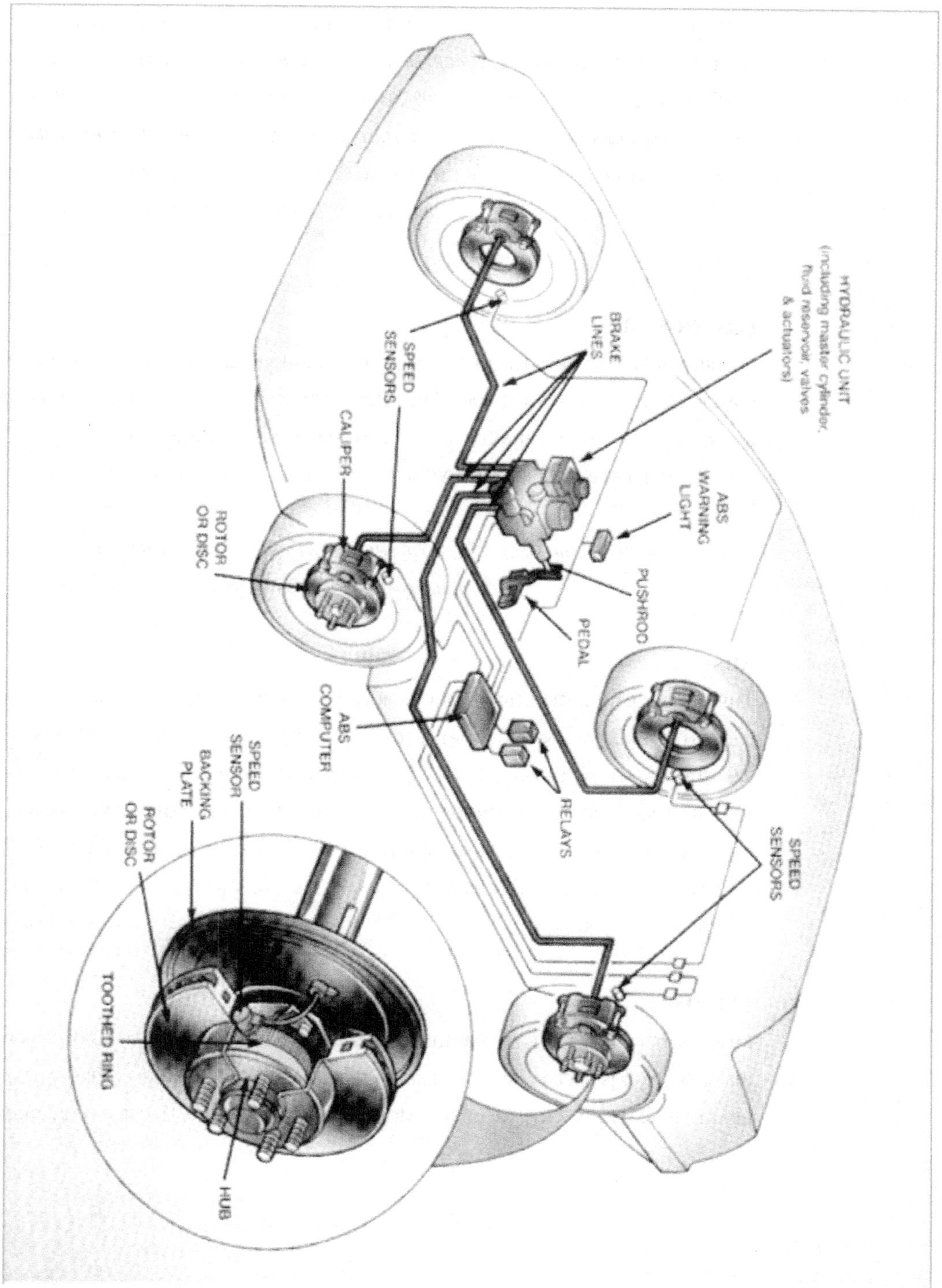
HYDRAULIC UNIT
(including master cylinder,
fluid reservoir, valves
& actuators)
ABS
WARNING
LIGHT
BRAKE
LINES
SPEED
SENSORS
PUSHROD
CALIPER
ROTOR
OR DISC
PEDAL
ABS
COMPUTER
RELAYS
SPEED
SENSORS
SPEED
SENSOR
BACKING
PLATE
ROTOR
OR DISC
TOOTHED RING
HUB

***NOTE:** YOUR VEHICLES FRONT BRAKES DO AN AVERAGE OF 75% (SOME VEHICLES DO 60%, VARYING FROM MANUFACTURER TO MANUFACTURER) OF YOUR BRAKING. THE REAR BRAKES DO AN AVERAGE OF 25% (SOME OTHER VEHICLES DO AN AVERAGE OF 40%, VARYING FROM MANUFACTURER TO MANUFACTURER); IF THE REAR IS HAVING PROBLEMS OR OUT OF ADJUSTMENT, IT IS POSSIBLE THAT YOU WILL PREMATURELY WEAR ON THE FRONT BRAKES. TAKE CARE OF YOUR DRUM BRAKING SYSTEMS, WITH ADJUSTMENTS AND LUBRICATION TO THE REAR SHOES EVERY 15,000- 30,000 MILES.*

POWER ASSIST

POWER ASSIST IS TO HELP THE DRIVER USE THE HYDRAULIC BRAKES EASILY. THERE ARE TWO (2) TYPES OF POWER ASSIST. THE VACUUM BOOSTER: THIS PART USES THE ENGINE'S VACUUM TO HELP PRESSURIZE THE HYDRAULIC PART OF THE BRAKING SYSTEM. HYDRO BOOST: THIS PART USES THE CAR'S POWER STEERING SYSTEM TO HELP PRESSURIZE THE HYDRAULIC PARTS OF THE BRAKING SYSTEM.

***NOTE**: MODERN VEHICLES HAVE ONE OF THESE SYSTEMS. IF ONE OF THESE SYSTEMS FAILS, THE BRAKE PEDAL WILL BE HARD AND THE VEHICLE WILL BE HARD TO STOP.*

ABS

THE ANTILOCK BRAKE SYSTEM IS INCORPORATED INTO THE BRAKE HYDRAULIC SYSTEM. IT IS COMPLEX IN ITS NATURE AND HAS AN ARRAY OF SENSORS TO MONITOR THE VEHICLES SPEED, BRAKE HYDRAULIC PRESSURES, AND WHEEL SKID. ALL OF THIS INFORMATION IS RELATED BACK TO A COMPUTER TO HELP WITH TRANSMISSION SHIFT, GAS ECONOMY, AND MOST IMPORTANTLY, TO HELP THE VEHICLE FROM GOING INTO A SKID WHILE UNDER BRAKING, THUS GIVING THE DRIVER MORE CONTROL. WHEN BRAKING, THE ABS SYSTEM WILL PULSE THE BRAKES IN A RHYTHM SO THAT YOUR CAR'S WHEELS WON'T "LOCK UP". THIS WILL HELP TO AVOID A BRAKING SKID.

FLUIDS

MOST MODERN DAY VEHICLES BRAKING SYSTEMS USE EITHER A DOT 3 OR A DOT 5 BRAKE FLUID. DOT 5 IS OIL BASED AND IS USED ON MOST GERMAN VEHICLES. DOT 3 IS A MORE ENVIRONMENTALLY FRIENDLY BRAKE FLUID (IT IS WATER SOLUBLE). MOST MODERN DAY VEHICLES USE A DOT 3 BRAKE FLUID.

BRAKE FLUID MAINTENANCE

Not many manufacturers will recognize a brake fluid flush as maintenance. It should be changed about once every 2-3 years or 20,000 – 30,000 miles, depending on your driving. By doing this, it ensures moisture stays out and helps hydraulic units from failing.

WHEEL BEARINGS

Your bearings are what your vehicle rolls on, just like roller skates. Some bearings are serviceable (repack the bearings), most modern bearings are sealed, non-serviceable, and many have ABS components incorporated into them. If a wheel bearing is starting to fail, you could hear a rolling noise while driving and could cause potential failures with other components and systems, including ABS sensors, suspension, brakes, axles, and uneven tire wear.

CHAPTER 11

SUSPENSION

SUSPENSION

THE SUSPENSION PLAYS A CRUTIAL ROLE IN HOW YOUR VEHICLE RIDES, HANDLES, AND OPERATES. THE SUSPENSION IS BASICALLY A SYSTEM OF SPRINGS AND SHOCK ABSORBERS ON A VEHICLE THAT REDUCES THE IMPACT OF BUMPS AND UNEVEN RUNNING SURFACES ON THE OCCUPANTS AND GIVES THE WHEELS BETTER CONTACT TO THE ROAD. DEPENDING ON DESIGN AND AGE OF THE VEHICLE MAKES THE DIFFERENCE BETWEEN YOUR VEHICLE RIDING LIKE A TANK, HIGH PERFORMANCE PIECE OF EQUIPMENT, OR A SOFT BLANKET RIDING IN THE CLOUDS. THE SUSPENSION IS CONSISTED OF THREE SYSTEMS. THE FIRST WOULD BE YOUR TIRES; THE SECOND WOULD BE THE STEERING AND RIDE CONTROL.

THE NEXT PAGE SHOWS AN EXPOSED VIEW OF CRUCIAL SUSPENSION COMPONENTS. AS YOU CAN SEE ON THE DISPLAYED VEHICLE, THE SUSPENSION LOOKS WELL BALANCED. THIS IS TRUE ON ANY VEHICLE.

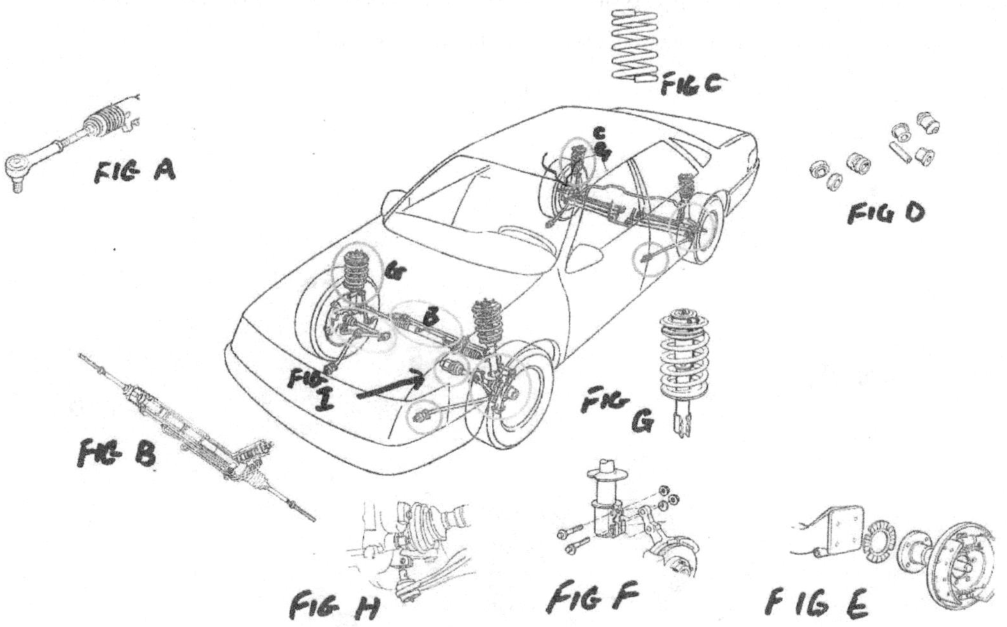

FIG **A**: OUTTER TIE ROD END FIG **B**: RACK & PINION UNIT FIG **C**: SPRING FIG **D**: BUSHINGS FIG **E**: A HUB ASSEMBLY AND BEARING UNIT FIG **F**: STRUT BOLTS UPPER HUB ASSEMBLY FIG **G**: STRUT ASSEMBLY FIG **H**: LOWER HUB AND BALL JOINT CONNECTION FIG **I**: C.V. AXLE

STEERING

THE STEERING CONSISTS OF LINKAGES, RACK & PINION OR STEERING GEAR, BUSHINGS, AND PIVOT POINTS. THE STEERING STARTS AT YOUR STEERING WHEEL AND ENDS AT A PLACE (OR STEERING KNUCKLE/ SPINDLE) CLOSE TO YOUR TIRES. AS YOU TURN THE WHEEL THERE IS A SHAFT THAT IS ATTACHED TO A LINKAGE THAT IS CONNECTED TO A GEAR BOX OR A RACK & PINION. THE GEAR BOX OR RACK IN PINION WILL ALLOW FOR EASY GEAR TRANSFER GIVING THE DRIVER LEVERAGE FOR EASY STEERING. THE RACK & PINION/GEARBOX IS CONNECTED TO A PIVOT POINT BY THE WHEEL

BASICALLY, YOU MANUALLY TURN THE WHEEL AND IT IS CONNECTED ELECTRICALLY OR MECHANICALLY TO A STEERING BOX OR RACK & PINION THAT SITS UPON PIVOT POINTS. THE BUSHINGS AND LINKAGES ATTACH TO THE VEHICLE'S FRAME OR LOWER BODY, TO ALLOW FOR VERTICAL TIRE TRAVEL.

AS SHOWN IN FIGURE B., THE RACK & PINION HAS A SHAFT ON THE TOP AND TWO SOCKETS ON EACH END KNOWN AS THE INNER TIE ROD ENDS. WHEN YOU TURN THE STEERING WHEEL, IT WILL ROTATE THE SHAFT LEFT AND RIGHT. THE GEAR IN THE MECHANISM PUSHES THESE SOCKETS (INNER TIE RODS) IN AND OUT OF THE HOUSING.

FIGURE A. SHOWS WHAT WOULD BE CONSIDERED AN OUTER TIE ROD END. THE OUTER TIE ROD END IS ATTACHED TO BOTH ENDS OF THE RACK & PINION, AS SHOWN IN FIGURE B.

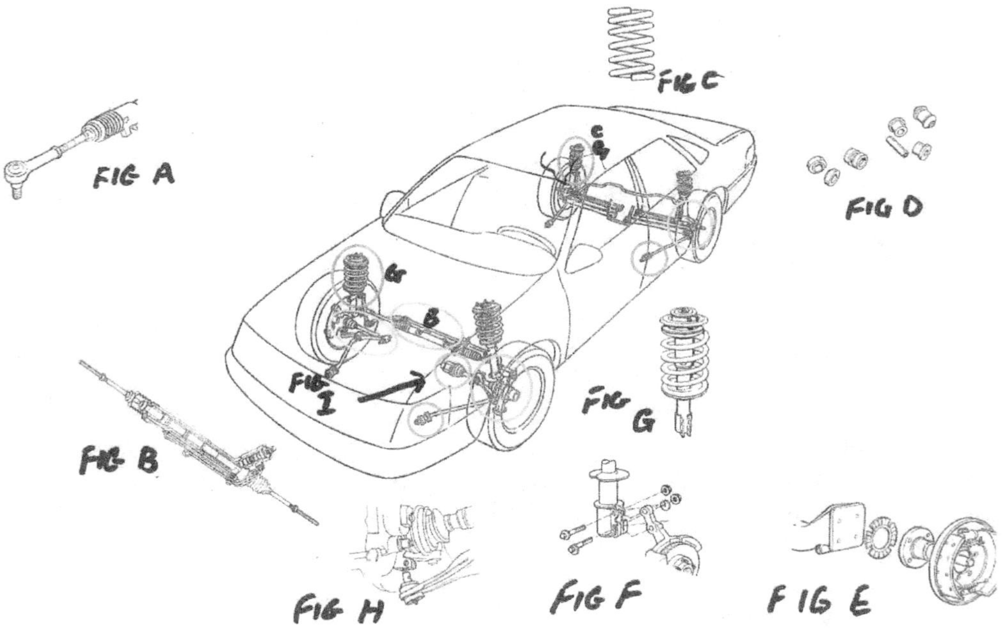

FIG **A**: OUTTER TIE ROD END FIG **B**: RACK & PINION UNIT FIG **C**: SPRING FIG **D**: BUSHINGS FIG **E**: A HUB ASSEMBLY AND BEARING UNIT FIG **F**: STRUT BOLTS UPPER HUB ASSEMBLY FIG **G**: STRUT ASSEMBLY FIG **H**: LOWER HUB AND BALL JOINT CONNECTION FIG **I**: A C.V. AXLE

POWER STEERING

YOUR VEHICLES POWER STEERING UNIT IS NOT THAT COMPLICATED. IT BASICALLY CONSISTS OF A PUMP, AND A FEW LINES THAT ATTACH TO YOUR RACK & PINION OR YOUR STEERING BOX. THIS UNIT HELPS THE DRIVER IN STEERING BECAUSE OF THE ADDED HYDRAULIC PRESSURE.

RIDE CONTROL

SPRINGS

MANY PEOPLE BELIEVE THAT IF YOU WERE TO REPLACE YOUR SHOCKS OR STRUTS THAT IT WILL BRING UP THE RIDE HEIGHT OF THE VEHICLE. THIS IS A BAD MISCONCEPTION. THE VEHICLE SPRINGS, SHOWN IN FIGURE C, AND CLOSE TO ALL FOUR WHEELS, ARE WHAT SUPPORT THE VEHICLE'S RIDE HEIGHT AND GIVE THE VEHICLE SUSPENSION ITS BOUNCE.

SHOCKS AND STRUTS

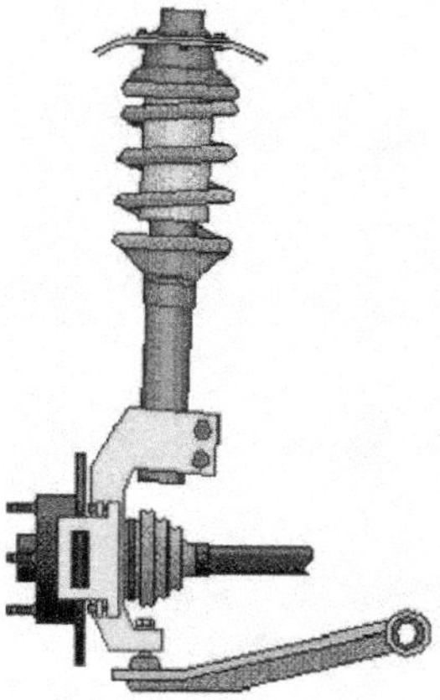

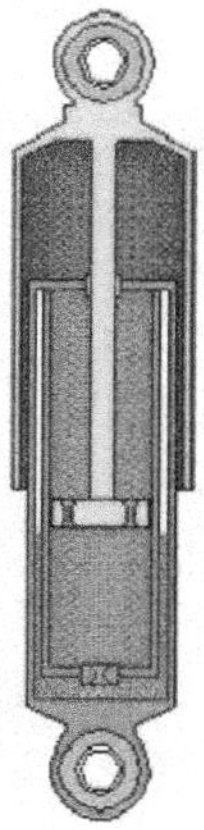

YOUR SHOCKS AND STRUTS ARE WHAT GIVE STABILITY TO THE CAR'S BOUNCE. AS YOUR VEHICLE'S GROSS WEIGHT IS BEING THROWN AROUND FROM THE FRONT TO THE REAR AND SIDE TO SIDE DUE TO BRAKING AND CORNERING, YOUR SPRINGS WILL COLLAPSE TO SOFTEN THE BLOW OF DISTRIBUTED WEIGHT. YOUR SHOCKS AND STRUTS ARE WHAT STABILIZE THE BOUNCE OF THE SPRING.

THIS SET UP IS ALSO DESIGNED TO KEEP YOUR TIRES PUSHED TO THE GROUND AT HIGH SPEEDS OR DURING BRAKING. YOUR SHOCKS, STRUTS, AND SPRINGS PLAY A CRUCIAL ROLE IN TIRE WEAR, PREMATURE BRAKE WEAR, PREMATURE SUSPENSION WEAR, AND VEHICLE HANDLING. IF YOUR CAR'S SHOCKS OR STRUTS ARE WEAK OR LEAKING DUE TO AGE, THEY WILL NOT SUPPORT THE VEHICLE UP PROPERLY, OVER USE OTHER SUSPENSION COMPONENTS AND NOT KEEP THE TIRES LOCATED WHERE THEY SHOULD BE.

LET'S SAY THESE STRUTS ARE WEAK ON YOUR VEHICLE AND YOU GO INTO A PANIC BRAKE. YOUR VEHICLE WILL NOSE DIVE DUE TO A WEAK SUSPENSION. THIS OVERHEATS YOUR BRAKES, CAUSING THEM NOT TO STOP

PROPERLY AND YOUR REAR TIRES WILL NOT KEEP IN FULL CONTACT WITH THE ROAD. THIS SCENARIO CAN EASILY BECOME A CATASTROPHE.

***NOTE: SOME CARS WILL TAKE STRUTS, SOME OTHER CARS WILL TAKE SHOCKS, AND SOME MAY TAKE BOTH. SHOCKS AND STRUTS ARE RECOMMENDED TO START BEING REPLACED AT 60,000 MILES. I TRY TO TAKE A LITTLE MORE REALISTIC APPROACH TO THIS. I RECOMMEND HAVING THEM REPLACED AT 75,000 TO 85,000 MILES AS LONG AS THEY ARE NOT LEAKING BEFORE THEN.**

CV JOINTS AND AXLES

YOUR CV (CONSTANT VELOCITY) JOINTS ARE BASICALLY PROPELLER SHAFTS. THEY ARE WHAT PROPEL THE TIRES IN THEIR SPIN MOTION. THESE CAN BE A STRAIGHT AXLE OR A SHAFT WITH JOINTS AT EACH END ALLOWING IT TO BE FLEXIBLE. THERE WILL BE A MINIMUM OF AT LEAST TWO AXLES FOR A VEHICLE. ON A REAR WHEEL DRIVE CAR, MOST OF THE TIME, THE AXLES WILL BE A SOLID AXLE AND WILL LEAD FROM THE DIFFERENTIAL TO THE WHEEL. ON A FRONT WHEEL DRIVE VEHICLE, THEY ARE GENERALLY CV JOINTS LEADING FROM THE TRANSMISSION TO THE HUB ASSEMBLY/WHEEL.

CHAPTER 12

TIRES & WHEEL ALIGNMENTS

WHEEL ALIGNMENTS

A WHEEL ALIGNMENT ADJUSTS THE ANGLES OF THE WHEELS SO THAT THEY ARE POSITIONED CORRECTLY RELATIVE TO THE VEHICLE'S FRAME. THIS ADJUSTMENT **MAXIMIZES THE LIFE OF YOUR TIRES** AND PREVENTS YOUR CAR FROM VEERING TO THE RIGHT OR LEFT WHEN DRIVING ON A STRAIGHT, LEVEL ROAD. THESE ADJUSTMENTS REQUIRE SPECIAL EQUIPMENT AND **SHOULD BE PERFORMED BY A QUALIFIED TECHNICIAN.** THE BEST TIME TO DO AN ALIGNMENT IS AFTER YOU HAVE HAD ANY SUSPENSION COMPONENTS CHANGED, OR NEW TIRES HAVE BEEN INSTALLED.

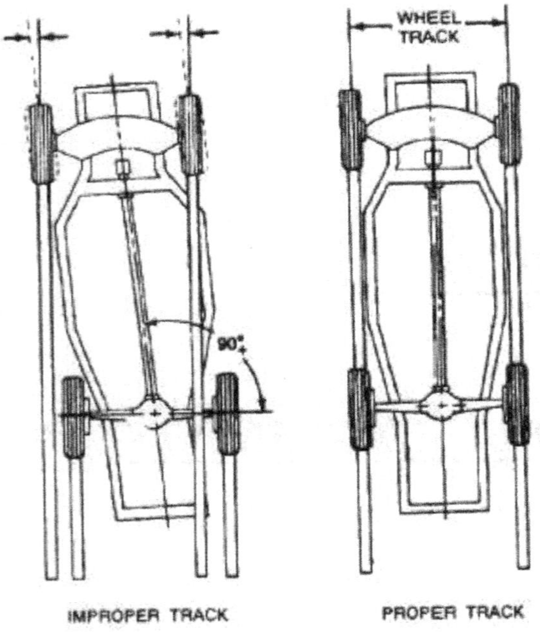

REAR WHEELS MUST TRACK CORRECTLY

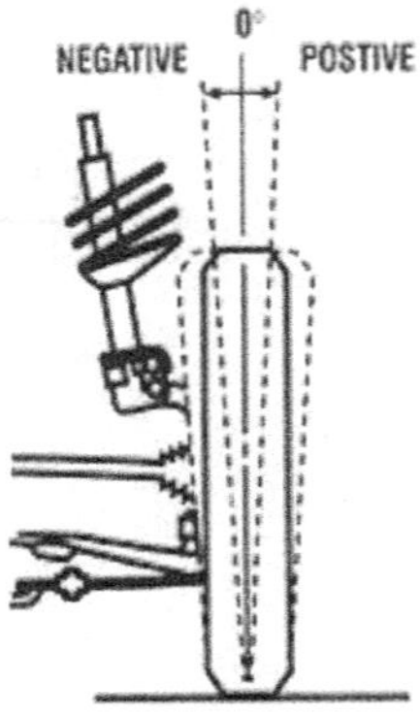

CAMBER ADJUSTMENT

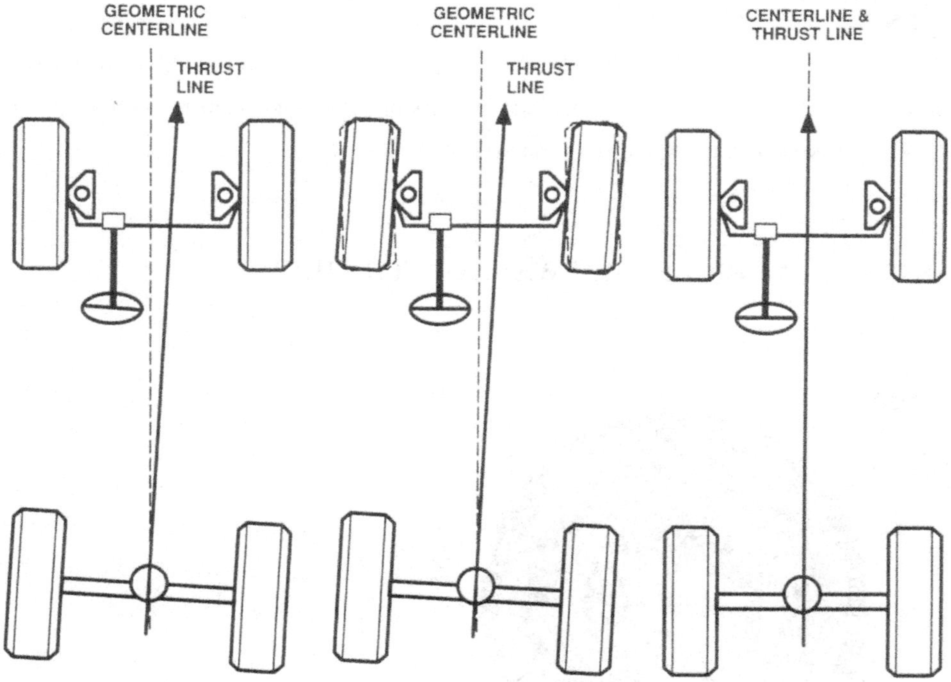

Geometric Centerline Alignment
Toe on each front wheel is measured and adjusted using the geometric centerline of the vehicle as a reference.

Geometric centerline alignment has been used for many years and may provide a satisfactory alignment if the rear wheels are positioned squarely with the geometric centerline of the vehicle.

However, if the vehicle's rear wheels (either solid axle or independent suspension) create a thrust line that is not parallel to the geometric centerline, the front end steering geometry will be off center and the steering wheel will be cocked as the vehicle moves in a straight direction.

Thrust Line Alignment
Aligning the front wheels to the vehicle's thrust line is a significant improvement over aligning to the geometric centerline.

In the thrust line method, rear individual toe is measured (but not adjusted). The thrust line created by the rear wheels is used as a reference for aligning the front wheels.

As a result, the operator is assured of a straight steering wheel as the vehicle moves straight ahead.

Total Four–Wheel Alignment
Total four–wheel alignment is the ultimate wheel alignment service. Individual rear toe is measured, then adjusted to the factory specifications. This adjustment brings the thrust line of the rear wheels parallel to the vehicle's geometric centerline.

The front wheels are then aligned to the rear wheel thrust line.

Total four–wheel alignment results in all four wheels being parallel and the steering geometry being centered as the vehicle moves in a straight line.

10

TIRES

Tires can be confusing, if you make them out to be confusing. Most of what you really need to understand about tires are written right on the side of the tire. Here is a little info to help you understand all you should need to know about tires.

PASSENGER VEHICLE - SIDEWALL OUTER CIRCLE

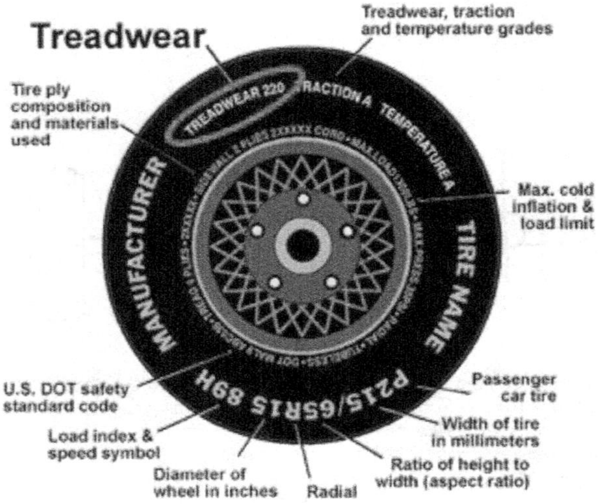

P

The "P" indicates the tire is for passenger vehicles.

Nominal Width

This three-digit number gives the width in millimeters of the tire from sidewall edge to sidewall edge. In general, the larger the number, the wider the tire.

Aspect Ratio

This two-digit number, known as the aspect ratio, gives the tire's ratio of height to width. Numbers of 70 or lower indicate a short sidewall for improved steering response and better overall handling on dry pavement.

R

The "R" stands for radial. Radial ply construction of tires has been the industry standard for the past 30 years.

Rim diameter code

This two-digit number is the wheel or rim diameter in inches. If you change your wheel size, you will have to purchase new tires to match the new wheel diameter.

Load index

This two- or three-digit number is the tire's load index. It is a measurement of how much weight each tire can support. You may find this information in your owner's manual. If not, contact a local tire dealer. Note: You may not find this information on all tires because it is not required by law.

Severe snow conditions

The "M+S" or "M/S" indicates that the tire has some mud and snow capability. Most radial tires have these markings; hence, they have some mud and snow capability.

Speed Rating

The speed rating denotes the speed at which a tire is designed to be driven for extended periods of time. The ratings range from 99 miles per hour (mph) to 186 mph. These ratings are listed below.

Note: You may not find this information on all tires because it is not required by law.

Q	99 mph	**H**	130 mph
R	106 mph	**V**	149 mph
S	112 mph	**W**	168 mph*
T	118 mph	**Y**	186 mph*
U	124 mph		

*For tires with a maximum speed capability over 149 mph, tire manufacturers sometimes use the letters ZR. For those with a maximum speed capability over 186 mph, tire manufacturers always use the letters ZR.

PASSENGER VEHICLE - SIDEWALL INNER CIRCLE

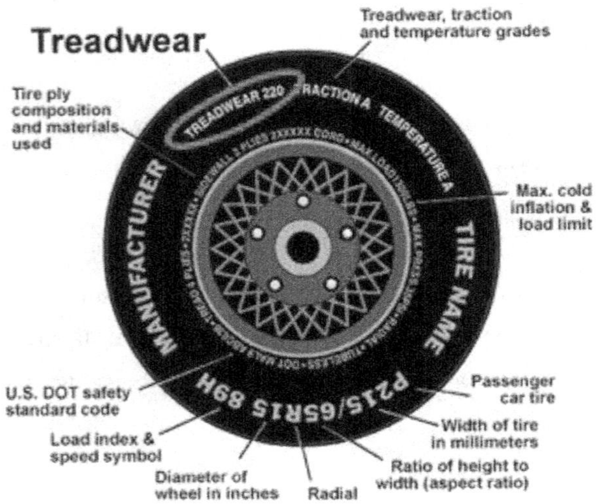

U.S. DOT Tire Identification Number

This begins with the letters "DOT" and indicates that the tire meets all federal standards. The next two numbers or letters are the plant code where it was manufactured, and the last four numbers represent the week and year the tire was built. For example, the numbers 3197 means the 31st week of 1997.

Tire Ply Composition and Materials Used

The number of plies indicates the number of layers of rubber-coated fabric in the tire. In general, the greater the number of plies, the more weight a tire can support. Tire manufacturers also must indicate the materials in the tire, which include steel, nylon, polyester, and others.

Maximum Load Rating

This number indicates the maximum load in kilograms or pounds that can be carried by the tire.

Maximum Permissible Inflation Pressure

This number is the greatest amount of air pressure that should ever be put in the tire under normal driving conditions

LIGHT TRUCKS - OTHER MARKINGS

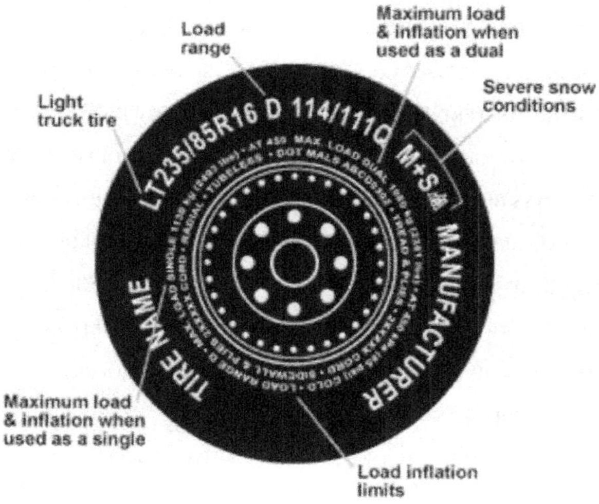

LT

THE "LT" INDICATES THE TIRE IS FOR LIGHT TRUCKS.

MAX. LOAD DUAL KG(LBS) AT KPA(PSI) COLD

THIS INFORMATION INDICATES THE MAXIMUM LOAD AND TIRE PRESSURE WHEN THE TIRE IS USED AS A DUAL, THAT IS, WHEN FOUR TIRES ARE PUT ON EACH REAR AXLE (A TOTAL OF SIX OR MORE TIRES ON THE VEHICLE).

MAX. LOAD SINGLE KG(LBS) AT KPA(PSI) COLD

THIS INFORMATION INDICATES THE MAXIMUM LOAD AND TIRE PRESSURE WHEN THE TIRE IS USED AS A SINGLE.

LOAD RANGE

THIS INFORMATION IDENTIFIES THE TIRE'S LOAD-CARRYING CAPABILITIES AND ITS INFLATION LIMITS.

*NOTE: TO **AVOID VIBRATIONS** OR SHAKING OF THE VEHICLE IT IS ESSENTIAL THAT THE TIRE IS PROPERLY BALANCED. THIS BALANCE IS ACHIEVED BY POSITIONING WEIGHTS ON THE WHEEL TO COUNTERBALANCE HEAVY SPOTS ON THE WHEEL-AND-TIRE ASSEMBLY.*

NITROGEN OR NOT

ONE NEW HOT ITEM THAT IS PART OF THE NEW AUTOMOTIVE TIRE INDUSTRY IS NITROGEN FILLED TIRES. WHEN THIS SERVICE FIRST CAME ABOUT, I THOUGHT THAT IT WAS A BOGUS SERVICE. I THOUGHT FACILITIES WERE SELLING SNAKE OIL OR WINTER AIR TO SUMMER AIR (FRIVOLOUS SERVICES) TO UNKNOWING CUSTOMERS. THE MORE THAT I RESEARCHED INTO NITROGEN, I DISCOVERED THAT THERE ARE DEFINITELY BENEFITS TO NITROGEN. THE AVIATION INDUSTRY HAS BEEN USING NITROGEN IN THEIR TIRES FOR YEARS. NITROGEN HAS THE ABILITY TO BE EXPOSED TO EXTREME TEMPERATURES, MINUS 30 DEGREES FAHRENHEIT TO A 130 DEGREES FAHRENHEIT, AND NOT BE AFFECTED BY THESE EXTREMES. THE KEY TO NITROGEN, AS OPPOSED TO REGULAR AIR, IS THAT NITROGEN ATOMS ARE LARGER THAN OXYGEN ATOMS. THEREFORE, THERE WILL BE FEWER LEAKS IN A TIRE. SO BASICALLY, IF YOUR TIRES CAN STAY AT THEIR PROPER INFLATION FOR A LONGER PERIOD OF TIME, THE TIRES WILL LAST LONGER.

NITROGEN WILL PROLONG THE LIFE OF THE TIRE, GIVE SAFER HANDLING, AND HELP WITH FUEL ECONOMY FOR THE VEHICLE.

2 TIRES AT A TIME?

NOTE: MANY PEOPLE THAT OWN A FRONT WHEEL DRIVE VEHICLE HAVE THE MENTALITY THAT WHEN THEY BUY TWO TIRES, THE LOGICAL THING TO DO IS HAVE THE NEW TIRES INSTALLED ON THE FRONT OF THE VEHICLE AND THEN HAVE THE BEST TWO TIRES PUT TO THE REAR OF THE VEHICLE. CONCLUSIVE STUDIES HAVE SHOWN THAT THIS IS FAR FROM THE TRUTH DUE TO THE MERE FACT THAT FRONT WHEEL DRIVE VEHICLE'S GROSS WEIGHT IS IN THE FRONT OF THE CAR. WHEN YOU PUT TIRES ON THE REAR OF A FRONT WHEEL DRIVE VEHICLE, YOU ARE MORE PRONE TO GO INTO A HIGH SPEED SPIN BECAUSE OF THE LACK OF TREAD ON THE REAR TIRES, USUALLY INDUCING AN ACCIDENT.

CHAPTER 13

HYBRID TECHNOLOGY

THE TECHNOLOGY BEHIND HYBRIDS

HYBRIDS ARE ONE OF THE MOST ADVANCED CARS ON THE MARKET TODAY. THEY COMBINE EXCEPTIONAL FUEL ECONOMY WITH NEAR-ZERO EMISSIONS.

HYBRIDS USE BOTH STAGNETIC AND KINETIC ENERGY TO POWER AND RECHARGE THEIR ELECTRICAL SYSTEMS. HYBRID SYSTEMS BASICALLY EXPLOIT THE ADVANTAGES OF BOTH THE ELECTRIC MOTORS AND GASOLINE INTERNAL-COMBUSTION ENGINES TO MAXIMIZE PERFORMANCE AND MINIMIZE EMISSIONS.

THERE ARE JUST A FEW BASIC ENGINEERING PRINCIPLES BEHIND HYBRID TECHNOLOGY. AN ELECTRIC MOTOR DEVELOPS MAXIMUM TORQUE FROM ITS STATE OF REST, WHICH MEANS IT'S PERFECT FOR POWERING A CAR AWAY FROM A STOPLIGHT FOR EXAMPLE. BY CONTRAST, A GASOLINE INTERNAL-COMBUSTION ENGINE DEVELOPS LITTLE TORQUE AT LOW SPEEDS BUT MAXIMUM TORQUE AT MEDIUM SPEEDS. IT'S PERFECT FOR MID-RANGE ACCELERATION AND HIGHWAY CRUISING.

HYBRID ENGINEERS CLEVERLY EXPLOIT THE COMPLEMENTARY POWER CHARACTERISTICS OF THE ELECTRIC MOTOR AND THE GASOLINE ENGINE. MOST HYBRIDS, UNDER GENTLE ACCELERATION, WILL USE THE ELECTRIC MOTOR TO PUSH THE CARS SPEED TO AROUND 40 MPH BEFORE THE INTERNAL-COMBUSTION ENGINE AUTOMATICALLY STARTS UP AND TAKES OVER ACCELERATION.

POWER FOR THE ELECTRIC MOTOR COMES FROM AN ON-BOARD HIGH-PERFORMANCE BATTERY THAT DEVELOPS A FANTASTIC AMOUNT OF WATTAGE. ONCE THE CAR IS UP TO HIGHWAY SPEED, THE GASOLINE ENGINE HAS POWER TO SPARE. IF YOU REMEMBER FROM HIGH-SCHOOL PHYSICS, IT TAKES LESS POWER TO KEEP A BODY IN MOTION THAN IT TAKES TO ACCELERATE THAT BODY UP TO SPEED. ON THE HIGHWAY, THE HYBRID'S GASOLINE ENGINE CAN SPLIT ITS POWER. THE GASOLINE ENGINE CAN USE PART OF ITS POWER TO DRIVE THE CAR AND PART OF ITS POWER TO DRIVE A GENERATOR THAT RECHARGES THE ON-BOARD HIGH-PERFORMANCE BATTERY. UNDER BRAKING OR WHEN DESCENDING A HILL, THE ELECTRIC MOTOR ITSELF ACTS AS A LARGE GENERATOR, HELPING TO SLOW THE HYBRID AND RECHARGE THE ON-BOARD HIGH-PERFORMANCE BATTERY.

A CLEVER PLANETARY GEAR SET UP USUALLY CONNECTING THE ELECTRIC MOTOR, GASOLINE ENGINE, AND TRANSMISSION. AT HIGHWAY SPEEDS, THE GENERATOR CAN SIMULTANEOUSLY RECHARGE THE ON-BOARD HIGH-PERFORMANCE BATTERY AND PROVIDES CURRENT FOR THE ELECTRIC MOTOR, WHICH IS USUALLY CONNECTED TO A CONTINUOUSLY VARIABLE TRANSMISSION.

THERE'S NO NEED FOR A STARTER. REMEMBER THE ELECTRIC MOTOR STARTS THE CAR OFF TO GET IT UP TO SPEED, AND THEN THE GENERATOR STARTS THE GASOLINE ENGINE TO TAKE OVER ACCELERATION.

MOST VEHICLES POWERED BY GASOLINE INTERNAL-COMBUSTION ENGINES USE MORE FUEL FOR STOP AND GO CITY DRIVING THAN FOR HIGHWAY CRUISING. BECAUSE HYBRIDS DO MUCH OF THEIR CITY DRIVING UNDER ELECTRIC POWER AND REGENERATIVE BRAKING, IT ACTUALLY HELPS RECHARGE THE ON-BOARD HIGH-PERFORMANCE BATTERY, HYBRIDS USE LESS FUEL IN THE CITY THAN ON THE HIGHWAY. THUS GIVING US A TECHNOLOGICALLY ADVANCED, GAS SAVING, ECONOMICAL VEHICLE.

HYBRIDS ARE THE WAVE OF THE FUTURE. CARS LIKE THESE ARE WHAT WILL SAVE OUR ENVIRONMENT FOR FUTURE GENERATIONS. IF YOU ARE THINKING ABOUT TRADING IN YOUR CAR, I HIGHLY RECOMMEND YOU LOOK INTO THE HYBRID MARKET. THEY ARE MORE AFFORDABLE THAN WHAT YOU THINK ESPECIALLY IF YOU ARE SAVING AN ARM AND A LEG ON GAS PRICES!

SECTION 3

MAINTENANCE 101

SECTION #3 OVERVIEWS MAINTENANCE DO'S AND DON'TS.

CHAPTER 14

MAINTENANCE

MAINTENANCE

IS THE GUY AT QUICK LUBE PLACE RIGHT?

SHOULD I DO MAINTENANCE OR SHOULD I NOT DO MAINTENANCE? THAT IS THE QUESTION THAT MANY PEOPLE ASK. SOME PEOPLE HAVE THE MINDSET AND THINK WHEN THEY ARE DOING MAINTENANCE THAT THEY ARE HAVING REPAIRS DONE. OTHER PEOPLE DON'T UNDERSTAND THAT WHEN YOU DO MAINTENANCE TO A VEHICLE AND ALL OF ITS SYSTEMS, IT WILL PROLONG THE LIFESPAN OF THAT SYSTEM. THIS DOES NOT MEAN THAT REPAIRS WON'T HAVE TO BE DONE. WHEN IT COMES TO MAINTENANCE ON YOUR VEHICLE, IT IS A GOOD IDEA TO KEEP ON TOP OF A GOOD REGULAR MAINTENANCE SCHEDULE. HOWEVER, MANY PEOPLE DON'T CARE ABOUT THE MAINTENANCE OF THEIR CAR. THEY HAVE THE ATTITUDE, WHEN IT BREAKS, THEN I WILL FIX IT. THE ONLY THING WRONG WITH THIS TYPE OF MENTALITY, IS WHEN YOU LET IT BREAK DUE TO LACK OF MAINTENANCE, THE REPAIR BILL IS SEVERELY HIGHER.

SO, IS THE GUY AT QUICK LUBE RIGHT?

IN THIS SCENARIO, WE WILL SAY THAT YOUR CAR HAS 57,000 MILES ON IT. YOU NEED AN OIL CHANGE AND YOU WILL NEED IT QUICK! SO YOU DRIVE OVER TO YOUR LOCAL QUICK LUBE PLACE. THE GUY AT THE LOCAL QUICK LUBE PLACE PULL YOUR CAR IN, AND STARTS THE OIL CHANGE. ONE OF THE OTHER EMPLOYEES COMES UP TO YOU AND SAYS THAT YOU WILL NEED A LOT OF WORK DONE. ALMOST $350 WORTH OF MAINTENANCE SERVICE! IS THAT GUY TRYING TO STEAL YOUR MONEY, OR JUST TRYING TO TELL YOU WHAT IS WRONG?

WELL, I HATE TO SAY IT, BUT THE GUY AT THE QUICK LUBE PLACE IS PROBABLY RIGHT. HE MAY ALSO BE MISSING SOME OTHER THINGS THAT SHOULD BE DONE AS WELL.

I'VE SAID IT ONCE AND I'LL SAY IT AGAIN, "MOST PEOPLE DO NOT DISTINGUISH BETWEEN MAINTENANCE AND REPAIR". IF YOU MAINTAIN THE SYSTEMS IN YOUR CAR, YOU WILL HAVE FEWER REPAIRS.

I TELL PEOPLE THIS TO PUT IT INTO PERSPECTIVE FOR THEM, "YOU EITHER PAY $100 TO HAVE YOUR TRANSMISSION FLUSHED (NOT A FILTER CHANGED AND FLUID TOPPED OFF), OR YOU PAY $3,000 WHEN IT BREAKS DOWN, ALL BECAUSE YOU DID NOT HAVE THE FLUID CHANGED".

MAINTENANCE ON A VEHICLE WILL VARY FROM MANUFACTURER TO MANUFACTURER, CHANGE FROM CAR TO CAR, AND FROM YEAR TO YEAR.

SO, IS THE GUY AT QUICK LUBE RIGHT? WE WILL NEED TO INVESTIGATE TO FIND OUT!

**NOTE: JUST BECAUSE THE OIL CHANGE GUY IS RIGHT ABOUT THE SERVICES, DOES NOT MEAN THAT THE WORK MUST BE DONE RIGHT AWAY, YOU ALSO HOLD THE RIGHT NOT TO HAVE THE WORK DONE AT THAT FACILITY.*

WHAT IS THE MANUFACTURER'S MAINTENANCE GUIDE?

YOU SHOULD ALWAYS TRY TO FOLLOW YOUR MANUFACTURER'S MAINTENANCE GUIDE. SO, WHAT IS THE MANUFACTURER'S MAINTENANCE GUIDE? IT IS A BOOK OR CHAPTER IN OR WITH YOUR OWNER MANUAL. IT IS A GUIDE OR REFERENCE TO LET YOU KNOW WHEN SERVICES SHOULD BE DONE. THE MANUFACTURER'S BUILT THE CARS AND THEY KNOW THE BEST "TIMES" OR INTERVALS TO HAVE CERTAIN SYSTEMS SERVICED. PRICES WILL VARY FROM COMPANY TO COMPANY AND SYSTEM SERVICING WILL VARY FROM MANUFACTURER TO MANUFACTURER. MOST OF THE TIME THE MANUAL IS PRETTY GOOD ABOUT "WHEN" AND "WHAT" TO DO BUT THERE ARE A FEW THINGS THAT ALMOST EVERY MANUFACTURER MISSES OR JUST DOESN'T PUT IT IN THEIR BOOKS FOR THE MERE FACT OF JOB SECURITY.
THINK ABOUT IT! IF THERE ARE NO SERVICES DONE TO THAT SYSTEM, IT WILL NEED TO BE REPAIRED!

**NOTE: NEVER USE SOMEONE ELSE'S MANUFACTURER'S GUIDE FOR YOUR VEHICLE! YOU MAY DO SERVICES TOO SOON, THAT DON'T NEED TO BE DONE OR NOT GET THE SERVICING DONE AT ALL!*

THE BIG INTERVALS

FOR MOST CARS/LIGHT TRUCKS, YOU WILL USUALLY HAVE FOUR (4) MAJOR SERVICES DURING A 120,000 MILE LIFE SPAN. THESE INTERVALS ARE AT 30,000, 60,000, 90,000, AND 120,000 MILES. AT THE 30, 60, AND THE 90,000 MILES, YOU SHOULD CHECK THE PARTS, COMPONENTS, SYSTEMS, AND FLUIDS TO INSURE THAT THERE WON'T BE ANY POTENTIAL PROBLEMS, EVERYTHING IS LUBRICATED, AND PROPERLY PROTECTED. ANY CAR OVER 120,000 MILES SHOULD HAVE A GOOD OVERALL CHECK EVERY 6 MONTHS DUE TO ITS AGE.
THE NEXT EIGHT PAGES ARE EXAMPLES OF A 30, 60, AND 90,000 MILE CHECK UP INTERVALS. THE FIRST SIX PAGES ARE THE INTERVALS FOR THE SAME AMERICAN VEHICLE. THE LAST TWO PAGES ARE A 60,000 MILE CHECK UP FOR A FOREIGN VEHICLE. YOU CAN TELL THE DIFFERENCE BETWEEN THE AMERICAN INTERVALS AND THE FOREIGN. THE TIMING BELT & SPARK PLUGS NEEDS TO BE REPLACED AT 60,000 ON THE FOREIGN CAR. THIS ADDS AN AVERAGE OF $400 TO $800 TO THE BILL.

AMERICAN CAR

30,000 MILE OR 48,000 KM

CHECK

COOLANT ***(E)***

FLUID- A/T

FLUID- MT

FLUIDS

CHECK AND ADD WASHER FLUID.

LIGHTING AND TRACTION CONTROL

INSPECT

BRAKES AND TRACTION CONTROL

CONSTANT VELOCITY JOINT BOOTS ***(CV BOOTS)***

DRIVE BELT ***(E)***

EVERY 30,000 MILES OR 24 MONTHS.

*EXHAUST GAS RECIRCULATION (E.G.R. SYSTEM)****(E)***

EXHAUST SYSTEMS ***(E)***

*FUEL TANK****(E)***

INSPECT CAP AND LINES ALSO.

HOOD LATCH

SEALS AND GASKETS, DRIVE AXLES

THROTTLE CABLE/LINKAGE

LUBRICATE

PARKING BRAKE CABLE

GUIDES, LINKAGE AND CONTACT POINTS ONLY.

SHIFT LINKAGE, A/T

SHIFT LINKAGE, M/T

STEERING AND SUSPENSION

LUBRICATE AND INSPECT COMPONENTS

REPLACE

*AIR FILTER ELEMENT **(E)***

*ENGINE OIL **(E)***

EVERY 3,000 MILES OR 3 MONTHS.

*OIL FILTER, ENGINE **(E)***

EVERY OIL CHANGE.

*POSITIVE CRANKCASE VENTILATION **(E)***

REPLACE INLET FILTER

ROTATE

TIRES

(S)= SERVICE WARRANTY REQUIREMENT

(E)= EMISSION WARRANTY REQUIREMENT

(B)= BOTH SERVICE AND EMMISSION WARRANTY REQUIREMENTS

AMERICAN CAR

60,000 MILE OR 96,000 KM

CHECK

COOLANT ***(E)***

FLUID- A/T

FLUID- MT

FLUIDS

CHECK AND ADD WASHER FLUID.

LIGHTING AND TRACTION CONTROL

INSPECT

BRAKES AND TRACTION CONTROL

CONSTANT VELOCITY JOINT BOOTS ***(CV BOOTS)***

DRIVE BELT ***(E)***

EVERY 30,000 MILES OR 24 MONTHS.

*EXHAUST GAS RECIRCULATION (EGR SYSTEM)****(E)***

EXHAUST SYSTEMS ***(E)***

*FUEL TANK****(E)***

INSPECT CAP AND LINES ALSO.

HOOD LATCH

SEALS AND GASKETS, DRIVE AXLES

THROTTLE CABLE/LINKAGE

LUBRICATE

PARKING BRAKE CABLE

GUIDES, LINKAGE AND CONTACT POINTS ONLY.

SHIFT LINKAGE, A/T

SHIFT LINKAGE, M/T

STEERING AND SUSPENSION

LUBRICATE AND INSPECT COMPONENTS

REPLACE

AIR FILTER ELEMENT ***(E)***

ENGINE OIL ***(E)***

EVEY 3,000 MILES OR 3 MONTHS.

OIL FILTER, ENGINE ***(E)***

EVERY OIL CHANGE.

POSITIVE CRANKCASE VENTILATION ***(E)***

REPLACE INLET FILTER

(S)= SERVICE WARRANTY REQUIREMENT

(E)= EMISSION WARRANTY REQUIREMENT

(B)= BOTH SERVICE AND EMMISSION

WARRANTY REQUIREMENTS

AMERICAN CAR

90,000 MILE OR 144,000 KM

CHECK

COOLANT ***(E)***

FLUID- A/T

FLUID- MT

FLUIDS

CHECK AND ADD WASHER FLUID.

LIGHTING AND TRACTION CONTROL

INSPECT

BRAKES AND TRACTION CONTROL

CONSTANT VELOCITY JOINT BOOTS ***(CV BOOTS)***

DRIVE BELT ***(E)***

EVERY 30,000 MILES OR 24 MONTHS.

*EXHAUST GAS RECIRCULATION (EGR SYSTEM)****(E)***

EXHAUST SYSTEMS ***(E)***

*FUEL TANK****(E)***

INSPECT CAP AND LINES ALSO.

HOOD LATCH

SEALS AND GASKETS, DRIVE AXLES

THROTTLE CABLE/LINKAGE

LUBRICATE

PARKING BRAKE CABLE

GUIDES, LINKAGE AND CONTACT POINTS ONLY.

SHIFT LINKAGE, A/T

SHIFT LINKAGE, M/T

STEERING AND SUSPENSION

LUBRICATE AND INSPECT COMPONENTS

REPLACE

AIR FILTER ELEMENT ***(E)***

ENGINE OIL ***(E)***

EVEY 3,000 MILES OR 3 MONTHS.

OIL FILTER, ENGINE ***(E)***

EVERY OIL CHANGE.

POSITIVE CRANKCASE VENTILATION ***(E)***

REPLACE INLET FILTER

ROTATE

TIRES

(S)= SERVICE WARRANTY REQUIREMENT

(E)= EMISSION WARRANTY REQUIREMENT

(B)= BOTH SERVICE AND EMMISSION

WARRANTY REQUIREMENTS

<u>FOREIGN CAR</u>

60,000 MILES OR 96,000 KM

INSPECT

BRAKES HOSES/LINES

BRAKES AND TRACTION CONTROL

INSPECT FRONT AND REAR BRAKES

COOLING SYSTEM

INSPECT COOLING SYSTEM HOSES AND CONNECTIONS.

DISTRIBUTOR CAP

EXHAUST CAP

FLUIDS

FUEL SUPPLY LINE

IDLE SPEED

IGNITION CABLES

IGNITION ROTOR

PARKING BRAKE SYSTEM

STEERING AND SUSPENSION

TIE-ROD ENDS, STEERING GEAR BOX, AND BOOTS. SUSPESION COMPONENTS, DRIVESHAFT BOOTS.

WATER PUMP

INSPECT/ ADJUST

DRIVE BELTS

REPLACE

AIR FILTER ELEMENT ***(E)***

ENGINE OIL ***(E)***

FLUID-A/T

FLUID- M/T

OIL FILTER, ENGINE ***(E)***

SPARK PLUG ***(E)***

TIMING BELT

(S)= SERVICE WARRANTY REQUIREMENT

(E)= EMISSION WARRANTY REQUIREMENT

(B)= BOTH SERVICE AND EMMISSION

WARRANTY REQUIREMENTS

AS YOU CAN SEE, MAINTENANCE TO YOUR VEHICLE CAN BE A LITTLE MORE COMPLEX THAN WHAT IT SEEMS DUE TO THE COMPLEX NATURE OF TODAY'S MODERN DAY VEHICLES. BUT FOLLOWING THE GUIDE MAKES IT EASY!

ALL I CAN SAY ABOUT MAINTENANCE IS, IT IS THE BEST WAY TO KEEP YOUR CAR RUNNING, IN GOOD SHAPE, & HELPS LOWER THE COST OF FUTURE REPAIRS. BUT OVER HALF THE CUSTOMERS I ENCOUNTER THINK IT'S UNIMPORTANT. WHY WOULD YOU NEGLECT THE VEHICLE YOU DEPEND ON? I SUGGEST THAT YOU LOOK THROUGH YOUR MAINTENANCE GUIDE AND SEE WHAT YOU OR THE SHOP YOU HAVE BEEN GOING TO HAS MISSED.

CHAPTER 15

MAINTENANCE NOTES

GENERAL

ON THE NEXT FEW PAGES I MADE A LIST OF MAINTENANCE NOTES FOR JUST ABOUT EVERY CAR/ LIGHT TRUCK OUT THERE (DON'T FOLLOW MY NOTES FOR YOUR MAINTENANCE GUIDE!! FIND YOUR OWN!!! USE MY NOTES AS A REFERENCE ONLY!!). I HAVE ALSO MADE SOME NOTES ON SOME THINGS THAT MANY MANUFACTURES /SHOPS WILL MISS, OR THAT SHOULD BE TAKEN CARE OF ON EVERY CAR BUT STILL SEEMS TO BE MISSED.

**NOTE: NEVER USE SOMEONE ELSE'S MANUFACTURER'S GUIDE FOR YOUR VEHICLE! YOU MAY DO SERVICES TOO SOON, THAT DON'T NEED TO BE DONE OR NOT GET THE SERVICING AT ALL!*

**NOTE: JUST BECAUSE THE OIL CHANGE GUY IS RIGHT ABOUT THE SERVICES, DOES NOT MEAN THAT THE WORK MUST BE DONE RIGHT AWAY, YOU ALSO HOLD THE RIGHT NOT TO HAVE THE WORK DONE AT THAT FACILITY.*

**NOTE: IF YOU HAVE AN ENGINE THAT HAS A LONG OR LARGE TUBE FOR OIL FILL UP'S AND YOU HAVE A YELLOW FOAM FORM ON THE CAP THIS DOES NOT MEAN THAT THE HEAD GASKET IS BLOWN. AS ENGINE EMULSIFICATION OCCURS, THE LONG OR LARGE TUBE FOR OIL FILL UP'S WILL COLLECT THAT EMULSIFICATION ON THE TOP OF THAT CAP. HAVE A HYDRO CARBON TEST DONE ON THE ENGINE TO TRULY SEE IF THE HEAD GASKET IS BLOWN.*

**NOTE: AN "INLINE FOUR OR SIX" CYLINDER WOULD HAVE FOUR (4) OR SIX (6) CYLINDERS IN A ROW. A V6 WOULD HAVE THE CYLINDERS IN A "V" PATTERN. A V8 WOULD BE THE SAME WAY AS A V6, BUT WITH TWO (2) MORE CYLINDERS*

NOTE: WHEN A CAR/TRUCK IS IN THE AIR, WITH THE WHEEL OFF THE GROUND, IF THE TIRES IN THE FRONT ONLY SPIN, IT IS CONSIDERED A "FRONT WHEEL DRIVE". IF ONLY THE REAR WHEELS SPIN IT IS A "REAR WHEEL DRIVE" AND IF ALL FOUR ARE SPINNING (OR HAS THE CAPABILITY OF) IT IS A "FOUR WHEEL DRIVE". THESE ARE THE WHEELS THAT PROPEL THE CAR FORWARD & BACKWARDS.

4 X 4 & REAR WHEEL DRIVE NOTE: IF YOUR VEHICLE IS A REAR WHEEL DRIVE, OR A FOUR WHEEL DRIVE YOU WILL NEED TO CHANGE THE REAR DIFFERENTIAL FLUID EVERY 30 TO 60 THOUSAND MILES (DEPENDING ON FLUID TYPES.-SYNTHETIC OR NOT) ON A FOUR WHEEL DRIVE YOU WILL ALSO NEED TO CHANGE THE FRONT DIFF. AND TRANSFER CASE FLUIDS.

OIL CHANGES

NOTE: PAY ATTENTION TO THE TYPE OF OILS YOUR VEHICLE TAKES. THERE IS A REASON THAT I SAY THIS. YOUR ENGINE BEARING DOESN'T RIDE ON ANYTHING BUT A BEAD OF OIL!!

EXAMPLE;

5W30 OIL MOLECULES ARE LET'S SAY ONLY THIS BIG: ***O***

AND WE WILL SAY THAT 5W20 OIL MOLECULES ARE ONLY THAT BIG: ***o***

IF YOUR ENGINE HAS A 5W20 OILING SYSTEM AND YOU PUT 5W30 OIL IN IT, IT WILL WORK, BUT NOT WELL. THE MOLECULES ARE TOO BIG TO BE ABLE TO PROPERLY LUBRICATE THE ENGINE.

THE OIL PUMP WILL HAVE TROUBLE PICKING THE OIL UP TO THE TOP OF THE ENGINE BECAUSE THE OIL IS TOO HEAVY. THIS COULD CAUSE SERIOUS ENGINE DAMAGE OVER THE COURSE OF TIME. 5W30, 5W20, 10W30 SYNTHETICS, WHAT'S THE BIG DEAL, THEY ALL WORK. DON'T USE THE WRONG OIL IN YOUR CAR FOR 50,000 MILES OF THE CARS LIFE AND GET MAD AT IT BECAUSE IT HAS ISSUES. NOT THAT IT'S A BAD CAR, THEY'RE JUST BAD OWNERS.

NOTE: OVER THE COURSE OF TIME, OIL GASKETS AND SEALS WILL BREAK DOWN, WEAKEN, AND BECOME BRITTLE. WHEN THESE PARTS START TO LEAK, IT COULD CAUSE SIGNIFICANT DAMAGES TO THE ENGINE. YOU CAN HELP TO PREVENT FAILURE OF THESE SEALS AND GASKETS BY JUST KEEPING UP ON YOUR OIL CHANGES AND COOLANT FLUSHES

NOTE: CHANGE OIL EVERY 3,000 TO 10,000 MILES DEPENDING ON THE TYPE OF FLUID YOU ARE USING.

NOTE: IF YOU HAVE A BRAND NEW CAR, YOU SHOULD CHANGE AT LEAST THE OIL FILTER (IF NOT THE OIL AS WELL) AT 500 MILES, AND AGAIN AT 1,500 MILES, THEN YOU CAN START YOUR REGULAR INTERVALS. WHY DO I SAY THIS? YOUR ENGINE IS NEW! MOST OF ITS WEAR OR SEAT IN TIME WILL HAPPEN WITHIN THE FIRST 500 MILES. SEAT IN WEAR WILL HAPPEN WITHIN THE FIRST 1,500 MILES.

TIMING BELT/ CHAIN

TIMING BELT SHOULD BE CHANGED ANYWHERE BETWEEN THE MILEAGES OF 60,000 MILES TO 90,000 MILES REALLY DEPENDING ON THE MANUFACTURER AND THE ENVIRONMENT. MANY TIMING BELTS WILL RUN THE WATER PUMP AS WELL. WHEN IT COMES TIME TO REPLACE THE TIMING BELT I WOULD ALSO RECOMMEND TO HAVE THE WATER PUMP REPLACED AND ANY OIL SEALS AS WELL, DUE TO THE HEAVY LABOR TIME INVOLVED IN REPLACING THE TIMING BELT. THE TIMING BELT IS A BELT AND WILL DRY OUT, CRACK AND BREAK. A TIMING CHAIN WILL STRETCH AND ALMOST NEVER BREAKS, BUT THE CHAIN GUIDE WILL WEAR OUT! IF YOU HAVE NOT HAD THIS COMPONENT CHANGED AT 100,000 MILES, I WOULD RECOMMEND TO HAVE IT REPLACED.

TRANSMISSION

MAINTENANCE TIPS/SUGGESTIONS: *OWNER'S MANUAL RECOMMENDATIONS ON TRANSMISSION FLUID CHANGES VARY CONSIDERABLY AND MAY GO AS HIGH AS 100,000 MILES OR MORE. FOR BEST RESULTS, HAVE YOUR CAR'S TRANSMISSION FLUID CHANGED EVERY 30,000 MILES. ALWAYS USE THE TYPE OF FLUID SPECIFIED BY YOUR CAR'S MANUFACTURER. THIS INFORMATION CAN BE FOUND IN THE OWNER'S MANUAL OR ON THE END OF THE TRANSMISSION DIPSTICK (IF YOUR CAR HAS ONE!!). THE OVERWHELMING MAJORITY OF TRANSMISSION FAILURES ARE HEAT-RELATED, AND AUTOMATIC TRANSMISSION FLUID BREAKS DOWN RAPIDLY WHEN SUBJECTED TO HIGH TEMPERATURES. DRIVING CONDITIONS SUCH AS TRAILER TOWING, QUICK STOPS AND STARTS, ASCENDING AND DESCENDING MOUNTAINS, AND WHEEL-SPINNING IN SLIPPERY CONDITIONS ARE BUT A FEW SCENARIOS THAT CAN DEVASTATE THE LIFE OF THE TRANSMISSION FLUID.*

TO AVOID MAJOR TRANSMISSION FAILURES,

I RECOMMEND: A TRANSMISSION FLUID FLUSH (NOT A FILTER CHANGE & FLUID TOP OFF!!) A FEW THOUSAND MILES BEFORE THE MANUFACTURER'S RECOMMENDATION. THIS IS THE BEST WAY TO TAKE CARE OF THE SYSTEM.

NOTE: SOME NEW CARS HAVE WHAT THEY CALL A "SEALED TRANSMISSION" WHERE YOU WILL NEED TO "HOOK-UP" A COMPUTER JUST TO GET THE FLUID LEVELS. MOST SHOPS TODAY DON'T HAVE THE EQUIPMENT TO SERVICE THAT TRANSMISSION. HAVE THESE CARS SERVICED AT THE DEALER ONLY. YOU COULD PAY AS MUCH AS $300.00 FOR THAT TRANSMISSION SERVICE.

BRAKES

**NOTE: NOT MANY MANUFACTURERS WILL RECOGNIZE A BRAKE FLUID FLUSH AS MAINTENANCE. IT SHOULD BE CHANGED ABOUT ONCE EVERY 2-3 YEARS OR 20,000 – 30,000 MILES, DEPENDING ON YOUR DRIVING. BY DOING THIS, IT ENSURES MOISTURE STAYS OUT AND HELPS BRAKE HYDRAULIC UNITS FROM FAILING*

****NOTE:*** *YOUR VEHICLE'S FRONT BRAKES DO AN AVERAGE OF 75% (SOME VEHICLES DO 60%, VARYING FROM MANUFACTURER TO MANUFACTURER) OF YOUR BRAKING. THE REAR BRAKES DO AN AVERAGE OF 25% (SOME OTHER VEHICLES DO AN AVERAGE OF 20-40%, VARYING FROM MANUFACTURER TO MANUFACTURER); IF THE REAR IS HAVING PROBLEMS OR IS OUT OF ADJUSTMENT, IT IS POSSIBLE THAT YOU WILL PREMATURELY WEAR ON THE FRONT BRAKES. TAKE CARE OF YOUR REARS WITH ADJUSTMENTS AND LUBRICATION EVERY 15,000 MILES.*

**NOTE: IT IS A GOOD IDEA TO HAVE YOUR BRAKES LOOKED AT (TWICE, I WILL EXPLAIN THIS LATER) EVERY SIX MONTHS, CLEAN AND ADJUST THE REAR SHOES (IF APPLICABLE) AND HAVE THEM INSPECTED (THERE IS A DIFFERENCE) ONCE A YEAR.*

**NOTE: ALWAYS HAVE A SECOND OPINON ON YOUR BRAKES, THIS WILL HELP TO DETERMINE IF YOU ARE BEING LIED TO OR NOT.*

**NOTE: WHEN YOU HAVE THE BRAKES"LOOKED AT", THAT IS ALL THE SHOP SHOULD DO, IS LOOK. WHEN YOU HAVE THE BRAKES INSPECTED, THE SHOP WILL USE TOOLS TO MEASURE COMPONENTS AND CHECK FOR ISSUES TO COME.*

FUEL SYSTEMS

**NOTE: THE ENGINE COMBUSTION "BURN" WILL LEAVE CARBON IN THE INTAKE VALVE AND CYLINDER, CAUSING CARBON ISSUES & PERFORMANCE PROBLEMS.*

RECOMMENDATION: *HAVE YOUR FUEL SYSTEM CLEANED (INTAKE, THROTTLE PORT, FILTERS &CYLINDERS) EVERY 20 TO 30,000 MILES.*

****NOTE: HAVE YOUR FUEL FILTER CHANGED EVERY 30,000 MILES IF IT IS AN EXTERNAL FUEL FILTER. IF YOUR FUEL FILTER FITS INSIDE THE FUEL TANK, CHANGE IT EVERY 70,000 MILES OR SO. IF THE FUEL FILTER IS IN THE GAS TANK, IT WILL COST MORE TO HAVE IT REPLACED.***

NOTE: THE CHEAP GAS AT YOUR GAS PUMPS WILL: USUALLY HAVE A "QUICK SPARK" AND "LOW ENERGY BURN" AS IT EXITS THE SYSTEM, IT WILL BE MORE PRONE TO RE-IGNITE. THE MOST EXPENSIVE GAS WILL: USUALLY- TAKE A BIT MORE SPARK TO RELEASE THE HIGH ENERGY IT HOLDS SO IT IS HARD ON IGNITION SYSTEMS. I RECOMMEND THAT YOU USE THE MID-RANGE GAS FOR AN AVERAGE VEHICLE DUE TO ITS AVERAGE IGNITION AND MID-RANGE ENERGY BURN. ALWAYS CHECK WITH YOUR MANUFACTURERS RECOMMENDATIONS.

COOLANT

COOLANT SHOULD BE CHANGED EVERY 30,000 MILES IF THE COOLANT IS GREEN (I WOULD EVEN DO IT AS EARLY AS 25,000 MILES), IF THE COOLANT IS ANY OTHER COLOR I WOULD

CHANGE IT EVERY 60,000 MILES JUST TO BE ON THE SAFE SIDE. WHATEVER FACILITY YOU HAVE THE COOLANT CHANGED AT, MAKE SURE THEY USE THE MANUFACTURERS RECOMMENDED COOLANT.

SYNTHETICS! SYNTHETICS!

YOU COULD ALMOST WRITE A BOOK ON THE OUTSTANDING PROPERTIES OF SYNTHETICS! SYNTHETIC OILS DELIVER EXTRAORDINARY LUBRICATION IN DIESEL, GASOLINE ENGINES, AND TRANSMISSION FOUND IN COMMERCIAL, FLEET, PERSONAL VEHICLES, AND ALMOST ALL OTHER ASPECTS OF THE SYSTEMS IN YOUR VEHICLE. IT WITHSTANDS THE STRESS OF HIGHER HEAT, HIGHER ACID LEVELS, EXCESSIVE SOOT, AND CARBON FOUND IN EGR EQUIPPED ENGINES. SYNTHETIC OILS CONSISTENTLY OUTPERFORM CONVENTIONAL OILS AND ARE EXCELLENT FOR LONG-LASTING PERFORMANCE AND PROTECTION.

SPARK PLUGS

NOTE: WHEN REPLACING THE SPARK PLUGS MAKE SURE YOU USE THE SAME SPARK PLUGS THAT CAME FROM THE MANUFACTURER ONLY!!! IF YOU DON'T, YOU WILL HAVE ODD ISSUES IN THE FUTURE. LET ME GIVE YOU A QUICK EXAMPLE OF WHY I SAY THIS.

THERE ARE THREE TYPES OF SPARK PLUGS THAT ARE STANDARD FOR THE INDUSTRY, A COPPER PLUG, A PLATINUM PLUG, AND AN IRIDIUM PLUG. THE COPPER PLUG IS A STANDARD PLUG AND WILL WORK WELL ON SOME CARS FOR ABOUT 25,000 MILES. A PLATINUM PLUG HAS A BIT HIGHER HEAT RATING AND WILL LAST ABOUT 75,000 MILES. THE IRIDIUM PLUG IS A GREAT PLUG AND WILL LAST ABOUT 110,000 MILES. SOME CUSTOMERS WILL HAVE A CAR THAT CALLS FOR IRIDIUM OR PLATINUM PLUG, SOME OF THESE CUSTOMERS WILL TRY TO SAVE A FEW DOLLORS BY REPLACING THE IRIDIUM OR PLATINUM PLUG WITH A STANDARD PLUG.

MOST SHOPS WILL BE OKAY WITH THAT CHOICE AND WILL ADVISE YOU IN A AROUND ABOUT WAY (WITHOUT PUSHING THE SALE) TO USE THE RIGHT PLUG. THE REASON THAT THEY ARE OKAY WITH YOUR CHOICE IS BECAUSE A STANDARD PLUG WILL BURN OUT QUICKLY!!! WHEN YOU COME BACK TO THAT SAME SHOP WITH A PROBLEM THEY WILL SAY "SIR/ MRS. WE TOLD YOU TO PUT IRIDIUM PLUGS AND YOU DIDN'T DO IT! YOU WILL NOW HAVE TO DO THE JOB OVER AND PAY $$???" WHO KNOWS? MOST LIKLEY THE SAME PRICE THAT WAS QUOTED WHEN YOU HAD YOUR FIRST VISIT TO THAT SHOP.

DIAGNOSES & CHECK ENGINE LIGHTS

NOTE: I DON'T KNOW OF ANY COMPUTER THAT "TIES" INTO THE CARS COMPUTER SYSTEMS AND TELLS YOU WHAT IS WRONG!!! THE COMPUTERS THAT INTERFACE WITH YOUR CAR COMPUTER LEADS THE SHOP IN THE DIRECTION OF WHAT MIGHT BE WRONG!

NOTE: VEHICLE COMPUTER SYSTEMS HAVE NO REAL MAINTENANCE, MAYBE A LIGHT RESET EVERY NOW AND AGAIN. IF THERE IS A LIGHT THAT HAS BEEN RESET AND IS STILL COMING ON HAVE IT CHECKED OUT!

POWER STEERING FLUID

**NOTE: NOT MANY MANUFACTURERS WILL RECOGNIZE A POWER STEERING FLUID FLUSH AS MAINTENANCE. IT SHOULD BE CHANGED EVERY 30,000 – 60,000 MILES DEPENDING ON FLUID TYPE.*

TIRES

NOTE: TIRE MAINTENCE IS EASY. CHECK THE AIR EVERY WEEK AND DO ROTATIONS EVERY 3,000-5,000 MILES.

*NOTE: TO **AVOID VIBRATION** OR SHAKING OF THE VEHICLE, IT IS ESSENTIAL THAT THE TIRES ARE PROPERLY BALANCED. THIS BALANCE IS ACHIEVED BY POSITIONING WEIGHTS ON THE WHEEL TO COUNTERBALANCE HEAVY SPOTS ON THE WHEEL-AND-TIRE ASSEMBLY.*

SECTION 4

DON'T JUST GO, KNOW WHAT YOU ARE LOOKING FOR

SECTION # 4 OVERVIEWS INFORMATION AND OPINIONS ON AUTOMOTIVE FACILITY, WORKERS IN THE AUTOMOTIVE FIELD, SHOP TICKETS AND SHOP OPERATIONS.

***CHAPTER* 16**

WHAT TO EXPECT, WHAT IS TO BE EXPECTED

WHAT TO EXPECT

PEOPLE WILL PICK AN AUTOMOTIVE REPAIR FACILITY FOR MANY REASONS. A FAMILY MEMBER MAY HAVE TOLD THEM ABOUT A SHOP, OR THEY MAY HAVE CALLED AROUND TO A FEW SHOPS, AND THEY PICK ONE SHOP IN PARTICULAR. THEY MAY HAVE PICKED THAT SHOP BECAUSE THE COMPANY ADVERTISED A GREAT PRICE, OR THEY HAVE THE ATTITUDE OF "WHEN I NEED AN OIL CHANGE, I WILL GO TO AN OIL CHANGE PLACE. WHEN I NEED BRAKES, I WILL GO TO A BRAKE PLACE." THERE IS NOTHING WRONG WITH DOING WHAT FEELS RIGHT. BUT LET'S GET REAL FOR A MINUTE. WHEN IT COMES TO AUTOMOTIVE, DOING WHAT FEELS RIGHT CAN SOMETIMES COST YOU AN ARM AND A LEG. REMEMBER WITHIN FIVE YEARS OF YOU OWNING A NEW CAR IT IS POSSIBLE THAT YOU COULD SPEND WELL OVER $10,000 DOLLARS ON MAINTENANCE & REPAIRS!! SO YOU DON'T WANT TO MAKE AN INFORMED DECISION, YOU NEED TO MAKE AN INFORMED DECISION. HOWEVER, TO MAKE AN INFORMED DECISION, YOU NEED TO KNOW AS MUCH AS POSSIBLE ABOUT THE AUTOMOTIVE WORLD AND WHAT TO EXPECT FROM IT.

SO I AM JUST GOING TO GIVE YOU SOME INFORMATION IN THIS SECTION AND A KIND OF "DO'S AND DON'TS LIST" IN THE NEXT SECTION. THIS WAY YOU WILL HAVE A SMALL REFERENCE GUIDE AND HOPEFULLY ALONG THE WAY YOU WILL PICK UP A LITTLE COMMON KNOWLEDGE WHEN IT COMES TO AUTOMOTIVE BUSINESS OPERATIONS.

YOU WILL NEED TO EXPECT A FEW THINGS WHEN YOU WALK INTO AN AUTOMOTIVE FACILITY. YOU WILL ALSO NEED TO HAVE THE UNDERSTANDING THAT THERE WILL BE A FEW THINGS EXPECTED OF YOU.

WHEN IT COMES TO AUTOMOTIVE FACILITIES YOU WILL NEED TO UNDERSTAND THAT ANY AUTOMOTIVE FACILITY IS A BUSINESS. WHOEVER OPENED THAT FACILITY YOU ARE TAKING YOUR VEHICLE TO, DID NOT OPEN THE DOORS FOR THE FUN OF IT!! THE OWNERS WENT INTO BUSINESS TO DO ONE THING AND ONE THING ONLY: **MAKE MONEY**!

NOW, SOMETIMES THESE OWNERS/WORKERS ONLY CARE ABOUT MONEY. ON THE OTHER HAND, SOMETIMES THESE OWNERS/WORKERS JUST WANT TO OPEN (OR WORK FOR) A BUSINESS THAT DOES GOOD WORK AT A FAIR PRICE. REGARDLESS OF ANY ATTITUDES THAT THE OWNERS/WORKERS MAY HAVE, THEY ALL NEED TO HAVE A SUCCESSFUL BUSINESS TO BE ABLE TO REACH THEIR OWN PERSONAL GOALS.

THE KEY TO A SUCCESSFUL BUSINESS IS KNOWING HOW TO RUN A SMART, EFFICIENT OPERATION. THIS RINGS TRUE WITH ANY BUSINESS, SO WHEN IT COMES TO AN AUTOMOTIVE FACILITY THE OWNERS ARE PREPARING FOR SUCCESS!! SUCCESS CAN BE TOUGH TO DEFINE, ALTHOUGH MANY PEOPLE DEFINE SUCCESS ON HOW MUCH MONEY WAS MADE IN AN ALLOWED AMOUNT OF TIME. BASICALLY MAKE AS MUCH MONEY, AS FAST AS YOU CAN! WITH THAT SAID, IT SHOULD EXPLAIN A LITTLE MORE OF WHY OPERATIONS AT AN MANY AUTOMOTIVE FACILITIES CAN SOMETIMES BE LESS THAN FAVORABLE.

***NOTE**: NOW I'M NOT SAYING THAT ALL AUTOMOTIVE FACILITIES ARE BAD. I DID NOT WRITE THIS BOOK TO TALK BAD ABOUT ALL AUTOMOTIVE BUSINESS. I WROTE THIS BOOK FOR TWO REASONS: #1 I COULD HELP SOME GOOD PEOPLE SAVE SOME MONEY AND #2 I COULD STOP FEELING LIKE THE BAD GUY WORKING FOR AN UNFORGIVING COMPANY. SO I AM GOING TO TELL THE CONSUMERS "THE WAY IT IS", SO THEY CAN MAKE A TRULY INFORMED & EDUCATED DECISION. THIS WAY THE CONSUMERS HAVE THE PLEASURE OF CHOOSING TO TALK BAD ABOUT AN AUTOMOTIVE FACILITY IF THEY WANT TO!!*

UNFAVORABLE SALES EXAMPLE

LET ME GIVE YOU AN EXAMPLE OF ONE UNFAVORABLE SALES TACTIC.

EXAMPLE: MANY SHOP OWNERS KNOW THAT THE BEST WAY TO INCREASE THE REVENUE AT THEIR FACILITY IS TO EDUCATE THE CUSTOMER. THIS FACT IS VERY TRUE! IF YOU HAVE AN EDUCATED CUSTOMER WALK INTO A SHOP HE OR SHE WILL BE MORE LIKELY TO SPEND MORE MONEY ON THEIR CAR. THE REASON EDUCATED CUSTOMER SPEND MORE ON THEIR CAR THAN EVERYONE ELSE, IS BECAUSE THEY KNOW WHAT'S GOING ON WITH THEIR CAR. SO, MANY AUTOMOTIVE FACILITIES WILL TRY TO EDUCATE THEIR CUSTOMERS WHILE THEY ARE AT THE SHOP. THIS SCENARIO SEEMS LIKE A GOOD DEAL FOR EVERYONE, BUT IT'S NOT!! I SAY THIS BECAUSE WHEN YOU EDUCATE A CUSTOMER ABOUT THEIR CAR AT THE SHOP, MOST CUSTOMERS WILL UNDERSTAND THE IMPORTANCE OF CERTAIN SERVICES, GET CONFUSED, AND LOSE FOCUS OF WHAT THE REAL ISSUES ARE. THIS IS ONE TACTIC THAT MANY OF THE AUTOMOTIVE FACILITIES WILL USE TO INCREASE SHOP PROFIT. BUT THESE SHOPS WILL STAND BEHIND THE IDEA OF "WE ARE INFORMING THE CUSTOMER SO THEY CAN MAKE A MORE INFORMED DECISION". I SAY "BULL!"

I FEEL LIKE MANY SHOPS WILL USE SALES TACTICS THAT ARE COMPARABLE TO A MAGIC SHOW. A LITTLE SLEIGHT OF HAND, MIRRORS, AND SMOKE TO TRICK YOUR EYES AND MIND TO MAKE SEE AND THINK THINGS THAT ARE JUST NOT REALITY.

I AM GOING TO TRY TO PROPERLY EDUCATE YOU AND GIVE YOU SOME TOOLS TO USE, SO YOU CAN STOP THE MAGIC SHOW.

REMEMBER!!! IT IS MY MISSION TO HELP YOU SEE THROUGH ALL OF THE CLOAK AND DAGGER OF THE AUTOMOTIVE WORLD IN THE HOPES THAT YOU WILL HAVE A GOOD UNDERSTANDING OF WHAT IS REALLY GOING ON WITH THE AUTOMOTIVE INDUSTRY, YOUR CAR AND YOUR POCKETBOOK, IN THE HOPES THAT YOU WILL NEVER BE TAKEN AGAIN!

WHAT IS TO BE EXPECTED

SO WHAT IS TO BE EXPECTED OF YOU, WHEN DOING BUSINESS WITH AN AUTOMOTIVE FACILITY? ARE YOU EXPECTED TO KNOW ALL THE IN AND OUTS TO THE AUTOMOTIVE WORLD? ARE YOU EXPECTED TO KNOW ALL THE TECHNICAL GARBAGE ABOUT YOUR CAR? ARE YOU EXPECTED TO KNOW AS MUCH AS A MASTER TECHNICIAN? THE ANSWERS ARE NO, NO AND NO.

HOWEVER SOME OF THE PEOPLE WHO WORK IN THE AUTOMOTIVE INDUSTRY EXPECT YOU TO HAVE A LITTLE COMMON KNOWLEDGE AND SENSE! ANTICIPATE THIS TYPE OF ATTITUDE FROM MORE THAN ONE FACILITY. SOME AUTOMOTIVE WORKERS WILL EXPECT YOU TO KNOW HOW SHOPS OPERATE, UNDERSTAND WHY YOUR CAR IS HAVING ISSUES AND WHY THE SHOP IS CHARGING THE PRICES THEY ARE CHARGING. YOU ARE EXPECTED TO MAKE AN INFORMED DECISION AND YOU ARE ALSO EXPECTED TO KNOW THERE ARE A FEW UNWRITTEN RULES. SOME OF THESE RULES ARE COMMON KNOWLEDGE, OTHER RULES YOU WILL NEED TO KNOW.

ARE YOU REALLY EXPECTED TO KNOW ALL OF THIS STUFF???? AGAIN, THE ANSWER IS NO!! YOU ARE REALLY NOT EXPECTED TO DO OR KNOW ANYTHING. ALL YOU REALLY NEED TO DO IS SHOW UP AND PAY THE BILL. BUT IF YOU EXPECT TO SAVE SOME OF YOUR GOOD MONEY, YOU SHOULD EXPECT TO KNOW SOME OF THIS STUFF.

KNOW YOUR CAR

THE FIRST RULE THAT YOU SHOULD KNOW IS **KNOW YOUR CAR!!!** KNOW THE YEAR, MAKE, MODEL, ENGINE SIZE, TYPE OF OIL, MAINTENANCE LIST, ETC. YOU DON'T HAVE TO KNOW THE STUFF BY HEART, JUST HAVE IT WRITTEN DOWN SOMEWHERE. IF YOU ARE NOT SURE ABOUT YOUR INFORMATION CALL THE DEALER AND ASK FOR MANUFACTURERS SPECIFICATIONS. I KNOW WHAT SOME OF YOU ARE SAYING, "WHY SHOULD I NEED TO KNOW THAT INFORMATION? THIS IS WHAT THE TECHNICIANS AT THE SHOPS ARE FOR." THIS OUTLOOK IS A BAD VIEW TO HAVE. LET ME EXPLAIN.

THIS IS AN EXAMPLE OF WHAT HAPPENS AT THE INITIAL WALK-IN. SAY YOU GO IN FOR AN OIL CHANGE AND YOU ARE THE AVERAGE RUN-OF-THE-MILL CUSTOMER. THE GUY AT THE COUNTER OF THE AUTOMOTIVE FACILITY ASKS YOU WHAT YEAR AND WHAT TYPE OF CAR YOU HAVE. YOU SAY "I DON'T KNOW" OR YOU SAY "IT'S THAT GREY (WHATEVER MAKE YOUR CAR IS), BUT I DON'T KNOW THE YEAR". IMMEDIATELY THAT WORKER KNOWS THAT YOU ARE "CLUELESS" WHEN IT COMES TO AUTOMOTIVE!! THEREFORE, THIS WORKER IS GOING TO TRY TO WRITE YOU A REPAIR ESTIMATE 3-PAGES LONG. HE WILL ALSO TRY TO CONVINCE YOU THAT YOU NEED ALL THAT WORK DONE! HOWEVER, (WITH CONFIDENCE) IF YOU WALK INTO THE OFFICE OF A REPAIR FACILITY AND YOU SAY "I DRIVE A (WHATEVER YEAR AND MODEL YOUR CAR MAY BE)" AND YOU TELL THE EMPLOYEE AT THE SHOP THAT "MY CAR TAKES "X" PINTS OF 5W20", HE WILL BE LESS LIKELY TO TRY TO SELL YOU UNNEEDED SERVICES.

SO IT WOULD BE A GOOD IDEA TO HAVE A LITTLE KNOWLEDGE ABOUT YOUR CAR. I SUGGEST FINDING OUT AS MUCH AS POSSIBLE, THIS WAY YOU DO NOT APPEAR UNINFORMED AND VULNERABLE.

CHAPTER 17

WHO ARE YOU DEALING WITH?

WHO ARE YOU DEALING WITH?

BEFORE YOU PICK OUT SOME SHOPS, YOU WILL NEED TO TAKE INTO CONSIDERATION OF WHAT AND WHO YOU ARE DEALING WITH. I HAVE COMPILED A FEW INDUSTRY PROFILE REPORTS TOGETHER TO GIVE YOU MORE INSIGHT INTO THE AUTOMOTIVE FACILITIES, OWNERS AND MANAGERS. ALL OF THE REPORTS SHOWED ME THAT OVERALL, MOST PRIVATE SHOP OWNERS IN THE U.S. AUTOMOTIVE REPAIR INDUSTRY ARE TYPICALLY:

1) MORE EDUCATED THAN WHAT THEY HAVE BE IN YEARS PAST. THE REPORTS FOUND 97% OF SHOP OWNERS ARE HIGH-SCHOOL GRADUATES, AND MANY HAVE COMPLETED OTHER FORMS OF HIGHER LEARNING. ABOUT 14% OF SHOP OWNERS EVEN HAVE COLLEGE DEGREES, 20% HAVE GRADUATED FROM A VOCATIONAL SCHOOL AND 3% FINISHED POST-GRAD SCHOOL.

2) MOST OWNERS STARTED WORKING FOR PAY IN THE REPAIR INDUSTRY AROUND AGE 19.

3) MANY WILL ALSO RUN A FAMILY-OWNED BUSINESS. ONLY ONE-FIFTH OF INDEPENDENT SHOPS (20%) ARE NOT FAMILY-OWNED.

4) EACH WEEK, THE TYPICAL SHOP OWNER/ MANAGER SPENDS ABOUT 22% OF THEIR TIME REPAIRING VEHICLES, 21% OF THE TIME WORKING WITH CUSTOMERS, 21% MANAGING THE BUSINESS, 18% OF THE TIME DIAGNOSING VEHICLE PROBLEMS AND 11% OF THE TIME WORKING WITH SUPPLIERS.

WORKFORCE AND EARNINGS

THE AVERAGE NUMBER OF FULL-TIME EMPLOYEES AT TODAY'S SHOPS IS 3.7, ABOUT 46% OF SHOPS THAT YOU GO TO EMPLOY A PART-TIME STAFF (ONE OR TWO PEOPLE).THE AVERAGE NUMBER OF TECHNICIANS PER SHOP IS "3". SHOPS ARE NOT ONLY EMPLOYING MORE PEOPLE, BUT ANNUAL SALARIES HAVE GROWN FOR THE MORE EXPERIENCED STAFF IN THE LAST FEW YEARS. RESEARCH SHOWS THAT AVERAGE ANNUAL EARNINGS FOR MANAGERS CONSIDERED "MOST EXPERIENCED" IS ANYWHERE FROM $42,000 TO 60,000. MANAGER SALARIES CONSIDERED "LEAST EXPERIENCED" AVERAGES FROM $32,000 TO $36,000 A YEAR.

HOURLY WAGES, ACCORDING TO STATISTICS RELEASED FROM THE U.S. DEPARTMENT OF LABOR (WWW.BLS.GOV), SHOWS AVERAGE WAGES FOR THE "MOST EXPERIENCED" TECHNICIAN RANGE FROM $40,000 TO $60,000. THE WAGES FOR THE "LEAST EXPERIENCED" TECHNICIANS RANGED FROM $25,000 TO $30,000 ANNUAL.

THE MIDDLE 50% OF TECHNICIANS EARNED BETWEEN $10.61 AND $19.84 AN HOUR. THE LOWEST 10% EARNED LESS THAN $8.14 AND THE HIGHEST 10% EARNED MORE THAN $25.21 AN HOUR.

THE U.S. DEPARTMENT OF LABOR ALSO REPORTS THAT AUTOMOTIVE SERVICE TECHNICIANS AND MECHANICS (FROM BOTH INDEPENDENT AND DEALERSHIP BUSINESSES) HELD ABOUT 818,000 JOBS IN 2009 (DOWN FROM 840,000 IN 2008). THIS TOTAL INCLUDES THOSE WHO WORK FOR RETAIL AND WHOLESALE AUTOMOTIVE DEALERS, INDEPENDENT REPAIR SHOPS OR AUTOMOTIVE SERVICE FACILITIES AT DEPARTMENT,

AUTOMOTIVE OR HOME SUPPLY STORES. OTHERS FOUND EMPLOYMENT AT GASOLINE STATIONS, TAXI BUSINESSES, AUTOMOTIVE LEASING BUSINESSES AND GOVERNMENT LOCATIONS.

THE AUTOMOTIVE SERVICE ASSOCIATION'S (ASA) RESEARCH DEPARTMENT, WHICH RECENTLY DEVELOPED A BRIEFING PAPER PRESENTING TRAINING, RETENTION AND RECRUITING CONCERNS FOR THE AUTOMOTIVE INDUSTRY, RELEASED A BREAKDOWN OF THE TECHNICIANS CURRENTLY EMPLOYED.
ACCORDING TO ASA, THIS TECHNICIAN POOL IS COMPRISED AS FOLLOWS:

- 26.6% AS AUTOMOTIVE MECHANICAL TECHNICIANS
- 25.9% ARE EMPLOYED BY NEW CAR DEALERS
- 6.6% ARE EMPLOYED BY AUTO, HOME SUPPLY STORES
- 4.4% BY GASOLINE SERVICE STATIONS
- 2.76% BY AUTOMOTIVE SERVICES OTHER THAN REPAIR
- 2.67% BY LOCAL GOVERNMENTS
- 1.8% BY PARTS SUPPLIERS
- 1.46% ARE SELF-EMPLOYED, SECONDARY JOBS
- 1.24% BY DEPARTMENT STORES
- 1% BY AUTOMOTIVE RENTAL COMPANIES
- 0.43% BY PUBLIC AND PRIVATE EDUCATIONAL SERVICES

ASA SAID IT EXPECTS THE NUMBER OF AUTOMOTIVE TECHNICIANS TO GROW BY 18% OR 151,050 OVER THE NEXT 10 YEARS. THOUGH THE ASSOCIATION PREDICTS GASOLINE SERVICE STATIONS WILL CONTINUE TO SEE A DECREASE IN THE NUMBER OF TECHNICIAN POSITIONS THROUGH 2010, AUTOMOTIVE REPAIR SHOP POSITIONS ARE EXPETCED TO INCREASE FROM 26.6% TO 29%. DEALERSHIP SLOTS ARE PREDICTED TO DROP FROM 25.9% TO 24.7% DURING THAT PERIOD.

THE ONE THING THAT THE ASA DID NOT CONSIDER IS "GENERATION X". YOU MAY NOT REALIZE IT, BUT THE "BABY BOOMERS" GENERATION MAKES UP ABOUT 50% OF THE WORKFORCE, SO AS THEY RETIRE THE AUTOMOTIVE INDUSTRY WILL NEED TO FIND THE NEXT GENERATION OF POTENTIALLY SKILLED WORKERS. GENERATION X IS A LITTLE CLOSER TO THEIR PARENTS THAN ANY OTHER GENERATION. THEIR PARENTS HAVE BEEN INSPIRED BY IDEALISTIC VIEWS LIKE DR. SPOCK "YOU DON'T HAVE TO MAKE STRAIGHT A'S, JUST DO YOUR BEST". THIS HAS CREATED A DIFFERENT WAY OF THINKING FOR THE NEXT GENERATION. THE NEXT GENERATION HAS SEEN HOW MANY HOURS THEIR PARENTS HAVE WORKED AND THEY DON'T WANT TO WORK LIKE THAT. THEY WORK TO LIVE, NOT LIVE TO WORK LIKE PRIOR GENERATIONS. THE NEXT GENERATION ALSO FEELS THAT THEY ARE ENTITLED TO JOB PERKS LIKE MORE VACATION TIME, PROMOTIONS, AND RAISES WITHIN THE FIRST FEW YEARS OF EMPLOYMENT. THESE ISSUES ARE A CHALLENGE FOR BUSINESS OWNERS.

CHAPTER 18

SHOPS

SHOPS

THE AVERAGE GENERAL REPAIR FACILITY HAS 4.4 BAYS, HAS 3.7 FULL-TIME EMPLOYEES, EMPLOYS 3 TECHNICIANS, HAS BEEN IN BUSINESS 24.3 YEARS, CHARGES $58.53 TO $90.00 AS THEIR AVERAGE HOURLY LABOR RATE, AND HAS AN ESTIMATED VALUE OF INVENTORY (BELTS/HOSE, PLUGS/WIRES, REFRIGERANTS/OILS, ETC.) OF ABOUT $8,000-$10,000 DOLLARS.-THIS TELLS US THAT ALL SHOPS WILL NOT HAVE ALL THE PARTS FOR EVERY CAR!-.

TYPES OF SHOPS

PERCEPTION IS REALITY!! EACH SHOP WILL PROMOTE CERTAIN IMAGES, TO MAKE THEM LOOK LIKE THE BEST PLACE FOR YOU TO TAKE YOUR CAR. SOME AGENDAS AND IMAGES ARE GOOD, SOME ARE GREAT AND SOME YOU JUST DON'T WANT ANYTHING TO DO WITH. IT'S HARD TO FIND AN AUTOMOTIVE REPAIR FACILITY WHEN YOU'RE NOT EXACTLY SURE WHAT YOU ARE LOOKING FOR.

WHEN PICKING AN AUTOMOTIVE FACILITY, MANY PEOPLE WILL JUDGE THE SHOP OR BUSINESS FOR ALL THE WRONG REASONS. SOME PEOPLE WILL GO TO A SHOP BY JUST ASKING A FEW FRIENDS, OTHERS WILL LOOK FOR THE BEST DEALS OR COUPON. OTHER PEOPLE MAY GO TO A CERTAIN REPAIR FACILITY BECAUSE THE SHOP WILL ONLY WORK ON THAT TYPE OF CAR. THESE ARE ALL GREAT THINGS TO LOOK FOR, BUT FOR THE MOST PART THEY ARE UNEDUCATED DECISIONS.

THE FACT OF THE MATTER IS THAT YOU ONLY REALLY HAVE FOUR (4) AUTOMOTIVE REPAIR FACILITY OPTIONS. YOU HAVE THE DEALER, AFTER-MARKET, INDEPENDENT, AND THE SO-CALLED "TECHNICIAN GUY DOWN THE STREET"! THAT'S IT! WHERE ELSE ARE YOU GOING TO TAKE YOUR CAR FOR REPAIRS? THESE SHOPS MAY COME IN MANY SHAPES AND FORMS. (A QUICK LUBE PLACE, THE DEALERS, A BRAKE PLACE, TIRE SHOPS, AND SO ON.) SO, IT MAY SEEM THAT YOU HAVE MANY CHOICES. IN REALITY, YOU ONLY HAVE THE FOUR TYPES OF SHOP TO PICK FROM. THIS IS A COLD HARD REALITY, BUT IT'S A FACT. ON A WHOLE, THE ARRAY OF SHOPS THAT YOU HAVE TO PICK FROM MAY BE VAST, BUT THE TYPE OF SHOPS ARE FEW AND FAR BETWEEN. THIS CAN MAKE PICKING THE RIGHT SHOP FOR YOUR NEEDS A HARD TASK.

HOWEVER, WITH A LITTLE KNOW HOW YOU WILL BE ABLE TO PICK THE SHOP THAT WILL BE ABLE THE SUIT YOUR NEEDS THE BEST. AFTER KNOWING HOW TO MAKE AN EDUCATED & SOUND JUDGMENT ON WHAT TYPE OF SHOPS TO TAKE YOUR CAR TO, IT SHOULD REALLY ONLY COME DOWN TO THREE THINGS, PRICE, CUSTOMER SERVICE AND "ARE YOU COMFORTABLE?".

THE DEALER

DEALERSHIPS ARE WHERE THE CAR MANUFACTURES DISTRIBUTE THEIR NEW CARS. BASICALLY, THE MANUFACTURES WILL MAKE THE CARS AND THE DEALERS WILL SELL THE VEHICLES TO THE GENERAL PUBLIC. DEALERSHIPS ARE WHERE YOU BUY NEW CARS, AND USED CARS. -YOU CAN ALSO BUY AN EXTENDED WARRANTY OR STAY WITH THE MANUFACTURER'S WARRANTY. - YOU CAN EVEN BUY ACCESSORIES AND UPGRADES FROM THE FACTORY FOR YOUR NEW VEHICLE. THE DEALERSHIP IS ALSO ONE OF THE FEW PLACES THAT YOU WILL BE ABLE TO HAVE MANUFACTURER'S RECALLS AND WARRANTY WORK DONE AS WELL.

THE DEALER CAN BE REAL GOOD AT FINDING ODD AND TECHNICAL PROBLEMS WITH OLDER OR NEWER VEHICLES. THE DEALERS WILL WORK CLOSELY WITH THE MANUFACTURERS OF THE VEHICLE TO GIVE THE CUSTOMERS, (YOU) BETTER SERVICE. BECAUSE THE DEALER WORKS WITH THE MANUFACTURER OF THE VEHICLE, THE "DEALER" SHOULD HAVE ALL THE RIGHT PARTS, EQUIPMENT, AND INFORMATION FOR YOUR VEHICLE! BUT THE DEALER MAY NOT HAVE THE TECHNICAL ATTRIBUTES TO MEET YOUR DEMANDS.
MOST DEALERS (THAT I HAVE SEEN) HAVE ONLY A FEW (2-3) TOP TECHNICIANS! THE REST ARE ONLY MID TO ENTRY LEVEL TECHNICIANS! I'M NOT SAYING THAT THESE MID- TO ENTRY LEVEL TECHNICIANS ARE BAD TECHNICIANS, I'M JUST SAYING THAT YOU MAY NOT ALWAYS HAVE THE BEST TECHNICIANS WORKING ON YOUR VEHICLE. LET ME EXPLAIN.
AT MANY DEALERSHIPS, YOU MAY NEVER GET TO MEET THE TECHNICIAN THAT IS WORKING ON YOUR CAR! A GOOD EXAMPLE IS: YOU DON'T KNOW IF THE TECHNICIAN WHO IS WORKING ON YOUR CAR AT THAT DEALERSHIP (CHEVROLET OR TOYOTA FOR EXAMPLE), IS THE NEW TECHNICIAN THAT THEY JUST HIRED OR IF HE IS A TECHNICIAN FROM (DODGE), THAT WAS JUST HIRED AS A (CHEVY/FORD TOYOTA) CERTIFIED TECHNICIAN! YOU ALSO DON'T KNOW IF HE IS THE TECHNICIAN THAT IS AN 18 YEAR OLD KID THAT HAS BEEN WORKING FOR THAT DEALERSHIP FOR THE PAST 6 MONTHS, OR IF HE IS THE TECHNICIAN THAT HAS BEEN WORKING THERE FOR PAST 20 OR 30 YEARS AND KNOWS ALL OF THE INS AND OUTS OF YOUR CAR!

YOU SHOULD ALSO KEEP IN MIND THAT, SOMETIMES WITH NEWER CARS, THE DEALERSHIP IS THE ONLY OPTION THAT YOU HAVE FOR REPAIRS. (THE CARS ARE TOO NEW TO GET PARTS, INFORMATION, OR EQUIPMENT FROM ANYWHERE ELSE.) ON THE OTHER HAND I HAVE ALSO RUN INTO THE PROBLEM WHERE DEALERSHIPS WILL NOT HAVE ACCESS TO OLDER CAR PARTS. USUALLY IF THE CAR IS 20 YEARS OR OLDER, A DEALERSHIP WILL STOCK AND DEAL WITH FEW PARTS.
HOWEVER THE DEALERS WILL ALSO HAVE THE RIGHT PARTS FOR YOUR CAR. DEALERSHIPS GET THEIR PARTS FROM THE MANUFACTURER. -WHEN YOU BUY YOUR PARTS FROM THE COMPANY THAT MADE YOUR CAR, IT WILL BE RARE THAT YOU WILL GET THE WRONG PARTS-.

BECAUSE OF THE DEALER'S OVERHEAD, MANY PEOPLE EXPECT TO PAY A HIGHER PRICE FOR REPAIRS. THIS MAY BE TRUE IN SOME CASES BUT, MANY DEALERSHIPS HAVE INTEGRATED PACKAGE DEALS OR LOWERED THEIR PRICES ON SOME SERVICES TO CATCH SOME OF THE AFTERMARKET BUSINESS.

SO, LET'S SUM THIS UP. THE DEALER HAS ALL THE KNOWLEDGE, ALL THE RIGHT PARTS AND EQUIPMENT, BUT WILL THEY KNOW HOW TO USE WHAT IS AVAILABLE TO THEM? YOU MAY NEVER KNOW.

AFTER-MARKET

AFTER-MARKET AUTOMOTIVE IS DIVERSE AND COMPLEX IN ITS NATURE. AFTER-MARKET AUTOMOTIVE SHOULD BE RELIEF PRICING FROM THE DEALER. HOWEVER WITH TODAY'S STANDARDS, SOMETIMES YOU COULD PAY MORE FOR AN AFTER-MARKET REPAIR THAN WHAT YOU WOULD AT A DEALER.

AFTER-MARKET AUTOMOTIVE HAS ITS GOODS AND ITS BADS. THE GOODS ARE THAT THEY MAY BE CLOSER TO YOUR HOME, PARTS/LABOR ARE USUALLY CHEAPER THAN THE DEALER, WARRANTIES ARE BETTER MOST OF THE TIME AND YOU HAVE AN ARRAY OF SHOPS AND TECHNICIANS TO CHOOSE FROM. YOU MAY ALSO FIND A FEW AFTERMARKET CORPORATIONS AT A NATIONAL LEVEL. THIS CAN BE GREAT IF YOU DO A LOT OF TRAVELING.

THE BADS ARE THAT YOU HAVE A WIDE ARRAY OF SHOPS AND TECHNICIANS TO CHOOSE FROM. AFTER-MARKET ALSO MAY NOT HAVE ALL THE RIGHT PARTS, EQUIPMENT AND INFORMATION FOR YOUR VEHICLE! YOU ARE MORE LIKELY TO BE LIED TO AS WELL. THIS IS DUE TO THE WAY SOME OF THE EMPLOYEES ARE PAID (COMMISSION AND/OR FLAT RATES.) THEY ALSO MAY DO SOME EXTRA SERVICES THAT MAY NOT NECESSARILY NEED TO BE DONE, SO BEWARE!

I WOULD CLASSIFY ANY "AFTER-MARKET" SHOP AS SOME TYPE OF CORPORATION OR FRANCHISES.
THIS MEANS THAT WHEN GOING FROM ONE SHOP TO ANOTHER SHOP, (UNDER THE SAME NAME) YOU SHOULD RECEIVE THE SAME LEVEL OF PRICES, PARTS, AND CUSTOMER SERVICE. THESE CONSISTENCIES CAN BE LIMITED IN MANY ASPETCS OF THE FIELD. THERE COULD BE A LIMITED ACCESS OF NAME BRAND PARTS, LIMITED SERVICES FROM AREA TO AREA, MAN POWER, SHOP SIZE, AND PRICES. THE REASONS FOR THESE INCONSISTENCIES COMES DOWN TO PEOPLE AND MONEY. LET ME GIVE AN EXAMPLE.
WE WILL SAY THAT A CORPORATION WOULD LIKE TO START SELLING FRANCHISE RIGHTS TO INDEPENDENT OWNERS. BASICALLY, THE INDEPENDENT OWNER ANNUALLY PAYS A CORPORATION FOR THE RIGHT TO USE THEIR CORPORATE NAME, THUS REAPING IN THE BENEFITS OF THAT CORPORATE NAME. -THE BENEFITS COULD RANGE ANYWHERE FROM ADVERTISING, TO TECH-SUPPORT.- THEN WE WILL SAY THAT CORPORATION DECIDES TO HAVE A SALE ON A CERTAIN SERVICE. THIS COULD GO ANY WAY FOR THE CUSTOMER. IF THE CUSTOMER WALKS INTO A CORPORATE STORE HE/SHE WILL RECEIVE THE DISCOUNTED SERVICES WITH

MINIMAL ISSUES. HOWEVER, IF THE CUSTOMER WALKS INTO THE FRANCHISE STORE AND THEY DON'T HAVE THE PROPER EQUIPMENT TO DO THE JOB, THAT CUSTOMER MAY OR MAY NOT GET THE SERVICE OR THEY WILL RECEIVE POOR SERVICES.

THE BEST WAY I CAN RELATE AFTERMARKET AUTOMOTIVE TO EVERYONE WOULD BE SHOES. IF YOU GO AND PRICE OUT A HIGH PRICED NAME BRAND RUNNING SHOE, YOU WILL FIND THEM TO BE EXPENSIVE. THEN GO DOWN THE STREET AND LOOK IN THE DISCOUNT SHOE STORE. (REMEMBER, WE ARE TALKING FUNCTIONALITY WHEN IT COMES TO AUTOMOTIVE REPAIR, NOT STYLE.) AT THE DISCOUNT SHOE STORE YOU MAY FIND A GREAT PAIR OF SHOES THAT FITS YOUR NEEDS FOR HALF THE PRICE OF THE NAME BRAND SHOES. YOU MAY EVEN FIND OUT THAT THE DISCOUNTED SHOES HAVE MORE BENEFITS AND FEEL BETTER ON YOUR FEET THAN THE NAME BRAND SHOES. BUT THE DISCOUNTED SHOES JUST DON'T HAVE THAT NAME BRAND. ON THE OTHER HAND YOU MAY FIND THE DISCOUNTED SHOES TO BE CRAP, AND YOU STILL HAD TO BUY THE SHOES LACES.

THE ONE NICE THING ABOUT AFTERMARKET AUTOMOTIVE IS THEY WANT YOU, TO BE THEIR CUSTOMER. THESE GUYS ARE IN COMPETITION WITH EVERY ONE! THEY ARE NOT LIKE THE DEALER. IF THE DEALER IS THE ONLY ONE WHO CAN DO A CERTAIN SERVICE TO YOUR CAR, THERE IS NO COMPETITION FOR THAT SERVICE. AFTERMARKET NEEDS TO WORK TO GET YOUR TRUST, AND THEN YOUR MONEY. THEY ARE MORE WILLING TO LET YOU MEET THE TECHNICIAN, AND SHOW YOU THE ISSUES THAT YOU MAY BE HAVING WITH YOUR CAR. AFTERMARKET WANTS YOU TO FEEL COMFORTABLE! SO, SOMETIMES THEY WILL BE WILLING TO BEND OVER BACKWARDS FOR YOU.

INDEPENDENT SHOPS

INDEPENDENT SHOPS ARE JUST LIKE AFTERMARKET SHOPS, BUT THEY LACK CORPORATE STRUCTURE. THESE SHOPS ARE USUALLY LOCAL, AND MOST OF THE TIME THEY WERE STARTED BY A REALLY GOOD TECHNICIAN.

I CONSIDER INDEPENDENT FACILITIES TO HAVE OWNERSHIPS CLAIMS TO LESS THAN FIVE LOCATIONS. MOST OF THE TIME THESE ARE SHOPS THAT HAVE ONLY ONE LOCATION, AND ONE OWNER.

THESE SHOPS ARE GREAT BECAUSE THEY WERE USUALLY OPENED BY A TECHNICIAN WHO FELT THAT THEY HAD A LARGE ENOUGH CUSTOMER BASE TO START THEIR OWN SHOP. THE OWNER USUALLY STARTED THE SHOP WITH THE INTENT TO GIVE THEIR CUSTOMERS AN HONEST OPINION AND PRICE. BUT QUICKLY FOUND IT HARD TO DO CHEAP BUSINESS AND PAY THE BILLS.

INDEPENDENT SHOPS HAVE THEIR GOODS AND BADS AS WELL. THE NICE THING ABOUT AN INDEPENDENT SHOP IS THAT YOU USUALLY ONLY HAVE ONE PERSON TO DEAL WITH. THIS CAN BE GREAT IF YOU WOULD LIKE TO

SEE THE SAME PERSON EVERY TIME YOU GO INTO A SHOP. HOWEVER, THIS CAN BE BAD IF YOU HAVE AN ISSUE WITH THAT SHOP.

LET'S SAY YOU HAVE ANY ISSUE WITH AN INDEPENDENT REPAIR FACILITY. YOU GO IN TO MAKE A COMPLAINT TO THE OWNER. AT THAT TIME, IF THE OWNER FEELS THAT YOU'RE COMPLAINT HAS NO MERIT, (AND THEY KNOW THEIR LEGAL RIGHTS) THEY CAN EASILY TELL YOU TO GET LOST! AFTER YOU SPEAK WITH THE OWNER AND THE PROBLEM IS NOT SOLVED, YOU HAVE NO ONE ELSE TO COMPLAIN TO! THIS IS UNLIKE AN AFTERMARKET CORPORATE STRUCTURE. IF YOU HAPPEN TO HAVE ISSUES WITH AN AFTERMARKET REPAIR SHOP YOU CAN ALWAYS COMPLAIN TO THE MANAGER. IF NOTHING IS DONE ABOUT YOUR ISSUE, YOU CAN COMPLAIN TO SOMEONE ELSE. –LIKE THE MANAGER'S BOSS-.

THE OTHER DISADVANTAGE TO AN INDEPENDENT SHOP IS ITS SIZE. LIKE I SAID, MANY OF THESE SHOPS HAVE ONLY ONE LOCATION. ONE LOCATION CAN BRING MANY ISSUES. PRICING CAN BE ONE OF THESE ISSUES. - WHEN YOU HAVE A LARGE CORPORATION, THEY WILL GET A "PRICE BREAK" ON PARTS DUE TO THE FACT THAT THEY ARE BUYING IN QUANTITY- MANY TIMES A SMALLER SHOP CANNOT COMPETE WITH CORPORATE PRICING.

THE LAST ISSUE IS THERE IS: ONLY ONE LOCATION!! THIS CAN BE GREAT IF YOU NEVER LEAVE THE AREA YOU LIVE IN. ONE LOCATION CAN BE REAL BAD IF YOU LEAVE YOUR TOWN AND HAVE AN ISSUE WITH SOMETHING THAT WAS JUST REPAIRED.

THE TECHNICIAN GUY DOWN THE STREET

THE "TECHNICIAN GUY DOWN THE STREET" IS SOMETIMES A NICE WAY TO GO. THE ADVANTAGES OF USING THE "TECHNICIAN GUY DOWN THE STREET" IS THAT MOST-LIKELY PARTS AND LABOR WILL BE INEXPENSIVE. IF HE IS A TRAINED TECHNICIAN, HE WILL GIVE YOU HONEST PRICES AND OPINION. BUT **BUYERS BEWARE.** THE ADVANTAGES OF USING THE TRAINED "TECHNICIAN GUY DOWN THE STREET" DOES NOT WEIGHT OUT HIS DISADVANTAGES. IF HE DOES WORK ON YOUR VEHICLE AND YOU ARE ACROSS TOWN, WHILE SOMETHING BREAKS DOWN THAT HE JUST WORKED ON, THERE WILL BE NO WARRANTY ON HIS LABOR. THERE IS NEVER A SOLID GUARANTEE WITH THE "TECHNICIAN GUY DOWN THE STREET".

ON A SECOND NOTE, IF HE IS AN UNTRAINED TECHNICIAN, HE COULD DO INSTALLATIONS WRONG, CAUSING SIGNIFICANT DAMAGES TO OTHER SYSTEMS THAT HE WILL NOT PAY FOR. EXAMPLE: THE "TECHNICIAN GUY DOWN THE STREET" IS WORKING ON YOUR WATER PUMP AND HE DECIDES TO TOP OFF THE SYSTEM WITH GREEN COOLANT WHEN IT SHOULD BE RED. THIS WILL CAUSE AT LEAST $500 DAMAGES TO THE COOLING SYSTEM ON MOST VEHICLES. – YOU KNOW THAT HE DID SOMETHING WRONG, BUT YOU HAVE NO ONE TO COMPLAIN TO. IF HE WILL NOT COVER THE COST OF HIS MISTAKES, YOU WILL HAVE TO TAKE HIM TO COURT AND PROVE YOUR CLAIM OF HIM DOING SOMETHING WRONG TO YOUR CAR.

The last thing that I have to say, about the "Technician Down The Street", is that I know a couple that needed a new clutch. So they decided to try to save some money and use the technician guy down the street. During the process of installation, a piece of metal landed in the "Technician Guy Down The Street's" eye. So he goes to the hospital, he sends them the bill from the hospital and turns around and sues them. They paid eight times more for that clutch then going to a regular shop and having it done with a warranty.

WHAT SHOPS DO WHAT?

Quick oil & lube places: almost all of maintenance fluid changes: oil changes, transmissions fluid changes & most flushes. Some others will do tire rotations, clean your car out and even get into topping off your A/ C. Not too many quick lube places will do repairs and most quick lube places will charge a little higher price, due to the fact that they do their work in a quick way, so you can get on your way!

Brake places: Most brake places will do more than just brakes. Brake places could do: most of the maintenance fluid changes. Brakes!! Brake places will even get into some repairs: C.V. axle, shocks, struts, A/C work, etc. Some will do alignments and most will do tire rotations & wheel balancing as well. I have found that with most brake places, they will do services and repairs at will. This means that one day they may do a clutch on car, and the next day they won't. Prices will vary from shop to shop.

Dealerships: Everything. I have also found that some dealer are charging some good prices on some services. They do this to try to catch some of the aftermarket business.

Body shops: Paint, and body work. Some will also do detail work, alignments and frame work. Most body shops do not want to do maintenance or repairs. Be ready to pay through the nose.

Specialty or custom shops: High performance applications, custom car, classic cars, and some can even build you a car from scratch. They will only build you a car if you have the money to pay out. Most of these shops services will vary and they will charge a little more for services than other shops for the mere fact that they specialize in certain services.

Tire shops: Tires!! Some will do alignment, custom wheels, maintenance, and repair services, as well. Prices and services will vary from company to company.

Exhaust places: Exhaust! Most will do custom exhaust jobs and some will do maintenance & repair services. Prices and services will vary from company to company.

Stereo places: Custom & aftermarket stereos, alarms. Some will even do window tint. Prices and services will vary from company to company.

Car washes: Car washes! Some car washes will do wax jobs and detail work. I have even seen some car washes doing maintenance and small repair services. Prices and services will vary from company to company.

Technician Guy Down The Street: Whatever price he wants, and whatever type of work he feels like doing.

***CHAPTER* 19**

SHOP LABOR TIMES & PARTS

SHOP LABOR TIMES

MOST PEOPLE DON'T REALIZE THAT IN THE AUTOMOTIVE WORLD, THAT WHEN IT COMES TO MECHANICAL REPAIRS, THERE ARE PRE-SET LABOR TIMES! ALL THIS MEANS, IS THAT WHEN YOU GO INTO A FACILITY FOR REPAIRS AND YOU NEED (LET'S SAY) A WATER PUMP FOR A 1993, MAKE "Y", MODEL "X", THE AUTOMOTIVE FACILITY HAS A PRE-SET LABOR TIME TO DO THAT INDIVIDUAL REPAIR.

FOR EXAMPLE, IF THE LABOR TIME FOR A REPAIR CALLS FOR 1.5 HOURS, YOU WOULD TAKE THAT FACILITY'S HOURLY RATE OF, (LET'S SAY $75) AND MULTIPLY THAT BY 1.5 WHICH WOULD EQUAL $112.50 DOLLARS IN LABOR, PLUS THE PRICE OF THE PART OR, IN THIS CASE, THE WATER PUMP. YOU MAY ALSO FIND ANOTHER SHOP AND THEIR LABOR RATE IS $65 AN HOUR, BUT THERE "BOOK LABOR TIME" IS 1.8 HOURS. AS YOU CAN SEE THE LABOR COST FOR THE JOB IS ACTUALLY MORE. THEY CHARGED $117.00 FOR THE SAME JOB! YOU WOULD THINK THAT GOING TO THE SHOP THAT CHARGES $65 AN HOUR WOULD BE THE CHEAPER PLACE TO GO TO. SO, NOT EVERY SHOP HAS THE SAME SET LABOR RATES. HOWEVER, EVERY SHOP SHOULD USE SOME TYPE OF LABOR GUIDE. THE MANUFACTURER SETS MOST LABOR TIME STANDARDS.

DIAGNOSTIC CHARGES

ON AVERAGE, 92% OF SHOPS THAT ARE OUT THERE, CHARGE A FEE FOR DIAGNOSTIC TIME. WHILE 45% OF MOST OTHER SHOPS THINK THE FEE IS DIFFERENT FROM THEIR REGULAR WORK TIME, 55% THINK IT IS NOT. THE REST OF THE SHOPS (75%) SAID THEY CHARGE DIAGNOSTIC TIME BY THE HOUR, WITH THE REMAINING 25% CHARGING A FLAT RATE. THE RANGE OF PER-HOUR LABOR RATE CHARGE WAS $58.53 TO $90.00

SO WHEN IS A DIAGNOSTIC FEE CHARGED?

A DIAGNOSTIC FEE IS USUALLY CHARGED FOR ONE OF TWO REASONS:

REASON ONE: THE SHOP HAS TO DO MORE THAN "JUST LOOK ". MANY AFTER-MARKET SHOPS WILL DO FREE VISUAL INSPECTIONS ON MOST OF YOUR CARS SYSTEMS!! WHY WOULD THESE SHOPS DO THIS? SHOPS DO THIS FOR ONE REASON AND ONE REASON ONLY, TO HAVE THE OPPORTUNITY TO HAVE YOU AS A CUSTOMER. BUT IF THE SHOP HAS TO DO MORE THAN GIVE YOUR CAR AN "OVERALL CHECK" THEY WILL CHARGE A DIAGNOSTIC FEE. A GOOD EXAMPLE WOULD BE LOOKING AT A TRANSMISSION. A SHOP CAN LOOK (FOR FREE) AT A TRANSMISSION ALL DAY LONG AND SAY SOMETHING IS WRONG WITH IT. BUT THE SHOP WON'T KNOW WHAT IS WRONG WITH THAT TRANSMISSION UNTIL THEY TAKE IT APART. THE DIAGNOSTIC FEE WOULD COVER THEIR LABOR TIME OF THE "TRANSMISSION DIAGNOSTIC DISASSEMBLY", IN CASE THE CUSTOMER DOES NOT WANT TO FIX THE PROBLEM OR THEY DON'T HAVE THE MONEY TO FIX IT.

REASON TWO: THE SHOP CAN ONLY FIND OUT WHAT IS WRONG WITH THE CAR BY FOLLOWING A LONG DIAGNOSTIC PROCEDURE. THESE PROCEDURES CAN SOMETIMES JUST BE COMPLEX STEPS TO FOLLOW. A GOOD EXAMPLE WOULD BE A CHECK ENGINE LIGHT. LET SAY THE "CHECK ENGINE LIGHT" COMES ON IN YOUR CAR. YOU TAKE YOUR CAR TO A SHOP AND THEY SAY "WE NEED TO RUN SOME DIAGNOSTIC." THE SHOP WILL "HOOK UP" A COMPUTER THAT WILL INTERFACE WITH YOUR CAR'S COMPUTER. YOUR CAR'S COMPUTER WILL GIVE THE SHOP A "CODE." WE WILL SAY THE CODE IS A "PO123." -YOU CAN FIND "CODE PO123" HALF WAY DOWN ON THE LEFT HAND SIDE OF THE NEXT PAGE. THE PAGE AFTER THAT IS JUST THE BEGINNING OF ALL THE THINGS THE SHOP WILL HAVE TO DO TOO, TO JUST FIND THE PROBLEM.-

Diagnostic Trouble Code (DTC)	Application	Key On Engine Off	Key On Engine Running	Continuous Memory
P0102	All	—	DC6	DC6
P0103	All	DC20	DC20	DC20
P0106	Probe	—	—	HH1
P0107	Probe	—	—	HH11
P0108	Probe	—	—	HH20
P0112	All	DA20	DA20	DA90
P0113	All	DA10	DA10	DA90
P0117	Vehicles W/O ECT Sensor	DL20	DL20	DL90
	All Others	DA20	DA20	DA90
P0118	Vehicles W/O ECT Sensor	DL10	DL10	DL90
	All Others	DA10	DA10	DA90
P0121	All	—	DH22	DH22
P0122	All	DH11	DH11	DH11
P0123	All	DH8	DH8	DH8
P0125	All	—	—	DA100
P0131	All	—	—	H27
P0133	All	—	—	H20
P0135	NGV	HA30	HA30	HA30
	All Others	H30	H30	H30
P0136	All	—	—	H80
P0141	NGV	HA30	HA30	HA30
	All Others	H30	H30	H30
P0151	All	—	—	H27
P0153	All	—	—	H20
P0155	NGV	HA30	HA30	HA30
	All Others	H30	H30	H30
P0156	All	—	—	H80
P0161	NGV	HA30	HA30	HA30
	All Others	H30	H30	H30
P0171	NGV	—	—	HA41
	All Others	—	—	H41
P0172	NGV	—	—	HA41
	All Others	—	—	H41
P0174	NGV	—	—	HA41
	All Others	—	—	H41
P0175	NGV	—	—	HA41
	All Others	—	—	H41
P0176	All	—	DE1	DE20
P0182	NGV	DB4	DB4	DB7

Test Step		Result		Action to Take
HD9	CHECK INJECTOR DRIVER SIGNAL			
	NOTE: This step requires a standard 12 volt test lamp. A properly operating system will show a dim glow on the Test Lamp. • Key off. • Breakout box installed. • Connect PCM to breakout box. • Connect Test Lamp between Test Pin 71 or 97 and suspect injector test pin. • Start engine. • **Does test lamp have a dim glow while running engine?**	Yes No	▶ ▶	GO to HD10. No light or bright light: REPLACE PCM. REMOVE breakout box. RERUN Quick Test.
HD10	CHECK FUEL PRESSURE			
	WARNING: THE FUEL SYSTEM WILL REMAIN PRESSURIZED WHEN ENGINE IS NOT RUNNING. TO PREVENT INJURY OR FIRE, USE CAUTION WHILE WORKING ON THE FUEL SYSTEM. • Key off. • Install fuel pressure gauge. • Start and run engine at idle. Record fuel pressure. • Increase engine speed to 2500 rpm and maintain for one minute. Note and compare fuel pressure. • **Is fuel pressure between 210-310 kPa (30-45 psi)?**	Yes No	▶ ▶	GO to HD11. DIAGNOSE and REPAIR cause of incorrect fuel pressure.
HD11	CHECK ABILITY OF FUEL SYSTEM TO HOLD FUEL PRESSURE			
	• Start and run engine at idle. Note fuel pressure. • Increase engine speed to 2500 rpm and maintain for one minute. • Look for fuel leaking at the fuel injector O-ring, fuel pressure regulator and the fuel lines to the fuel charging assembly. Service as necessary. • Turn engine off. • Key on, engine off. • **Does fuel pressure remain at specification within 16.5 kPa (5 psi) for 60 seconds?**	Yes No	▶ ▶	GO to HD12. DIAGNOSE and REPAIR cause of fuel pressure bleed down.
HD12	CHECK FUEL INJECTOR FOR FLOW AND LEAKAGE			
	• Refer to Warning, Caution and Handling at the beginning of Pinpoint Test HC to avoid fuel spillage and injury. • Verify that the flow rate for each fuel injector is within specification using Injector Flow Tester. • **Is flow rate for each fuel injector within specification?**	Yes No	▶ ▶	Fuel delivery system is not likely to have caused the Misfire DTC. GO to HD20 to diagnose the vacuum system. REPLACE or CLEAN the inoperative fuel injector(s) as required. RERUN Quick Test.

NOW SOME SHOPS WILL CHARGE A PRICE TO CHECK ANYTHING ON YOUR CAR, AND SOME "CODES" ARE EASY TO DIAGNOSE, BUT NOW YOU CAN SEE WHY MOST SHOPS CHARGE A PRICE FOR DIAGNOSTIC.

***NOTE:* I DON'T KNOW OF ANY COMPUTER THAT "TIES" INTO THE CAR'S COMPUTER SYSTEM AND TELLS YOU WHAT IS WRONG!!! THE COMPUTERS THAT INTERFACE WITH YOUR CAR'S COMPUTER LEADS THE SHOP IN THE DIRECTION OF WHAT MIGHT BE WRONG! THAT IS WHY MOST SHOPS CHARGE A "DIAGNOSIS FEE" DUE TO THE COMPLEXITY OF THE SYSTEM. I WILL TELL YOU A POSSIBLE WAY TO GET AROUND THIS "FEE" IN THE SETCIONS #5.**

WHY ARE PARTS SO MUCH?

SO WHY ARE SHOP PARTS SO EXPENSIVE? WHAT PEOPLE DON'T REALIZE IS THAT IT MAY TAKE MANUFACTURERS YEARS AND MILLIONS UPON MILLIONS OF DOLLARS TO DEVELOP JUST ONE MODEL OF A VEHICLE. SO WHEN A MANUFACTURER DEVELOPS A NEW VEHICLE FROM THE "GROUND UP", THEY WILL NEED TO DO RESEARCH & DEVELOPMENT ON THE PARTS & COMPONENTS THAT MAKE UP THAT VEHICLE. SO, TO LESSEN THE WORK LOAD ON THAT MANUFACTURER, SOMETIMES THE MANUFACTURERS WILL SUB-CONTRACT OUTSIDE COMPANIES TO HELP DEVELOP SYSTEMS FOR THAT VEHICLE. THE MANUFACTURER OR OUTSIDE CONTRACTING COMPANIES WILL FIGURE OUT THE COST OF MATERIALS PLUS LABOR. THIS IS WHAT WILL DETERMINE THE OVERALL COST OF THE VEHICLE AND PARTS THAT MAKE UP THAT VEHICLE. YOU HAVE THREE TYPES OF PARTS TO CHOOSE FROM.

FACTORY PARTS: THESE ARE PARTS THAT COME FROM ONE OF TWO PLACES, THE MANUFACTURER OF THE CAR OR THE COMPANY THAT DESIGNED A SYSTEM IN THE CAR.

AFTERMARKET: THESE ARE PARTS THAT ARE RE-DESIGNED OR MADE BY COMPANIES OTHER THAN THOSE COMPANIES WHO COLLABORATED TO BUILD THE CAR. THESE PARTS CAN BE BROKEN DOWN INTO THREE CATEGORIES: HIGH PERFORMANCE PARTS, PARTS THAT MEET OR EXCEEDS OME (ORIGINAL MANUFACTURED EQUIPMENT) SPECIFICATION, AND ECONOMY OR CHEAP PARTS.

JUNK YARD PART: USED PART.

THE OTHER THING THE MANY PEOPLE DON'T UNDERSTAND IS THAT ANY TIME A PRODUCT IS MADE, BY THE TIME THE PRODUCT IS SOLD TO THE GENERAL PUBLIC, THAT PRODUCT HAS A MINIMAL MARK UP OF FIVE TIMES THE COST OF MANUFACTURING. SO BASICALLY IF IT COSTS A DOLLAR TO HAVE A PRODUCT MADE, BY THE TIME YOU BUY IT THE PRODUCT WILL COST FIVE DOLLARS. WHY IS THIS? THINK ABOUT IT. THE STANDARD MARK UP FOR ANY BUSINESS IS TWO AND A HALF TIMES WHAT THE PRODUCT ORIGINALLY COSTS. SO, LET'S SAY A PART IS MADE AT A MANUFACTURER. THE MANUFACTURER SELLS THE PART TO A DISTRIBUTING COMPANY. THAT DISTRIBUTING COMPANY MARKS THAT PART UP TWO AND A HALF TIMES TO MAKE A PROFIT, COVER THEIR COST AND THEN SELLS THE PART TO A RETAILER. THE RETAILER MARKS THAT SAME PART UP TWO AND A HALF TIMES TO MAKE A PROFIT, COVER THEIR COST AND THEN SELLS THE PART TO CONSUMERS.

THE ISSUE WITH THE AUTOMOTIVE INDUSTRY IS THAT ANY PART COULD BE MARKED UP AS HIGH AS TEN TIMES FROM THE ORIGINAL MANUFACTURING PRICE!!! IF A PART IS MADE FROM AN OUTSIDE CONTRACTING COMPANY, THE PART COULD BE MARKED UP THREE TIMES THE COST OF WHAT IT WAS MADE FOR AND SOLD TO A DISTRIBUTER. THE DISTRIBUTER MARKS THE PART UP BY THREE TIMES WHAT THEY PAID FOR IT AND SELLS THE PART TO A RETAILER. THE RETAILER MARKS THE PART UP AND SELLS IT TO THE GENERAL PUBLIC OR TO A REPAIR FACILITY. IF A REPAIR FACILITY BUYS THAT PART, THEY TOO WILL HAVE THEIR MARK UP.

CHAPTER ***20***

SHOP ESTIMATES /BILLS & PAPER WORK

SHOP ESTIMATES /BILLS & PAPER WORK

AS A CUSTOMER, YOU WILL DEAL WITH MANY DIFFERENT TYPES OF SHOPS. WITH DIFFERENT TYPES OF SHOPS, YOU WILL HAVE DIFFERENT TYPES OF PAPER WORK. SO IT'S A GOOD IDEA TO AT LEAST KNOW THE BASICS ABOUT A REPAIR FACILITY'S PAPER WORK.

CHECK-IN: THIS IS THE PAPER WORK THAT LISTS YOUR PERSONAL INFORMATION; NAME, ADDRESS, ETC. THIS PAPER WORK WILL TELL YOU IF THERE IS A COST TO 'LOOK' AT WHATEVER ISSUES THAT THE CAR MAY BE HAVING. IT COULD ALSO LIST AN AGREED PRICE FOR CERTAIN SERVICES. IF A COMPANY HANDS OUT A COPY OF THIS PAPER WORK, IT IS A GOOD IDEA TO KEEP IT. *GREAT EXAMPLE: I HAVE SEEN CUSTOMERS CARS STOLEN FROM A FEW DIFFERENT SHOPS, AND THE CUSTOMER HAD NO "CHECK –IN" PAPER WORK. WITHOUT PAPER WORK, THE CUSTOMER COULD NOT PROVE & BLAME THE SHOP FOR THEIR CAR BEING STOLEN.*

INSPECTION: THE PAPER WORK THAT THE TECHNICIANS USE TO DOCUMENT THEIR FINDING DURING AN INSPETCION. THIS IS WHAT WILL BE USED TO "MAP" OUT THE ESTIMATES. THIS IS ALSO THE PAPER WORK THAT THE "JOB" IS SOLD FROM.

ESTIMATES: THIS IS THE PAPER WORK THAT SHOWS THE COST OF MAINTENANCE OR REPAIRS. REMEMBER, IT IS JUST AN ESTIMATE. THE ESTIMATE ONLY LISTS THAT COMPANY'S PRICE FOR PARTS AND LABOR. THIS DOES NOT MEAN THAT YOU HAVE TO PAY THAT PRICE!!!

INVOICE: YOU PAY THE PRICE ON THIS PAPER WORK; THIS IS YOUR BILL, YOUR PROOF OF PURCHASE AND WARRANTY!! IT IS A GOOD IDEA TO KEEP A COPY OF THIS AND DOCUMENT IT WITH OTHER VEHICLE PAPER WORK!! IF YOU DRIVE AWAY FROM A SHOP AND YOUR CAR'S WHEEL FALLS OFF, IT IS A GOOD IDEA TO HAVE PROOF THAT THE SHOP THAT YOU JUST LEFT, WORKED ON YOUR CAR. IT IS ALSO A GOOD IDEA TO KEEP FOR WARRANTY PURPOSES.

FOR SOME PEOPLE, UNDERSTANDING SHOP ESTIMATES, TICKETS AND BILLS CAN BE VERY CONFUSING. DON'T MAKE THE PAPER WORK OUT TO BE MORE THAN WHAT IT IS. IF THE ESTIMATES OR TICKET HAS A LOT OF SMALL WORK ON IT, THAT SMALL WORK CAN ADD UP TO A LOT OF MONEY VERY QUICKLY. DON'T BE AFRAID TO UNDERSTAND THE PAPERWORK. THERE IS BASICALLY ONLY TWO THINGS THAT ARE SURE TO BE ON A BILL, **PARTS** AND **LABOR**. THE REST OF THE BILL/ESTIMATES COULD BE MADE UP OF EPA DISPOSAL FEES, SHOP SUPPLIES, AND TAXES, (WICH YOU CAN'T DO ANYTHING ABOUT ANYWAY.)

LET'S TAKE A FEW TICKETS AND BREAK THEM DOWN & ITEMIZE THEM. THIS WAY YOU CAN GET A GRASP ON HOW IT ALL COMES TOGETHER. WE ARE GOING TO ACT LIKE WE ARE TAKING A CAR INTO "AVERAGE JOES" PRETEND SHOP FOR AN OIL CHANGE, ALIGNMENT, AND TUNE-UP. LET'S TAKE A LOOK AT "AVERAGE JOES" BILL!!

NOTE: WE WILL NOT LIST TAXES, OR SHOP SUPPLIES.

THE AVERAGE JOE'S SHOP

100 CLOSE TO YOUR HOME ROAD

INDEPENDENT SHOP $800 OUT OF YOUR POCKET

JANE DOE CUSTOMER

123 PRETTY LANE

YOU'RE CITY, YOUR STATE, 12345

DESCRIPTION:	HOURS:	QTY:	COST:
1. OIL CHANGE SPECIAL	0.3	N/A	$9.00
5W30 OIL		5	$10.95
OIL FILTER		1	$3.00
2. AIR FILTER		1	$15.95
3. ALIGNMENT 4-WHEEL	0.6		$49.95
4. TUNE-UP SPECIAL 4-CYL	0.5		$39.95
STANDARD PLUGS		4	$7.95
5. FUEL FILTER		1	$12.95
FUEL FILTER INSTALLATION	0.4		$30.00
6. FI CHEMICAL		1	$12.95
INJECTOR SERVICE	0.4		$29.95
		TOTAL	**$222.60**

NOTE: LEFT EYE, RIGHT EYE? YEARS AGO, A UNIVERSITY (I DO NOT REMEMBER THE UNIVERSITY) DID A STUDY OVER VISUAL STIMULATION AND ITS ASSOCIATION TO PEOPLE'S DECISION MAKING. ONE OF THE FINDS OF THE STUDY REVEALED THAT PEOPLE WERE MORE LIKELY TO AGREE TO A PRICE AS LONG AS THE PRICE WAS SEEN ON THE RIGHT SIDE OF THE PAPER OR SEEN WITH THE RIGHT EYE!

NOT A BAD PRICE BUT, AS YOU CAN SEE "AVERAGE JOES" SHOP KNOWS HOW TO MAKE A BUCK!

AS YOU CAN SEE, JUST HAVING A FEW THINGS DONE TO YOUR CAR (AND THIS STUFF IS BASIC MAINTENANCE) CAN ADD UP QUICKLY. WHAT YOU ARE LOOKING AT IS THE END BILL, LET'S NOT LOOK AT THAT FOR A MINUTE, LET'S LOOK AT THE BILL ITSELF. IF WE BREAK IT DOWN TO THE ITEMS THAT ARE LISTED, WE WILL SEE SIX SERVICES:

1. OIL CHANGE
2. AIR FILTER
3. ALIGNMENT
4. PLUGS
5. FUEL FILTER
6. FUEL CLEANING SERVICE

THAT'S IT! SIX SERVICES LISTED, SO WHAT'S PARTS AND LABOR? WHY SO MUCH? (LIKE I SAID, SMALL SERVICES CAN ADD UP QUICKLY.) LET'S LOOK AT THE BILL AGAIN, AND LET'S FOCUS ON PARTS AND HOW MANY OF THEM THERE ARE:

DESCRIPTION:	**HOURS:**	**QTY:**	**COST:**
1. OIL CHANGE SPECIAL	0.3		$9.00
5W30 OIL		***5 QTS.***	$10.95
OIL FILTER		***1***	$3.00
2. ***AIR FILTER***		***1***	$15.95
3. ALIGNMENT 4-WHEEL	0.6		$49.95
4. TUNE-UP SPECIAL 4-CYL	0.5		$39.95
STANDARD PLUGS		***4***	$7.95
5. ***FUEL FILTER***		***1***	$12.95
FUEL FILTER INSTALLATION	0.4		$30.00
6. ***FI CHEMICAL***		***1***	$12.95
INJECTOR SERVICE	0.4		$29.95
		TOTAL	**$222.60**

AS YOU CAN SEE, YOU ONLY HAVE SIX ITEMS HIGHLIGHTED AND LISTED IN THE PARTS CATEGORY:

1.	OIL	$10.95
2.	OIL FILTER	$3.00
3.	AIR FILTER	$15.95
4.	SPARK PLUGS	$7.95
5.	FUEL FILTER	$12.95
6.	FUEL CLEANING CHEMICALS	$12.95

TOTAL $63.75

AS YOU CAN SEE, YOU HAVE A TOTAL IN PARTS AT THE RATE OF $63.75.

NOW WE KNOW HOW MANY PARTS AND HOW MUCH WE ARE PAYING FOR THOSE PARTS. SO WHAT AND HOW MUCH IS LABOR? LET'S GO BACK TO THE ESTIMATE TO FIND OUT.

DESCRIPTION:	**HOURS:**	**QTY:**	**COST:**
1. ***OIL CHANGE SPECIAL***	***0.3***	N/A	$9.00
5W30 OIL		5	$10.95
OIL FILTER		1	$3.00
2. AIR FILTER		1	$15.95
3. ***ALIGNMENT 4-WHEEL***	***0.6***		$49.95
4. ***TUNE-UP SPECIAL 4-CYL***	***0.5***		$39.95
STANDARD PLUGS		4	$7.95
5. FUEL FILTER		1	$12.95
FUEL FILTER INSTALLATION	***0.4***		$30.00
6. FI CHEMICAL		1	$12.95
INJECTOR SERVICE	***0.4***		$29.95
		TOTAL	**$222.60**

AS YOU CAN SEE, THERE ARE ONLY FIVE ITEMS HIGHLIGHTED AND LISTED IN THE LABOR CATEGORY:

1.	OIL CHANGE SPECIAL	0.3	$9.00
2.	ALIGNMENT 4-WHEEL	0.6	$49.95
3.	TUNE-UP SPECIAL 4-CYL	0.5	$39.95
4.	FUEL FILTER INSTALLATION	0.4	$30.00
5.	INJECTOR SERVICE	0.4	$29.95
		TOTAL	**$158.85**

SO IN PARTS YOU HAVE $63.75 AND IN LABOR YOU HAVE A TOTAL OF $158.85. THIS GIVES A TOTAL OF $222.60, PLUS THE TAXES, AND SHOP SUPPLIES.

DEALERSHIPS TICKET/ESTIMATE

LET'S TAKE A LOOK AT THE TICKET FROM THE DEALER FOR THE SAME WORK REQUESTED. REMEMBER, ORIGINALLY THE REQUEST FOR SERVICES WERE: ALIGNMENT, OIL CHANGE, & A STANDARD TUNE UP.

AVERAGE DEALER

200 IN YOUR AREA

PICK POCKET U.S.A.

JANE DOE CUSTOMER

123 PRETTY LANE

YOURE CITY, YOUR STATE, 12345

DESCRIPTION:	**HOURS:**	**QTY:**	**COST:**
1. OIL CHANGE SPECIAL	0.4	N/A	$15.00
5W30 OIL SYN. BLEND		5	$21.95
OIL FILTER		1	$5.00
3. ALIGNMENT (4-WHEEL)	2.0		$179.95
4. TUNE-UP SPECIAL 4-CYL	0.8		$49.95
STANDARD PLUGS		4	$12.95
5. RECALL LABOR	0.5		$00.
6. RECALLED PART		1	$00.
		TOTAL	**$284.80**

As you can easily see, at the dealer you had less work done and you paid a lot more money for parts and labor, but you had a free recall done that didn't cost anything.

-A nice Benefit—

In parts you have a total of $39.95 and in labor (mostly the alignment), a total of $244.90. So why is the dealer price more than the other facility? Easy, the labor and the parts cost more.

I know what you're saying, "I understand why the oil is more, AND I understand that I am paying more at the dealer for quality parts and labor on the rest of the bill, but why am I paying almost three times as much for the alignment?" This answer lies in the labor times and the quality of labor. Is it different labor, is it a better service? The real answer will involve your personal scenario. Ask questions about the differences in services. You may find out that the dealer is doing a full alignment for the price of $179.95, as where the independent shop is only doing a partial alignment called a "setting the toe" for $49.95 You may also find out that the independent shop is doing full alignment for $49.95 and the dealer is only doing a "setting of the toe". It is a good idea to ask what is included in that service without telling the facilities about one another! Find out for yourself!

CHAPTER 21

WHY THE HARD PROCESS & THE ATTITUDE TO CUSTOMERS

WHY THE HARD PROCESS

BUSINESS CAN MAKE YOUR TRIP TO AN AUTOMOTIVE FACILITY A COMPLEX PROCESS. SO EXPETC TO FEEL A LITTLE FRUSTRATED. BUT DON'T LET ANY FACILITY MAKE THIS PROCESS A HARD ONE. WHEN YOU GO TO AN AUTOMOTIVE FACILITY FOR MAINTENANCE OR REPAIR THE PROCESS CAN BE BROKEN DOWN INTO THREE WORDS. **COMPLAINT, CAUSE, & CURE!!**

COMPLAINT: THE COMPLAINT IS WHATEVER ISSUES YOU MAY HAVE WITH YOUR CAR (OIL CHANGE, TUNE-UP, ETC.)

CAUSE: THE CAUSE IS WHATEVER ISSUE THAT MAY BE CAUSING THE COMPLAINT. (THE CAR'S COIL PACK IS BAD: IT'S JUST TIME FOR MAINTENANCE, ETC.)

CURE: THE CURE IS WHAT WILL CURE THE COMPLAINT & CAUSE. (THE PLUGS WERE REPLACED AND THE CAR RUNS GREAT, THE CAR HAD NEW BRAKES INSTALLED AND NOW THE CAR STOPS GREAT, ETC.)

THESE THREE STEPS SHOULD BE FOLLOWED AT ALL TIMES. IT SEEMS LIKE AN EASY PROCESS. SO WHY DOES IT SEEM SO HARD TO HAVE THESE THREE STEPS FOLLOWED? THE EASIEST WAY TO ANSWER THIS ISSUE IS IN TWO STATEMENTS: **BEST SALESMAN EVER & YOUR CAR NEEDS A LOT OF WORK.**

BEST SALESMAN EVER: THE EMPLOYEE/ OWNER, WHO IS OVER VIEWING YOUR VEHICLE'S ISSUES WITH YOU, WILL EVENTUALLY SPEAK WITH YOU ABOUT PRICE. WHEN THESE GUYS TALK TO YOU ABOUT PRICE, THEY WILL FOCUS ON WHAT IS WRONG WITH THE CAR FIRST, TELL YOU HOW BAD IT IS AND THEN SPEAK WITH YOU ABOUT THE PRICE. TRUST ME ON THIS ONE (70 PERCENT FOR THE TIME) THEY DON'T CARE WHAT IS WRONG WITH YOUR CAR!!! ALL THEY CARE ABOUT IS HOW MUCH MONEY YOU ARE GOING TO SPEND AT THAT FACILITY. IF THE OWNER SELLS MORE, HE WILL PROFIT MORE. IF THE EMPLOYEE SELLS MORE THIS USUALLY MEANS, THEY WILL EVENTUALLY RECEIVE A HIGHER PAY. NOW DON'T GET ME WRONG, THERE ARE SOME REALLY GOOD SHOPS/GUYS OUT THERE THAT REALLY DO CARE ABOUT YOU AND YOUR CAR. SO DON'T WORRY! I AM GOING TO TRY TO HELP YOU FIND OUT HOW TO FIND THESE "GOOD SHOP/GUYS"!!!!!!!

YOUR CAR NEEDS A LOT OF WORK: IF YOUR CAR NEEDS A LOT OF WORK, IT WILL MAKE THE "BEST SALES GUYS" JOB EASY. THE VEHICLE MAY NEED MANY SMALL REPAIRS, ONE MAJOR REPAIR OR THE CAR JUST HAS NOT BEEN TAKEN CARE OF. WHEN THESE EVENTS TAKE PLACE, IT WILL JUST MAKE IT EASY TO WRITE A HIGHER BILL.

IF THE SHOPS CAN GET YOU TO BUY SERVICES OR REPAIRS, THEIR PROFITS WILL GO UP, THEIR PAY COULD INCREASE, AND THEIR SHOP CAN BE SUCCESSFUL!!

ATTITUDE TO CUSTOMERS

I KNOW SOME OF YOU MAY BE THINKING ABOUT HOW GOOD YOUR EXPERIENCE WAS WITH THE LAST AUTOMOTIVE FACILITY YOU TOOK YOUR CAR TO. SOME OF YOU ARE THINKING HOW NICE THE SERVICE ADVISOR WAS, AND HOW HE EXPLAINED EVERYTHING IN DETAIL. SOME OF YOU ARE THINKING ABOUT THE TECHNICIAN YOU HAVE BEEN DEALING WITH FOR THE LAST FIVE YEARS & HOW HONEST HE IS. THE PEOPLE WHO WORK IN THE AUTOMOTIVE INDUSTRY KNOW THAT IF THEY WANT CUSTOMERS TO COME BACK FOR RETURN SERVICES, THEY WILL NEED TO BE EXTRA NICE TO THOSE CUSTOMERS. SO, THE ATTITUDE TO THE CUSTOMER AT MOST SHOPS WILL BE A GOOD ONE, BUT **DO NOT KID YOURSELF!!** MANY SHOPS WILL DO WHATEVER IT TAKES TWO MAKE A SALE.

TO HELP PUT WHAT I'M TRYING TO CONVEY TO YOU INTO PERSPETCIVE, I WOULD LIKE YOU TO TAKE A LOOK AT THE DRAFT PROCEDURE THAT I GOT FROM A COMPANY THAT WAS HAVING TROUBLE WITH THEIR SALES.

CHANGES TO INFRASTRUCTURE, & OUTLOOKS CAN INCREASE SHOP REVENUE AND CUSTOMER BASES.

INTRODUCTION:

CUSTOMERS ARE THE "BACK BONE" OF OUR LIVES! WHY WOULD I SAY THAT? EASY, WITHOUT THEM WE COULD NOT DO BUSINESS, AND WE WOULD NOT HAVE A PAY CHECK. BASICALLY WE NEED OUR CUSTOMER. THE REAL "Q'S" ARE HOW DO WE KEEP THE CUSTOMERS THAT WE HAVE, HOW DO WE GET NEW ONES, AND HOW DO WE GET A HIGHER TICKET AVERAGE?

THERE ARE A FEW WAYS WE CAN DRAW IN NEW CUSTOMERS, KEEP OUR OLD ONES, GET A HIGHER TICKET AVERAGE, AND STILL MAKE EVERYONE HAPPY. BUT WE NEED TO BE WILLING TO CHANGE OUR ATTITUDES AND SOME OF THE WAYS WE DO THINGS.

GREETINGS:

WHETHER WE ARE ON THE PHONE OR WE ARE IN PERSON WE NEED TO TRY TO MAKE ALL CUSTOMERS FEEL AT EASE WITH US AND HOW WE OPERATE. AT THE SAME TIME WE NEED TO DRAW THEM IN THE DOOR. (GET THEM TO COME IN AT ALL COST. WE WOULD LIKE THEM TO SPEND THEIR MONEY WITH US.) ONCE THEY ARE IN THE DOOR AND WE ARE CHECKING THEM IN, IN AN EASY WAY WE NEED TO BE ABLE TO ASK IF WE CAN HAVE AN OPPORTUNITY TO BE ABLE TO CHECK ANYTHING ELSE ON THE CAR.

EXAMPLE: #1"WOULD YOU LIKE US TO DO AN OVERALL CHECK OF YOUR CAR WHILE YOU ARE HERE TODAY????"

#2 "I SAW THAT YOUR CAR HAS 30K, 60K, OR 90K WOULD YOU LIKE US TO CHECK YOUR CAR'S USER MANUAL TO MAKE SURE THAT YOU HAVE KEPT UP WITH ALL THE MAINTENANCE? IT IS A COURTESY FROM US TO YOU. " (THIS GIVES US A CHANCE TO BE ABLE TO SELL THEM **ANYTHING** AND NOT COME OUT LOOKING LIKE THE BAD GUYS.)

NOTE: WHEN YOU PULL OUT THE CUSTOMER'S MAINTENANCE BOOK FROM THEIR CAR IT WILL HELP WITH SALES. #1BECAUSE WE WILL FIND SERVICES THAT THEY HAVE NOT DONE TO THE CAR.
#2BECAUSE THEY KNOW THAT WE ARE NOT LYING TO THEM ON WHAT NEEDS TO BE DONE AND WHAT DOES NOT.

MOST CUSTOMERS NEGLECT THEIR CARS, SO WHEN THEY COME IN TO YOUR SHOP AND YOU TAKE A LITTLE MORE TIME WITH THEIR CAR YOU WILL BE SURPRISED AT THE RESPONSE THAT YOU WILL HAVE. IF WE FIX, MAINTAIN, OR JUST TELL THEM WHAT IS GOING ON WITH THEIR CAR, THEY WILL BE HAPPY THAT THE WORK HAS BEEN DONE AND IT IS OUT OF THEIR WAY. NOW THEY DON'T HAVE TO DEAL WITH THE ISSUE AT A LATER TIME OR THEY KNOW THAT THE ISSUE WILL NEED TO BE RESOLVED IN THE NEAR FUTURE.

INSPECTIONS:

IT IS HARD TO TELL YOUR TECHNICIANS THAT YOU WOULD LIKE THEM TO CHECK THE CARS "YOU'RE WAY." THEY MAY TAKE OFFENSE TO THIS. BECAUSE THEY ARE THE TECHNICIANS, THEY ARE THE GUYS WHO KNOW!! LET THEM KNOW THAT THEY ARE DOING A GOOD JOB, AND TELL THEM THAT IT IS CHANGE IN COMPANY POLICIES. THIS WAY YOU DON'T GET "BEAT UP" BY YOUR GUYS TOO MUCH. BUT YOU MUST MAKE THEM DO IT "YOUR WAY" FOR THE MERE FACT THAT IF YOU NEVER SAY ANYTHING, NOTHING WILL EVER CHANGE!

JUST BECAUSE A CAR COMES IN FOR A BRAKE JOB DOES NOT MEAN THAT IT IS JUST A BRAKE JOB! HAVE YOUR TECHNICIANS CHECK EVERYTHING. EVEN IF YOU DON'T WRITE IT ALL UP, OR YOU DON'T DO IT ALL, JUST TELLING THE CUSTOMER ABOUT THEIR CAR PLANTS A SEED IN THEIR MIND TO LET THEM KNOW THAT THE CAR NEEDS WORK. YOUR CUSTOMERS WILL ALSO BE GRATEFUL THAT YOU LOOKED EVERYTHING OVER.

MAKE YOUR TECHNICIAN'S CHECK THE CAR THIS WAY!!!!

ALL BRAKE JOBS ARE TO BE TEST DRIVEN, UNLESS THE CAR IS GRINDING OR LEAKING FLUIDS. ONCE THE CAR HAS BEEN TEST DRIVEN, AND PULLED IN TO THE SHOP, YOUR TECHNICIANS SHOULD DO:

#1 DO A LIGHT CHECK.

#2 OPEN THE HOOD AND DO A "U" AROUND THE ENGINE COMPARTMENT (START AT THE DRIVER'S SIDE OF THE CAR AND LOOK AT ALL THE MAJOR COMPONENTS UNDER THE HOOD IN A "U" FASHION.) STARTING AT THE MASTER CYLINDER, NEXT THE AIR FILTER, TRANS FLUID, OIL, MANIFOLDS, BELTS, ETC. YOUR TECHNICIANS SHOULD BE CHECKING EVERYTHING AND HAVE THEM START MAKING ANY NOTES THAT NEED TO BE MADE.

#3 RACK THE CAR AND PUT IT ALL THE WAY UP IN THE AIR. STARTING AT THE BACK OF THE CAR LOOK FOR ANYTHING THAT IT MAY NEED, SHOCKS LEAKING, TIRES ARE BALD, BAD OIL LEAK WHATEVER THE CASE MAY BE.

#4 DROP THE CAR DOWN AND SHAKE THE FRONT TIRES LOOKING FOR ANY LOOSE PARTS.

#5 PULL THE WHEELS AND CHECK THE BRAKES, WRITING DOWN ANY AND **ALL** SPEC.

#6 CHECK MILE MAINTENANCE TO SEE IF THERE IS ANY SERVICES THAT CAN BE RECOMMENDED.

BY DOING THINGS IN THIS ORDER WE WILL NOT MISS ANY POTENTIAL SALES AND THE COSTUMERS WON'T FEEL LIKE WE ARE TAKING ADVANTAGE OF THEM.

AS YOU CAN SEE, IT'S ALL ABOUT PERCEPTIONS AND THE SALE!!! THE OTHER WAY TO LOOK AT THIS PROCEDURE IS THAT YOUR CAR GETS A GOOD OVERALL CHECK. I HAVE WORKED AT A FEW SHOPS WHERE I HAVE SOLD 2,000 DOLLARS WORTH OF WORK TO MANY CUSTOMERS, WHEN THEY CAME IN FOR JUST AN OIL CHANGE, SIMPLY, BY UTILIZING THIS PROCEDURE. THE SAD PART IS THAT THE CARS REALLY DID NEED ALL THAT WORK DONE. THE WORST PART OF THIS STORY IS THAT ALL OF THE CUSTOMERS COULD HAVE TAKEN A LITTLE BIT OF TIME TO PLAN, AND COULD HAVE SAVED A MINIMUM OF $500.00 DOLLARS. LIKE I SAID, EXPECT TO FEEL A LITTLE FRUSTRATED.

SETCION 5

WHAT YOU CAN DO?

SETCION #5 GIVES COST SAVING FACTS, TIPS, AND OPINIONS ON WHAT TO DO WHEN BUYING, OWNING, & SELLING A VEHICLE.

CHAPTER 22

THE LIST

THE PLAN

IN THE FIRST FEW SECTIONS OF THIS BOOK, I HOPEFULLY GAVE YOU A LITTLE INSIGHT INTO THE AUTOMOTIVE WORLD. BUT, THIS IS THE SETCION THAT WILL HOPEFULLY SAVE YOU SOME MONEY! I CAN'T BE FOR SURE THAT YOU WILL GET COST CUTTING PRICES EVERY TIME. HOWEVER I CAN ALMOST BET A SMALL FORTUNE THAT THE NEXT TIME YOU HAVE AN AUTOMOTIVE SITUATION ARISE, YOU WILL BE A LITTLE MORE AWARE OF WHAT IS HAPPENING TO YOUR CAR AND YOUR MONEY.

I AM GOING TO DO MY BEST TO GUIDE YOU THROUGH AN AUTOMOTIVE EXPERIENCE, BUT I CAN'T LIST EVERY PROBLEM, ISSUE, SCENARIO OR SITUATION THAT YOU COULD POSSIBLY ENCOUNTER. THAT WOULD BE NEXT TO IMPOSSIBLE. WHAT I WILL TRY TO DO IS GIVE YOU COMMON ISSUES AND SITUATIONS THAT MAY ARISE. I WILL ALSO TRY TO GIVE YOU MY KNOWLEDGE OF WHAT I KNOW TO BE FACT, OPINIONS FROM THE FIELD, AND OPINIONS OF WHAT I WOULD DO TO SAVE MONEY. HOPEFULLY THIS WILL GIVE YOU A GOOD MIND-SET. THIS WAY THE NEXT TIME YOU HAPPEN TO RUN INTO AN ODD AUTOMOTIVE SITUATION THAT I MAY NOT HAVE LISTED, YOU SHOULD KNOW THE BEST WAY TO HANDLE THAT SITUATION.

THE ONE THING THAT I DO NOT WANT TO DO, IS HAVE YOU TAKE UP A LOT OF YOUR "AT HOME OR WEEKEND TIME". I DON'T WANT TO TAKE YOUR PERSONALL TIME AWAY FROM YOU AND I REALLY DON'T WANT TO HAVE DAYS OF AN UNSETTLED AUTOMOTIVE ISSUE. TIME IS MONEY AND IF I TAKE A LOT OF YOUR TIME IT WOULD BE COUNTERPRODUCTIVE. THIS IS THE LAST THING THAT I WANT TO DO. BUT I HOPE YOU UNDERSTAND THAT IF YOU WANT TO SAVE MONEY YOU WILL NEED TO INVEST A LITTLE TIME.

THE PLAN THAT I AM GOING TO DISPLAY MAY TAKE SOME TIME TO SET UP BUT ONCE IT IS SET UP FOR YOUR NEEDS, IT WILL WORK QUICKLY AND MANY TIMES OVER FOR YOU. THE REAL GREAT THING ABOUT THIS PLAN IS IT WILL TAKE MINIMAL EFFORT ON YOUR PART. SEE, MANY PEOPLE FEEL THAT THE PROCESS OF THE AUTOMOTIVE EXPERIENCE CAN BE BROKEN DOWN INTO THREE (3) PARTS: 1. ACCESS TO A VEHICLE- BUYING NEW, OR USED CAR. 2. MAINTENANCE/REPAIRS TO THAT CAR 3. DEPARTURE FROM THAT CAR- SOLD IT, WRECKED IT, GAVE IT AWAY, ETC. IT SEEMS SIMPLE BUT, THE AUTOMOTIVE EXPERIENCE IS SO MUCH MORE THAN THAT.

THE "PLAN" I KEEP TALKING ABOUT IS DISPLAYED ON THE NEXT PAGE IN A FLOW CHART FORMAT. THIS CHART, JUST OVERVIEWS WHAT I HAVE LAID OUT IN THE NEXT FEW CHAPTERS. ONCE YOU READ THROUGH ALL OF THEM, YOU COULD MARK THIS PAGE AS A QUICK REFERENCE.

SINCE I AM A TECHNICIAN AT HEART, I WILL BE ABLE TO GIVE YOU MORE COST SAVING TIPS WHEN IT COMES TO MAINTENANCE AND REPAIR. HOWEVER I WAS ABLE TO COMPILE LARGE AMOUNTS OF INFORMATION ON EVERYTHING ELSE.

I SAID THAT I DIDN'T WANT TO TAKE MUCH OF YOUR TIME. SO, I HOPE I HAVE MADE THIS SECTION EASY TO UNDERSTAND BEING DIRECT AND TO THE POINT.

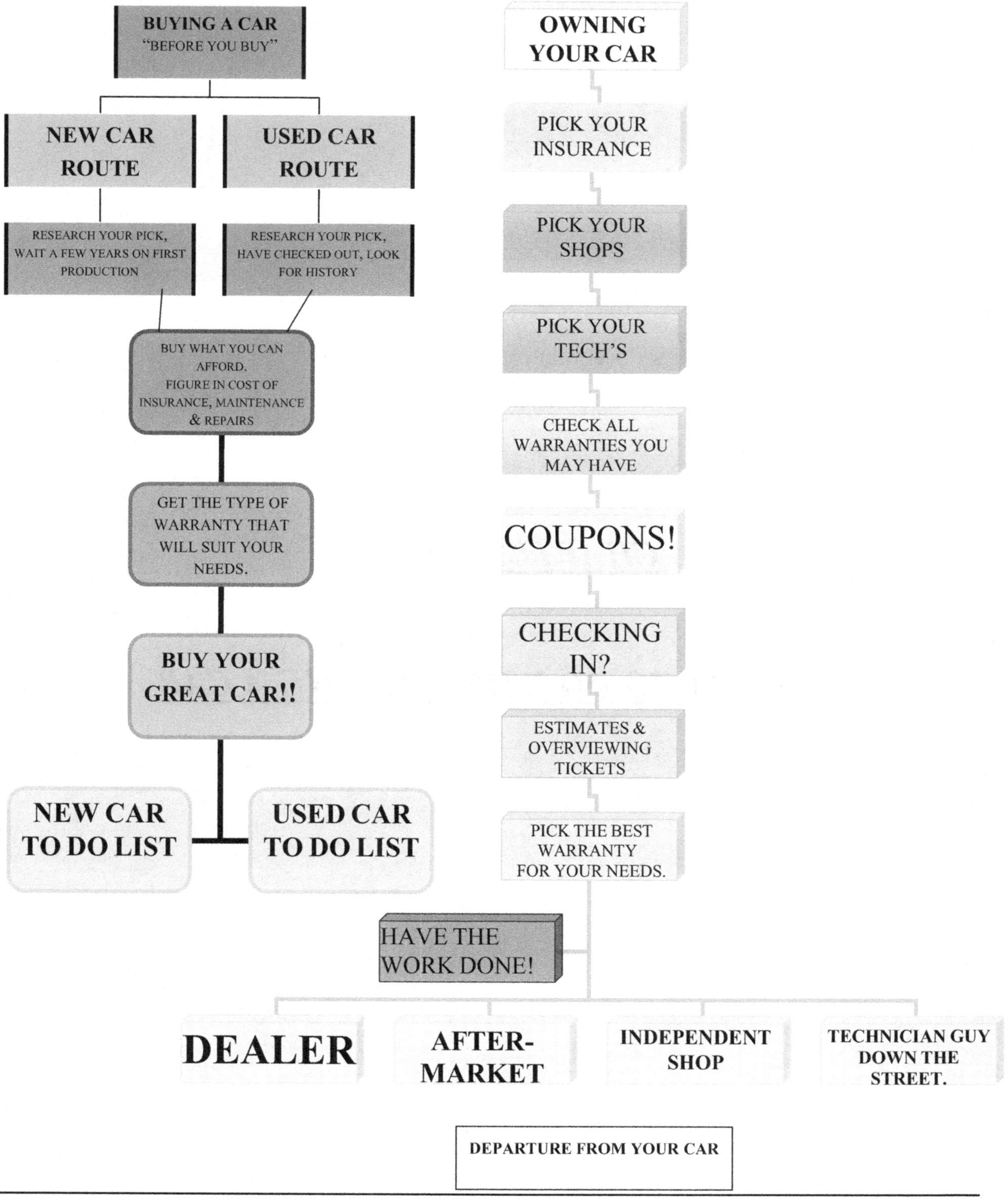
BUYING A CAR
"BEFORE YOU BUY"
NEW CAR ROUTE
USED CAR ROUTE
RESEARCH YOUR PICK, WAIT A FEW YEARS ON FIRST PRODUCTION
RESEARCH YOUR PICK, HAVE CHECKED OUT, LOOK FOR HISTORY
BUY WHAT YOU CAN AFFORD. FIGURE IN COST OF INSURANCE, MAINTENANCE & REPAIRS
GET THE TYPE OF WARRANTY THAT WILL SUIT YOUR NEEDS.
BUY YOUR GREAT CAR!!
NEW CAR TO DO LIST
USED CAR TO DO LIST
OWNING YOUR CAR
PICK YOUR INSURANCE
PICK YOUR SHOPS
PICK YOUR TECH'S
CHECK ALL WARRANTIES YOU MAY HAVE
COUPONS!
CHECKING IN?
ESTIMATES & OVERVIEWING TICKETS
PICK THE BEST WARRANTY FOR YOUR NEEDS.
HAVE THE WORK DONE!
DEALER
AFTER-MARKET
INDEPENDENT SHOP
TECHNICIAN GUY DOWN THE STREET.
DEPARTURE FROM YOUR CAR

CHAPTER ***23***

WHAT TO DO WHEN BUYING A CAR

BUYING A CAR

AUTOMOBILES ARE AN ESSENTIAL IN TODAY'S SOCIETY. YES, IT IS TRUE THAT SOME PEOPLE DON'T DRIVE AT ALL, BUT MOST AMERICANS OWN A VEHICLE. THE AUTOMOTIVE INDUSTRY IS VERY AWARE OF HOW BIG OF A ROLE YOUR AUTOMOBILE PLAYS IN YOUR LIFE. WITH SUCH A LARGE DEPENDENCE ON AUTOMOBILES, YOU WOULD THINK THAT THE GENERAL PUBLIC WOULD KNOW EVERYTHING ABOUT AUTOMOTIVE. BUT FOR UNKNOWN REASONS THIS IS NOT THE CASE. I HAVE MEET TOO MANY PEOPLE THAT ONLY KNOW HOW TO PUMP GAS AND DRIVE. THIS IS A SAD SITUATION.

IT'S NOT SAD THAT THESE PEOPLE DON'T KNOW ANYTHING ABOUT THEIR CAR. IT IS UNDERSTANDABLE THAT PEOPLE ARE BUSY WITH WORK, KIDS, LIFE AND JUST DON'T HAVE THE TIME TO STUDY MORE ABOUT THE SUBJECT OF AUTOMOTIVE. WHAT IS SAD IS TO KNOW THAT AT SOME POINT AND TIME THESE PEOPLE WILL BE TAKEN ADVANTAGE OF.

I KNOW SOME OF YOU ARE ASKING YOURSELF "HOW CAN I AVOID SHOPS ALTOGETHER?" THE ONLY WAY I KNOW HOW TO DO THAT IS: DRIVE RENTAL CARS OR TAKE ANOTHER MEANS OF TRANSPORTATION.
EVEN THOUGH PICKING OUT A CAR CAN BE A PAIN, THERE ARE WAYS TO PICK YOUR GREAT NEW OR USED CAR WISELY. HOWEVER, NO ONE CAN PICK A CAR FOR YOU DUE TO YOUR PERSONAL SITUATION. IT SHOULD BE PRIORITY TO YOU TO THAT YOU MAKE AN INFORMED DECISION.

NOTE BEFORE WE START ON NEW CARS: *WHEN YOU BUY A NEWER CAR, THERE ARE A FEW TERMS THAT YOU SHOULD BECOME FAMILIAR WITH. THESE TERMS ARE: WARRANTY, RECALLS, SILENT RECALLS, AND TSB.*

WARRANTY: *A WARRANTY CAN BE FROM THE MANUFACTURER OR YOU CAN BUY AN EXTENDED WARRANTY. A MANUFACTURER'S WARRANTY WILL COVER SOME OR ALL ISSUES WITH VEHICLE SYSTEMS. -USUALLY UP TO AN ALLOWED AMOUNT OF MILES-. BASICALLY IF A VEHICLE IS HAVING AN ISSUE, THE MANUFACTURER WILL PAY FOR THE REPAIRS. AN EXTENDED WARRANTY EXTENDS THE MANUFACTURER'S WARRANTY WITH A LARGER ALLOWED MILEAGE.*

RECALLS: *A RECALL IS WHERE THE MANUFACTURER MAKES IT PUBLIC THAT THERE WAS A MISTAKE WITH A CERTAIN PART OF THE CAR THAT NEEDS TO BE FIXED. THE MANUFACTURER'S WILL PAY FOR THIS REPAIR.*

SILENT RECALLS: *THIS IS WHERE THE MANUFACTURER WILL FIND A CERTAIN PROBLEM WITH A CAR, AND DECIDES NOT TO TELL ANYONE. THE MANUFACTURE WILL PAY FOR THIS REPAIR ONLY IF YOU ASK IF THERE IS A RECALL.*

TSB: *THESE ARE TECHNICAL SERVICE BULLETINS'. BASICALLY THESE ARE ISSUES THAT THE MANUFACTURER RECOGNIZES, BUT THEY WILL NOT PAY FOR THE REPAIRS. SOMETIMES, THESE ARE ALSO USED BY TECHNICIANS TO HELP THEM PINPOINT ISSUES AS WELL.*

NEW CAR

BEFORE YOU GO OFF AND BUY A NEW CAR YOU SHOULD DO SOME PLANNING. THIS SHOULD BE AN EASY PLAIN. ALL YOU REALLY NEED TO DO IS CHECK OUT A FEW THINGS AND USE YOUR HEAD.

1. THE FIRST THING YOU SHOULD THINK ABOUT IS WHAT TYPE OF CAR YOU WOULD LIKE TO SEE YOURSELF IN: A SPORTS CAR, FAMILY SEDAN, SUV ETC.

2. THE SECOND THING YOU SHOULD DO IS CHECK OUT FOUR OR FIVE (MAYBE EVEN MORE) MANUFACTURERS. NEXT, DO A MATCH COMPARISON OF PRICES, WARRANTIES, RECALLS ETC. MAYBE CHECK OUT SOME CONSUMER REPORTS FROM CAR MAGAZINES, OR EVEN THE INTERNET.

3. ONCE YOU HAVE PICKED OUT A FEW CARS THAT YOU LIKE THE NEXT THING YOU SHOULD IS THINK ABOUT AFFORDABILITY. THIS IS THE ONE FACTOR THAT MOST PEOPLE NEGLECT TO FIGURE IN OR FORGET TO STEP BACK AND LOOK AT THE "BIG PICTURE." YOU SHOULD NOT ONLY FIGURE IN THE COST OF YOUR PAYMENT AND GAS. YOU SHOULD ALSO FIGURE IN THE COST OF OPERATION. LOOK AT:

A. INSURANCE COST. YOU CAN ASK YOUR INSURER HOW PREMIUMS FOR THE VEHICLE YOU WANT COMPARE WITH SMALLER MODELS. PREMIUMS ARE HIGHER FOR MOST LUXURY, SPORT OR FOUR-WHEEL DRIVE MODELS BECAUSE OF REPAIR COSTS AND AUTO THEFT EXPERIENCE. CHECK THE INSURANCE INSTITUTE FOR HIGHWAY SAFETY'S WEB BROCHURE, "INJURY, COLLISION, AND THEFT LOSSES" AT WWW.HIGHWAYSAFETY.ORG.

B. MAINTENANCE. WHEN YOU ARE LOOKING AT YOUR FUTURE NEW CAR, TRY TO PULL OUT THE OWNERS MANUAL AND LOOK AT ITS MAINTENANCE LIST. TRY TO COMPARE IT TO OTHER CARS THAT YOU HAVE PICKED OUT. YOU COULD EVEN ASK THE DEALER TO MAKE A COPY OF IT SO YOU CAN TAKE IT HOME AN COMPARE IT TO OTHER CARS.

C. REPAIRS. I HAVE SEEN SO MANY PEOPLE SPEND $60,000 ON A CAR AND TURN AROUND AND COMPLAIN ABOUT THE COST OF REPAIRS. EXAMPLE: DON'T EXPECT TO DRIVE A HIGH-END LUXURY SPORTS CAR AND EXPECT TO PAY A TOTAL OF $100 FOR BRAKE REPAIRS. BE REALISTIC ABOUT THE CAR YOU WANT TO DRIVE AND BE PREPARED TO PAY FOR THE MAINTENANCE AND REPAIRS.

D. LOOK AT THE WARRANTY'S AGAIN. YOU MAY A FIND GREAT WARRANTY THAT REALLY SUITS YOUR NEEDS. YOU MAY FIND OUT THAT EVEN THOUGH YOU ARE PAYING MORE FOR A MONTHLY PAYMENT, YOU WILL SPEND A LOT LESS ON REPAIRS.

NOTE: *I SUGGEST THAT YOU WAIT A FEW YEARS BEFORE BUYING A FIRST YEAR PRODUCTION MODEL CAR. WHY? WELL IF THE CAR WAS BUILT FROM THE GROUND UP, THE COMPANY MAY NOT HAVE ALL THE "BUGS" WORKED OUT OF THE SYSTEM YET. AS A FEW YEARS PASS, THE MANUFACTURERS WILL GENERALLY FIX ENGINEERING ISSUES WITH THAT PRODUCTION MODEL.*

USED CARS

USED CARS TAKE A LITTLE MORE WORK, BUT YOU CAN STILL FIND A GREAT USED CAR IF YOU CHECK IT OUT PROPERLY. IF YOU DECIDE TO GO THE USED CAR ROUTE, YOU SHOULD DO EVERYTHING THAT IS INVOLVED IN BUYING A NEW CAR. THE ONE THING THAT YOU SHOULD ALWAYS DO BEFORE BUYING A USED CAR IS HAVE IT CHECKED AND I MEAN HAVE IT CHECKED OUT! YOU SHOULD LET THE USED CAR DEALERSHIP KNOW, THAT IF YOU CAN'T HAVE THE CAR CHECKED OUT BY SOMEONE ELSE—YOU WON'T BUY FROM THEM! THE USED CAR DEALERSHIP SHOULD BE OKAY WITH YOU HAVING THE CAR CHECKED BY SOMEONE ELSE. (IF NOT, THEN THEY MAY HAVE SOMETHING TO HIDE.) HAVE YOUR USED CAR CHECKED OUT BUY AT LEAST TWO REPAIR SHOPS. (SET UP AN APPONTMENT FOR TIME & COVIENANCE.) HAVE IT CHECKED OUT FROM TOP TO BOTTOM. ALSO MAKE SURE YOU HAVE THEM CHECK TO SEE IF THE CAR HAS BEEN IN AN ACCIDENT. IF A CAR WAS IN A SERIOUS ACCIDENT, IT MAY NEVER RIDE THE SAME.

THERE ARE MANY SYSTEMS AND PARTS THAT NEED TO BE CHECKED ON A USED CAR.

SEE IF MAINTENANCE HAS BEEN DONE:

OIL CHANGES
TIRE ROTATIONS
TRANS. FLUSHES
BRAKE FLUSHES
P/S FLUSHES
COOLANT FLUSHES

REAR WHEEL & 4 WHEEL DRIVE FLUSHES
REAR DIFF.
TRANSFER CASE
FRONT DIFF.

SEE IF THESE REPLACEMENTS OR REPAIRS NEED TO BE DONE:

FILTERS
ALIGNMENTS
TIRES
BRAKES
SUSPENSION
COMPONENTS
COOLING SYSTEM
BELTS
IGNITION
ELECTRICAL
AIR-CON.
LIGHTS
DASH & INTERIOR
ENGINE
TRANSMISSION
MISC.

NOTE: *THE ONE THING THAT YOU SHOULD HAVE CHECKED OUT ON A USED CAR (ESPECIALLY CARS WITH NO POWER TRAIN WARRANTY) IS THE ENGINE'S COMPRESSION. MANY SHOPS FORGET TO CHECK THIS OUT AND MANY PEOPLE HAVE NO IDEA WHAT IT IS. I WILL GIVE YOU A HINT, IT REALLY TELLS HOW STRONG THE ENGINE IS. THE LAST THING YOU WANT TO DO IS, BUY A CAR WITH NO WARRANTY AND HAVE THE ENGINE BLOW UP A WEEK LATER. YOU MAY HAVE TO PAY SOME CASH TO HAVE THE ENGINES COMPRESSION CHECKED, BUT YOU SHOULD PAY THE COST. IT WILL REALLY MAKE IT EASY DECIDING IF YOU WANT THE CAR OR NOT.*

IF YOU COME TO FIND OUT THAT THE CAR NEEDS $2,000 DOLLARS IN REPAIRS, WHY WOULD YOU PAY TOP DOLLAR FOR THAT CAR?

BEFORE YOU BUY THE CAR, YOU CAN TAKE THE REPAIR ESTIMATES BACK TO WHOEVER IS SELLING THE CAR AND DEMAND THAT THE COST OF THE CAR BE DROPPED BY THE TOTAL COST OF THE REPAIR ESTIMATE. YOU MAY NOT GET THE TOTAL OF THE COST OF REPAIR DROPPED, BUT IT'S A GREAT PLACE TO START IN WITH NEGOTIATIONS! MANY TIMES INDEPENDENT SELLERS WILL NOT DROP TOO MUCH ON THE PRICE, BUT A USED CAR DEALER WILL!!

ONCE YOU HAVE DONE YOUR RESEARCH ON WHAT TYPE OF CAR THAT YOU WANT, YOU CAN MAKE A LOGICAL DECISION AND GO BUY YOUR GREAT CAR!!

NOTE: *YOU CAN ALWAYS CHECK WITH AN AUTO DEALER, BANK OR LOOK UP YOUR VEHICLE'S VALUE IN KELLEY'S BLUE BOOK AT WWW.KBB.COM TO INSURE YOU ARE PAYING A FAIR PRICE FOR YOUR CAR.*

TO DO LIST

NEW CAR: OKAY SO THERE IS NO REAL LIST. JUST TAKE CARE OF YOUR CAR. FOLLOW YOUR MANUFACTURERS MAINTENANCE GUIDE AND KEEP RECORDS OF ALL REPAIRS AND MAINTENANCE. (I WILL SHOW YOU THE BEST WAY TO KEEP RECORDS IN CHAPTER # 30.) DON'T FORGET TO INVOLVE WASHES AND WAXES INTO YOUR MAINTENANCE TO KEEP THE PAINT FROM FADING. ENJOY YOUR NEW CAR.

USED CAR: DO EVERYTHING THAT I SUGGESTED TO DO WITH A NEW CAR. MAKE SURE THAT YOU DO ALL MAINTENANCE OR REPAIRS THAT NEED TO BE DONE AS WELL, THIS WAY YOU WILL MINIMIZE THE POSSIBILITY OF BREAKING DOWN. KEEP FOLLOWING YOUR MANUFACTURER'S MAINTENANCE GUIDE AND KEEP RECORDS OF ALL REPAIRS AND MAINTENANCE. (I WILL SHOW YOU THE BEST WAY TO KEEP RECORDS IN CHAPTER # 30) DON'T FORGET TO INVOLVE WASHES AND WAXES INTO YOUR MAINTENANCE AS WELL.

CHAPTER 24

INSURANCE

INSURANCE

I KNOW ABSOLUTELY NOTHING ABOUT INSURANCE. I AM NOT, NOR HAVE I EVER BEEN AN INSURANCE AGENT, BROKER, SALESMAN, OR CLAIMS ADJUSTER. ANY INFORMATION THAT YOU NEED TO FIND OUT, ASK AN INSURANCE AGENT!! I AM SURE THEY WILL BE WILLING TO ANSWER ANY QUESTIONS THAT YOU MAY HAVE. I DID HOWEVER, LOOK, ON THE INTERNET, FOUND A LOT OF INFORMATION AND I AM PASSING ON WHAT I KNOW ON TO YOU!! ENJOY!!

WAYS TO SAVE MONEY ON AUTO INSURANCE

HERE ARE SOME WAYS TO SAVE ON YOUR AUTO INSURANCE WITHOUT SACRIFICING YOUR INSURANCE NEEDS.

- **COMPARISON SHOP.** CHECK WITH SEVERAL INSURANCE COMPANIES AND AGENTS BEFORE MAKING A FINAL DECISION. CHANCES ARE THAT YOU'LL FIND DIFFERENCES IN SERVICE AS WELL AS PREMIUMS. SERVICE SHOULD BE A MAJOR FACTOR WHEN MAKING A DECISION ON AUTO INSURANCE. ALSO ASK QUESTIONS ABOUT THEIR CLAIMS HANDLING PROCESS; HOW LONG THEY'VE BEEN IN BUSINESS; AND THEIR FINANCIAL STABILITY OR RATING. ASK FRIENDS AND FAMILY FOR RECOMMENDATIONS AND SURF THE NET FOR COMPANY INFORMATION.
- **RAISE YOUR DEDUCTIBLES.** YOU CAN REDUCE YOUR PREMIUMS IF YOU SHOULDER MORE OF THE RISK. BY INCREASING YOUR DEDUCTIBLE, YOU ARE RESPONSIBLE FOR SMALL LOSSES, NOT YOUR INSURER. INCREASING YOUR DEDUCTIBLES FROM $200 TO $500 COULD REDUCE YOUR COLLISION AND COMPREHENSIVE PREMIUMS BY 15% - 30%.
- **CHOOSE THE RIGHT CAR.** BEFORE BUYING A CAR, ASK YOUR INSURER HOW PREMIUMS FOR THE VEHICLE YOU WANT COMPARE WITH SMALLER MODELS. PREMIUMS ARE HIGHER FOR MOST LUXURY, SPORT OR FOUR-WHEEL DRIVE MODELS BECAUSE OF REPAIR COSTS AND AUTO THEFT EXPERIENCE. CHECK THE INSURANCE INSTITUTE FOR HIGHWAY SAFETY'S WEB BROCHURE, "INJURY, COLLISION, AND THEFT LOSSES" AT *WWW.HIGHWAYSAFETY.ORG.*
- **CONTACT YOUR STATE'S DEPARTMENT OF INSURANCE FOR A FREE AUTO INSURANCE SHOPPER'S GUIDE.** IT PROVIDES ALL TYPES OF INFORMATION, INCLUDING AVERAGE AUTO PREMIUMS BY COMPANY.
- **ELIMINATE COLLISION AND COMPREHENSIVE COVERAGE.** THIS IS ESPECIALLY TRUE AS YOUR CAR GETS OLDER AND DEPRECIATES IN VALUE. A GENERAL RULE IS TO ELIMINATE THESE COVERAGES IF YOUR CAR IS WORTH LESS THAN $1000, BECAUSE IT MAY COST MORE TO INSURE IT THAN WHAT YOU'D COLLECT AFTER A CRASH. CHECK WITH AN AUTO DEALER, BANK OR LOOK UP YOUR VEHICLE'S VALUE IN KELLEY'S BLUE BOOK (*WWW.KBB.COM*). IN MOST STATES IT IS LAW TO KEEP YOUR AUTO LIABILITY COVERAGE INTACT.
- **ASK ABOUT DISCOUNTS.** MOST INSURANCE COMPANIES OFFER A MULTIPLE CAR DISCOUNT OR A DISCOUNT IF YOU ALSO CARRY HOMEOWNERS OR ANOTHER TYPE OF INSURANCE WITH THEM. SOME GIVE DISCOUNTS TO STUDENTS WITH GOOD GRADES, AND OTHERS OFFER A CREDIT IF A YOUNG DRIVER IS AWAY AT SCHOOL MORE THAN 100 MILES WITH OR WITHOUT A CAR, DEPENDING ON THE LOCATION.

SOME COMPANIES PROVIDE DISCOUNTS FOR AIRBAGS, DAYTIME RUNNING LIGHTS AND FACTORY-INSTALLED ANTI-THEFT DEVICES. SENIORS COMPLETING A STATE-APPROVED DEFENSIVE DRIVER COURSE ARE ALSO ELIGIBLE FOR DISCOUNTS.

- **ELIMINATE DUPLICATION OF COVERAGES**. SOME AUTO MEDICAL EXPENSE COVERAGES MAY DUPLICATE INSURANCE PROVIDED BY YOUR EMPLOYER. IF YOU BELONG TO AN AUTO CLUB THAT PROVIDES TOWING SERVICES OR IT'S PROVIDED BY THE AUTO MANUFACTURER, YOU DON'T NEED POLICY COVERAGE.
- **REDUCE YOUR DAILY DRIVING**. STATISTICS SHOW THAT THE MORE YOU DRIVE, THE MORE LIKELY YOU'D BE INVOLVED IN AN ACCIDENT----AND THE MORE YOU'LL PAY FOR INSURANCE. SOME COMPANIES OFFER DISCOUNTS TO THOSE DRIVING LESS THAN A PREDETERMINED NUMBER OF MILES ANNUALLY.
- **DRIVE DEFENSIVELY**. AN AT-FAULT ACCIDENT OR A MAJOR TRAFFIC VIOLATION CAN INCREASE PREMIUMS BY AS MUCH AS 40%. IN SOME CASES IT CAN PLACE YOU IN A HIGH-RISK CATEGORY. SOME COMPANIES REWARD POLICYHOLDERS FOR REMAINING ACCIDENT-FREE FOR A CERTAIN PERIOD OF TIME.
- **DOUBLE-CHECK HOW AND WHERE YOU PARK**. OFTEN THE COST OF VANDALISM AND AUTO THEFT IS OVERLOOKED, WHICH INVARIABLY COSTS US ALL. ALWAYS LOCK YOUR CAR AND PARK UNDER STREET LIGHTS.
- **AVOID FILING EXCESSIVE OR FRAUDULENT CLAIMS.** THE MORE CLAIMS YOU FILE, ESPECIALLY SMALL ONES THAT YOU CAN PAY YOURSELF, THE GREATER THE LIKELY HOOD THAT YOUR PREMIUMS WILL REFLECT THIS. PADDING INSURANCE CLAIMS REFLECTS ON THE PREMIUMS WE ALL PAY.

INSURANCE DISCOUNTS

MOST MOTORISTS CAN GENERATE SAVINGS ON INSURANCE BY MAINTAINING A SAFE DRIVING RECORD AND COMMUTING TO CERTAIN LIFESTYLE CHANGES. GOOD DRIVER DISCOUNTS CAN MEAN A SAVINGS IN THE 10% - 20% RANGE OFF THE BOTTOM LINE OF AN AUTO INSURANCE PREMIUM.

MOST INSURANCE COMPANIES OFFER AUTO INSURANCE DISCOUNTS, THOUGH THEY VARY FROM STATE TO STATE AND COMPANY TO COMPANY. AMONG THEM ARE:

- **DRIVER TRAINING DISCOUNT:** FOR YOUNG DRIVERS WHO HAVE ATTENDED DRIVER TRAINING COURSES.
- **GOOD STUDENT DISCOUNT:** LIMITED TO HIGH SCHOOL OR FULL-TIME COLLEGE STUDENTS OVER THE AGE OF 16, AND IS USUALLY CONTINGENT ON MAINTAINING A B OR BETTER GRADE AVERAGE. DISCOUNTS COULD RANGE FROM 5% - 25%.
- **MULTI-CAR DISCOUNT:** USUALLY AVAILABLE TO THOSE WHO INSURE TWO OR MORE CARS WITH THE SAME COMPANY.

- **Multiple policy discount:** Available from some companies to individuals carrying more than one policy (i.e., auto, home, life and/or health) with the same company. Savings should be in the 15% - 20% range.
- **Resident student discount:** Offered by some companies to an insured family includes a resident student, without a car, at a college more than 100 miles from home. A premium reduction might also be available for those taking a car, depending on the college location.
- **Safety feature discount:** Available from some companies to drivers of cars of air bags, since studies have should that there are reduced injuries to vehicle occupants. A few provide discounts for anti-lock brakes (ABS). Some companies have begun to phase out these discounts as most newer makes and models provide airbags and ABS systems as standard equipment.
- **Antitheft device discount:** Available from some companies to insures whose vehicles are equipped with alarms or disabling devices that reduce exposure to theft.
- **Nondrinker and/or nonsmoker discounts:** These are becoming increasingly more popular.
- **Completion of a state-approved senior driver defensive course:** Senior drivers 60 and older can obtain a discount by completing an accident prevention course.
- **Commuter or carpools:** If you drive just a few miles to take public transportation to work or carpool, ask if a mileage discount is available.

In general terms, a policy constitutes a contract by which a company promises to pay to, or on behalf of, an insured losses under specified conditions. The policy also provides certain services. Automobile insurance contracts usually spell out the dollar limits of coverage and the conditions applicable to a loss occurrence.

Note: ***This is a general description of coverage's that vary based to your specific auto policy. It's important to read the policy and discuss any limitations or exclusions with your insurance agent or company representative.***

CONTENTS OF POLICY

COVERAGE'S: EACH AUTOMOBILE INSURANCE POLICY PROVIDES SEVERAL TYPES OF COVERAGE, AND EACH, WHEN PURCHASED, HAS A SPECIFIC FUNCTION. COMMON COVERAGES ARE:

- **BODILY INJURY LIABILITY** – THIS PROTETCS YOU, UP TO THE DOLLAR AMOUNT STATED IN YOUR POLICY, AGAINST THE FINANCIAL CONSEQUENCES OF A LOSS ARISING FROM INJURY TO SOMEONE FROM AN AUTOMOBILE ACCIDENT FROM WHICH YOU ARE LEGALLY TO BLAME. DEFENSE COSTS ARE IN AN ADDITION TO THE LIMITS OF LIABILITY.
- **PROPERTY DAMAGE LIABILITY** – SIMILAR TO BODILY INJURY LIABILITY COVERAGE, EXCEPT THAT IT PROTECTS YOU AGAINST A CLAIM FOR DAMAGE TO ANOTHER AUTOMOBILE OR OTHER PROPERTY, IN AN ACCIDENT FOR WHICH YOU ARE LEGALLY LIABLE. THE PROTETCION AGAIN IS UP TO THE AMOUNT OF INSURANCE YOU PURCHASE. DEFENSE COSTS ARE IN ADDITION TO THE LIMITS OF LIABILITY.
- **MEDICAL PAYMENTS** – PAYS FOR MEDICAL OR FUNERAL EXPENSES, UP TO THE AMOUNT OF INSURANCE YOU PURCHASE, FOR YOU AND FOR OTHERS INJURED OR KILLED RIDING IN YOUR CAR, NO MATTER WHO CAUSED THE ACCIDENT. I T ALSO COVERS YOU AND RESIDENT MEMBERS OF YOUR FAMILY IF STRUCK BY A CAR AS A PEDESTRIAN OR IF RIDING IN ANOTHER CAR.
- **UNINSURED MOTORISTS (UM)** – PROVIDES INJURY COVERAGE TO THE INSURED DRIVER, RESIDENT MEMBERS OF YOUR FAMILY AND PASSENGERS, UP TO THE POLICY LIMITS, WHEN INVOLVED IN AN ACCIDENT CAUSED BY THE OWNER OR OPERATOR OF AN UNINSURED VEHICLE OR A "HIT-SKIP." THE NAME INSURED AND ALSO THE FAMILY MEMBERS ARE COVERED IF THEY ARE PEDESTRIANS AND STRUCK BY A UM VEHICLE.

UNINSURED MOTORISTS SHOULD BE A MUST ON EVERY POLICY!!

THIS IS A GREAT OPTION TO HAVE IF YOUR INSURANCE COMPANY OFFERS IT, ***TAKE IT!!***

- **UNDERINSURED MOTORISTS (UIM)** – PROVIDES INJURY COVERAGE TO THE INSURED DRIVER, RESIDENT MEMBERS OF YOUR FAMILY AND PASSENGERS, UP TO THE POLICY LIMITS, WHEN INVOLVED IN AN ACCIDENT WHEN THE AT-FAULT DRIVER'S POLICY LIMITS ARE LESS THAN YOUR UIM LIMIT.
- **UNINSURED MOTORISTS PROPERTY DAMAGE (UMPD)** – PROVIDES COVERAGE FOR YOUR VEHICLE IF INVOLVED IN AN ACCIDENT WITH A NEGLIGENT UNINSURED MOTORIST. INSURANCE COMPANIES ARE NOT REQUIRED TO OFFER UMPD TO THOSE CARRYING COLLISION COVERAGE, SINCE IT PROVIDES SIMILAR COVERAGE. COVERAGE AMOUNT IS USUALLY $7500 AND INCLUDES A DEDUCTIBLE NO HIGHER THAN $250.
- **COLLISION** – THIS COVERAGE PAYS FOR DAMAGE TO YOUR CAR CAUSED BY IMPACT WITH ANOTHER OBJECT OR AN OVERTURN, IRRESPETCIVE OF FAULT. THE COLLISION COVERAGE USUALLY

INCLUDES A DEDUCTIBLE. THIS MEANS THAT YOU PAY THE FIRST $100, $200 OR SO FOR REPAIRS TO YOUR CAR AND THE COMPANY PAYS THE REST.

- **OTHER THAN COLLISION** – THIS IS A CATCH-ALL COVERAGE THAT PAYS YOU FOR DAMAGE TO YOUR CAR CAUSED BY SOMETHING OTHER THAN COLLISION OR UPSET. PERILS COVERED UNDER "OTHER THAN COLLISION" MAY INCLUDE FIRE, THEFT, MISSILES, FALLING OBJECTS, LARCENY, EXPLOSION OR EARTHQUAKE, TORNADOS OR WINDSTORMS, HAIL, WATER, FLOOD, MALICIOUS MISCHIEF, VANDALISM, RIOT, CIVIL COMMOTION AND CONTACT WITH A BIRD OR ANOTHER ANIMAL, "OTHER THAN COLLISION" IS ALSO AVAILABLE WITH DEDUCTIBLES. IT IS ALSO KNOWN AS "COMPREHENSIVE" INSURANCE COVERAGE.
- **SUPPLEMENTARY PAYMENTS** – THIS PROVIDES FOR PAYMENT OVER THE LIMITS OF LIABILITY NOTED IN YOUR POLICY FOR EXPENSES INCURRED BY THE INSURANCE COMPANY, ALL COSTS TAXED AGAINST YOU IN A COURT SUIT, ATTORNEY'S FEES, BAIL BONDS (UP TO A CERTAIN AMOUNT) AND RELATED COSTS. IT ALSO COVERS REASONABLE EXPENSES YOU INCUR AT THE REQUEST OF THE COMPANY. MOST POLICIES COVER UP TO $200 A DAY FOR WAGE LOSSES IF ATTENDING A HEARING OR TRIAL AT THE COMPANY'S REQUEST.
- **DEFINITION:** THIS SECTION OF THE INSURANCE POLICY DEFINES SUCH TERMS AS WHO IS COVERED BY THE CONTRACT AND WHAT THE COMPANY DESCRIBES AS THE "COVERED AUTO."
- **EXCLUSIONS:** EXCLUSIONS CLARIFY THE INTENT OF THE INSURANCE POLICY BY EXPLAINING THE SITUATIONS IN WHICH THE POLICY WILL NOT COVER YOU OR THE INSURED VEHICLE. YOU MAY BE ABLE TO "BUY BACK" COVERAGE FOR CERTAIN EXCLUSIONS BY ADDING ENDORSEMENTS TO THE POLICY. POLICYHOLDERS SHOULD PAY SPECIAL ATTENTION TO THIS SECTION AND SHOULD BE AWARE THAT THE POLICY DOES NOT COVER ALL THINGS UNDER ALL CIRCUMSTANCES.
- **CONDITIONS:** THIS SECTION ESTABLISHES THE CONDITIONS WHICH MUST BE PRESENT OR COMPLIED BY WITH THE COMPANY AND/OR THE INSURED. EXAMPLES OF CONDITIONS INCLUDE TIME-PERIOD RESTRICTIONS, DUTIES, IN THE EVENT OF A CLAIM, PROOF OF LOSS, CANCELLATIONS, ETC.

***CHAPTER* 25**

COUPONS

COUPONS

THE BEST WAY FOR COMPANIES TO DRAW IN NEW CUSTOMER IS ADVERTISING. MANY TIMES IT WILL BE IN THE FORM OF A COUPON. COUPONS ARE GREAT, ONLY IF THEY APPLY TO YOU. IT IS KIND OF TOUGH TO FIND OUT WHAT COUPONS WORK FOR YOU, AND WHICH ONES DO NOT. -THIS IS ALSO WHY; IT IS GOOD IDEA TO KNOW A LITTLE ABOUT YOUR CAR. -

SEE, YOU MAY FIND A COUPON THAT IS GOOD FOR ONE OIL CHANGE AT THE PRICE OF $10.95! YOU THINK THIS IS GREAT PRICE SO YOU HOP IN YOUR CAR, DRIVE DOWN TO THE SHOP THAT HAS THAT COUPON ADVERTISED, AND COME TO FIND OUT YOUR OIL CHANGE IS GOING TO BE $29.95???? WHAT JUST HAPPENED? I HAD A COUPON? THEY SAID MY CAR DID NOT APPLY.

BEFORE YOU CALL OR DRIVE DOWN TO ANY COMPANY YOU SHOULD JUST LOOK. YOU CAN LEARN A LOT BY JUST LOOKING, AND HAVING A LITTLE INFORMATION ABOUT YOUR CAR. AFTER THAT, ALL YOU NEED TO DO IS READ THE "FINE PRINT." I HAVE A LIST OF COUPONS FROM THE INTERNET AND SUNDAY PAPER ACROSS THE COUNTRY. I AM GOING TO GO DOWN THE LIST AND PINPOINT THE ISSUES THAT I SEE, TO GIVE YOU EXAMPLES OF WHAT YOU SHOULD BE LOOKING FOR. OTHER THAT THE "FINE PRINT", COUPONS ARE A GREAT WAY TO SAVE SOME CASH!!

COUPON EXAMPLES:

ADD $2.50 FOR SHOP SUPPLIES, NO NAME BRAND ON THE OIL AND ITS ONLY GOOD FOR 10W30 OIL!! THIS COUPON WOULD BE GOOD IF YOU ARE GOING TO SELL YOUR CAR OR IF 5 QTS. OF 10W30 APPLIES TO YOUR CAR.

NOTE: *MOST NEW CARS TAKE A 5W30 OR 5W20 OIL.*

ADD $2.50 FOR SHOP SUPPLIES, BUT NOT A BAD PRICE. GOOD UP TO 5QTS. OF REGULAR 10W30, NAME BRAND OIL. A GREAT COUPON IF IT APPLIES TO YOUR CAR.

NO NAME BRAND ON THE OIL, 10W30 ONLY AND AN EPA FEE.

NO NAME BRAND ON THE SYNTHETIC BLEND OIL.

LOOKS LIKE THEY WILL GIVE YOU A GOOD PRICE ON A NO NAME BRAND OIL CHANGE, BUT IT ALSO LOOKS LIKE THEY WILL FIND ISSUES WITH THE 30, 60, 90K INSPECTION. TO ME, IT LOOKS LIKE THIS COMPANY IS GOING TO TRY TO SELL YOU EVERYTHING UNDER THE SUN.

WHAT! $74.95 FOR AN OIL CHANGE? ACTUALLY, IT IS A GOOD PRICE IF YOU DRIVE LARGER DIESEL TRUCK.

NOT A BAD PRICE, GOOD NAME BRAND OIL, AND SHOWS HOW MUCH YOU SAVE.

IT LOOKS LIKE THIS COMPANY NEEDS BUSINESS. THE OIL CHANGE IS A NO NAME BRAND OIL CHANGE WITH A TIRE ROTATION FOR A REAL CHEAP PRICE. THIS COMPANY MAY NOT GIVE A GREAT OIL CHANGE, BUT THEY COULD BE GREAT TO USE FOR OTHER REPAIRS, FOR THE MERE FACT THAT THIS COMPANY NEEDS THE BUSINESS. SO, THIS COMPANY MAY HAVE A CHEAPER REPAIR PRICE THAN EVERYWHERE ELSE.

LOOKS LIKE A GREAT PRICE FOR A FACTORY SCHEDULED MAINTENANCE, BUT, YOU SHOULD REALLY THINK ABOUT IT. EVERY CAR WILL BE DIFFERENT WHEN IT COMES TO MAINTENANCE. IT ALSO SAYS <u>STARTING AT $149.95, MOST CARS.</u> YOU SHOULD CHECK OUT YOUR OWN PERSONAL MAINTENANCE SCHEDULE, NOT SOMEONE ELSES.

WITH 15,000 MILES ON JUST ABOUT ANY CAR, THERE SHOULDN'T BE MORE THAN AN OIL CHANGE, MAYBE A FEW FILTER CHANGES, AND A TIRE ROTATION WITH A QUICK BRAKE CHECK.

THE 30,000 MILE SERVICE MAY BE GOOD BUT AGAIN CHECK OUT YOUR OWN PERSONAL MAINTENANCE SCHEDULE, DON'T HAVE SOMEONE ELSE CHECK IT FOR YOU.

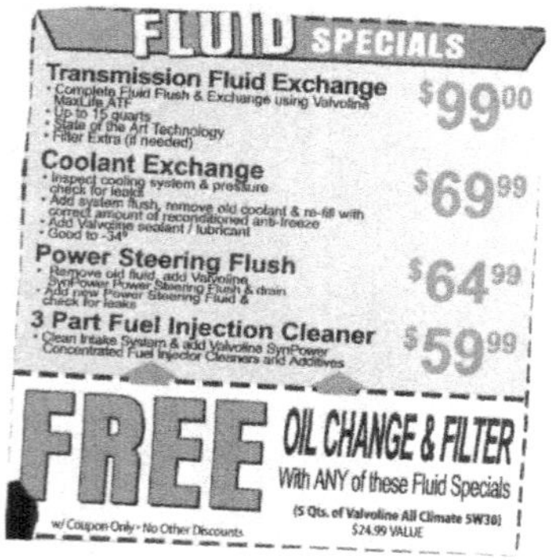

I LIKE THIS ONE! ALL PRICES ARE IN PLAIN VIEW AND YOU GET AN OIL CHANGE. – YOU CAN'T SEE IT BUT <u>IT IS</u> A NAME BRAND OIL CHANGE AS WELL-

I LIKE THIS ONE TOO. IT'S A NO NAME OIL CHANGE BUT, EVERYTHING THAT THEY DO WITH THAT SERVICE, IS IN PLAIN SIGHT.

THIS COUPON IS NOT A BAD PRICE FOR WHAT THEY ARE DOING, BUT EVERYTHING THAT THEY ARE DOING HAS NOTHING TO DO WITH YOUR FUEL SYSTEM. DOING THIS STUFF COULD HELP WITH YOUR FUEL MILEAGE, BUT IT IS BASICALLY AN OIL CHANGE, TIRE ROTATION, AND AN AIR FILTER PACKAGE.

NOT A BAD PRICE. THEY ARE ONLY CLEANING THE AIR INTAKE AND REPLACING THE AIR FILTER.

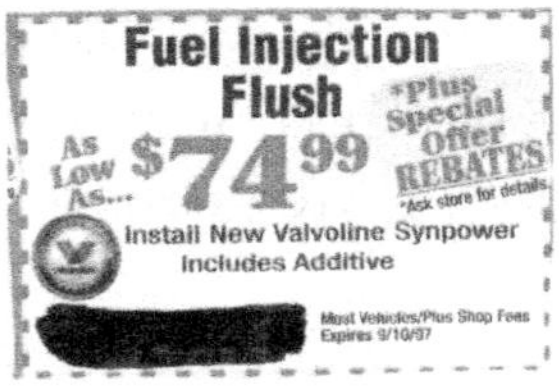

LOOKS LIKE A HIGH PRICE BUT, THEY ARE CLEANING YOUR FUEL INJECTION SYSTEM. IT IS ACTUALLY A GOOD SERVICE. JUST MAKE SURE TO CALL AND ASK IF THEY ARE CLEANING THE FUEL RAIL, AND NOT DOING THE SERVICE IN THE ABOVE COUPON.

$69.95 FOR FOUR PLUGS INSTALLED, EXTRA FOR PLATINUM PLUGS, IRIDIUM PLUGS AND ANYTHING OTHER THAN A 4-CYLINDER CAR. THERE IS NO NAME BRAND ON THE PLUGS AS WELL. BASICALLY, IT IS OKAY.

YOU CAN'T SEE IT BUT, THIS IS FOR A <u>4-CYLINDER CAR ONLY AND BOSCH PLUGS</u>. IF YOU DRIVE A 4-CYLINDER CAR THAT TAKES A BOSCH PLUG, THIS WOULD BE A GREAT COUPON.

$64.95 FOR THEM TO DO A CHECK. THEY ARE NOT EVEN ADDING FREON!

$19.95 FOR THEM JUST TO LOOK.

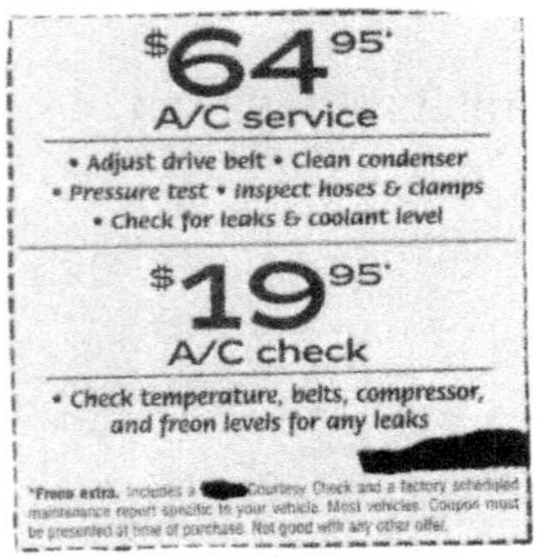

FOR $19.95 THIS COMPANY WILL DO THE SAME THING THE LAST COMPANY WAS DOING FOR $64.95. FREON IS STILL EXTRA.

SAME BASIC CHECK OUT AS THE LAST COUPON.

THEY LOOK LIKE THEY ARE CHEAPER THAN EVERYONE ELSE, BUT THEY ARE ONLY LOOKING AT THE SYSTEM. THEY ARE NOT DOING A PRESSURE CHECK, LIKE THE LAST TWO COUPONS.

FREE ALIGNMENT WITH FOUR TIRES. NOT TOO BAD, JUST CHECK THE PRICE ON TIRES, AND COMPARE WITH EVERYONE ELSE. YOU MAY FIND OUT THAT YOU CAN GET BOTH DONE FOR A CHEAPER PRICE.

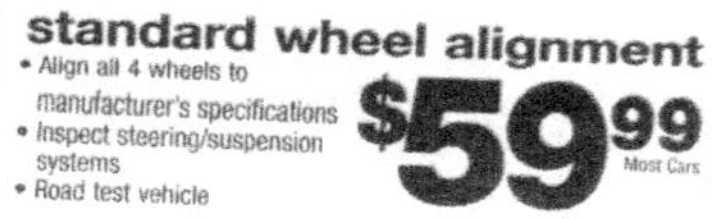

MOST CARS

AS LOW AS

DO NOT MISTAKE AN ALIGNMENT FOR A WHEEL BALANCE!!! OTHER THAN THAT THIS IS A GOOD COUPON.

WHENEVER A SHOP DOES AN INSPECTION ON A TRANSMISSION, THEY WILL ALMOST HAVE TO DISASSEMBLE IT TO FIND OUT WHAT IS WRONG. WITH THAT SAID, THERE IS NO REAL INSPECTION WITH THIS COUPON. THEY ARE ONLY LOOKING AT YOUR TRANSMISSION.

THIS IS A GOOD COUPON, ONLY IF YOU HAVE A TRANSMISSION LIGHT ON!!

$100 OFF? HOW MUCH IS THE REPAIR?

NOT A BAD PRICE ON A TRANSMISSION FLUSH. NO NAME BRANDS LISTED.

THIS IS NOT A TRANSMISSION FLUSH!!! IT IS A DRAIN AND FILL ONLY!! IF YOU HAVE A LOWER TRANSMISSION PAN GASKET LEAK, THIS WOULD BE A GREAT COUPON TO USE.

GOOD PRICE, JUST WATCH OUT FOR *AS LOW AS*

HOW MUCH WILL IT BE FOR THEM TO DO THE BRAKES?

OFF WHAT? THEY DON'T EVEN TELL YOU WHAT IS INCLUDED WITH THE SERVICE.

NO NAME BRAND ON PARTS.

RIGHT UNDER THE $68.00 YOU CAN SEE IT IS FOR LABOR ONLY.

AS LOW AS AND LABOR ONLY

STARTING AT AND, LABOR ONLY.

NO LABOR LISTED

NO NAME BRAND ON TIRES.

I LOVE IT! ALL SIZES AND PRICES ARE LISTED. THEY ARE ALSO NAME BRAND TIRES!

MAIL IN OFFER, YOU NEED TO BUY FOUR TIRES AND IT LOOKS LIKE YOU WILL HAVE TO JUMP THROUGH SOME HOOPS TO GET YOU'RE $50.00.

A FREE COMPUTER SCAN ONLY IF YOU FIX THE PROBLEM. OTHERWISE YOU WILL HAVE TO PAY THE DIAGNOSTIC FEE.

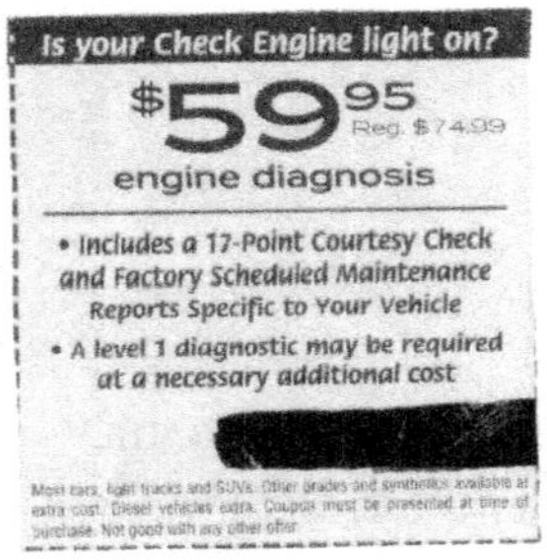

THE PRICE IS CLEAR AND THEY ARE TELLING EXACTLY WHAT THEY ARE DOING. BUT, THIS ALSO MEANS THEY WILL HAVE TO PROPERLY DIAGNOSE THE PROBLEM AND STAND BEHIND THEIR WORK. THEY ALSO PUT IN A SMALL NOTATION THAT WOULD REGULARLY BE IGNORED. ***A LEVEL 1 DIAGNOSTIC MAY BE REQUIRED AT A NECESSARY ADDITIONAL COST** *. THIS SHOULD BASICALLY MEAN, IF THE TIME LAPES GOES OVER AN HOUR AND THE SHOP CAN'T FIND THE PROBLEM, THE SHOP WILL START TO CHARGE EXTRA.

IF IT COST $500.00 TO DO THE T-BELT, YOU'RE NOT EVEN SAVING 10%. FIND OUT THE COST OF THE REPLACEMENT.

***CHAPTER* 26**

PICK YOUR SHOPS

PICKING SHOPS

ONE OF THE MOST COMMON QUESTIONS I HEAR IS, "WHERE SHOULD I TAKE MY CAR TO GET IT FIXED?" MY ANSWER IS TO TAKE IT TO A REPAIR FACILITY THAT (1) HAS A GOOD REPUTATION (ASK FRIENDS AND NEIGHBORS WHERE THEY TAKE THEIR VEHICLES), THAT (2) IS AFFILIATED WITH A GROUP SUCH AS AAA AND/OR HAS ASE CERTIFIED TECHNICIANS, AND (3) APPEARS TO BE CLEAN, FRIENDLY, AND COMPETENTLY MANAGED. (4) THE SHOP SHOULD ALSO ADHERE TO THE CODE OF ETHICS AND REPAIR STANDARDS PUT FORTH BY THE MOTORIST ASSURANCE PROGRAM (MAP) OFFICIAL WEBSITE.

WORD OF MOUTH IS PROBABLY THE BEST WAY TO FIND A SHOP. MOST REPAIR SHOPS IN THE UNITED STATES ARE OWNER-OPERATED, AND THOSE OWNERS KNOW THAT THE BEST WAY TO LOSE BUSINESS IS TO PROVIDE SHODDY WORK. THEIR SELF-INTEREST MAKES THEM WANT TO DO A GOOD JOB FOR YOU, BECAUSE IF THEY DO NOT, YOU WON'T BRING YOUR CAR BACK WHEN IT NEEDS SERVICE IN THE FUTURE. IN ADDITION, YOU MAY TELL THE PERSON WHO REFERRED YOU ABOUT YOUR BAD EXPERIENCE, AND THAT PERSON MAY DECIDE NOT TO GO BACK AND/OR NOT TELL ANY OF THEIR OTHER FRIENDS TO USE HIM. IT HAS BEEN SAID THAT "ONE SATISFIED CONSUMER WILL TELL JUST A FEW FRIENDS, BUT A CONSUMER THAT IS UNHAPPY TELLS AN AVERAGE OF TEN."

IT WILL BE TOUGH TRYING TO FIND THE RIGHT SHOP FOR ALL OF YOUR AUTOMOTIVE NEEDS. BUT, AFTER YOU HAVE LOOKED AT ALL OF THE POSSIBLITIES YOU SHOULD ALSO THINK ABOUT YOUR SITUATION. IF YOU DO A LOT OF TRAVELING, YOU SHOULD TRY TO TAKE YOUR CAR TO A SHOP THAT IS NATION WIDE. I WOULD ALSO THINK ABOUT THE PROBLEM THAT YOU MAY HAVE. DON'T TAKE AN ENGINE REPAIR TO A MUFFLER SHOP. OTHER THAN THAT, PICK THREE DIFFERENT SHOPS (IN THAT SAME FIELD. TIRES, BRAKES, ENGINE, ETC.) AND, COMPARE LABOR TIMES AND PART PRICES.

AFTER KNOWING HOW TO MAKE AN EDUCATED & SOUND JUDGMENT ON WHAT TYPE OF SHOPS TO TAKE YOUR CAR TO, IT SHOULD REALLY ONLY COME DOWN TO THREE THINGS, PRICE, CUSTOMER SERVICE, AND "ARE YOU COMFORTABLE?".

SAVE SOME TIME

THERE ARE A FEW THINGS THAT YOU CAN DO TO SPEED UP THE PROCESS OF PICKING SOME SHOPS OUT. THE BEST TIME TO TAKE YOU CAR TO JUST ABOUT ANY SHOP WILL BE MID- MONTH AND MID WEEK. THIS IS THE TIME MOST SHOPS WILL BE LESS BUSY. IF THEY ARE LESS BUSY, THEY SHOULD HAVE MORE TIME TO SERVE YOU!

YOU SHOULD ALSO:

1. THINK ABOUT WHAT YOUR REPAIRS OR MAINTENANCE CHECKS ARE.
2. THINK OF THE FACILITY YOU WOULD LIKE TO TAKE YOUR AUTOMOBILE TO.

   NOTE: DON'T TAKE YOUR AUTOMOBILE TO A BRAKE SHOP FOR ENGINE DIAGNOSTICS!
3. YOU CAN SAVE MOST OF YOUR TIME BY CALLING AROUND TO A FEW SHOPS AND ASKING THEM SPECIFIC QUESTIONS.

ASK:

1. HOW LONG IS THE WAIT?
2. WHAT ARE YOUR LABOR RATES?
3. WHAT ARE THE COST?
4. ASK IF THERE IS A CHEAPER PRICE OR OPTIONS ON PARTS. **LISTEN TO THE GUY TO SEE IF HE IS TOO BUSY, SEE IF HE CARES, TRY TO PAY ATTENTION TO HIS VOCABULARY AND HIS KNOWLEDGE.**

REMEMBER, YOU ONLY HAVE FOUR SHOPS TO PICK FROM:

1. **DEALER:** SOME WARRANTY
2. **AFTER-MARKET:** CHECK WARRANTY, SOME GOOD, SOME BAD
3. **INDEPENDENT:** WARRANTIES ON SOME STUFF, BUT ONLY AT THAT LOCATION
4. **GUY DOWN THE STREET:** NO WARRANTY, NO WARRANTY, NO WARRANTY!!!!!!!!

ALSO REMEMBER THERE ARE ONLY THREE THINGS THAT SHOULD HAPPEN. YOUR:

COMPLAINT: THE COMPLAINT IS WHATEVER ISSUES YOU MAY HAVE WITH YOUR CAR (OIL CHANGE, TUNE-UP, ETC.)

CAUSE: THE CAUSE IS WHATEVER ISSUE THAT MAY BE CAUSING THE COMPLAINT. (THE CARS COIL PACK IS BAD: IT'S JUST TIME FOR MAINTENANCE, ETC.)

CURE: THE CURE IS WHAT WILL CURE THE COMPLAINT & CAUSE, (THE PLUGS WERE REPLACED AND THE CAR RUNS GREAT, THE CAR HAD NEW BRAKES INSTALLED AND NOW THE CAR STOPS GREAT, ETC.)

THINK ABOUT WHAT PARTS YOU WOULD LIKE TO USE.

FACTORY PARTS: THESE ARE PARTS THAT COME FROM ONE OF TWO PLACES, THE MANUFACTURER OF THE CAR OR THE COMPANY THAT DESIGNED A SYSTEM IN THE CAR.

AFTERMARKET: THESE ARE PARTS THAT ARE RE-DESIGNED OR MADE BY COMPANIES OTHER THAN THOSE COMPANIES WHO COLLABORATED TO BUILD THE CAR. THESE PARTS CAN BE BROKEN DOWN INTO THREE CATEGORIES: HIGH PERFORMANCE PARTS, PARTS THAT MEET OR EXCEEDS O.M.E.(ORIGINAL MANUFACTURED EQUIPMENT) SPECIFICATION, AND ECONOMY OR CHEAP PARTS.

JUNK YARD PART: USED PART.

NOTE: *BEFORE YOU DECIDE TO PICK THE RIGHT SHOP FOR YOUR NEEDS, YOU SHOULD KNOW A LITTLE ABOUT THE WORKERS. THE FIRST THING THAT YOU WILL NEED TO REMEMBER IS THAT MOST OF THE GUYS THAT WORK IN THE AUTOMOTIVE INDUSTRY ARE OVERWORKED, THEY ARE EXPETCED TO KNOW EVERYTHING ABOUT YOUR VEHICLE, AND 60% OF THE TIME THEY ARE UNDERPAID. THE SECOND THING (YOU WILL HAVE TO REMEMBER) IS, WHEN YOU CALL A FACILITY OR DRIVE UP TO CHECK THE PLACE OUT, THE PEOPLE WHO WORK THERE DON'T ALWAYS HAVE A GOOD ATTITUDE BECAUSE THEY FEEL OVERWORKED, AND UNDERPAID. SO, BEFORE YOU PICK A SHOP YOU WILL NEED TO TAKE IN TO CONSIDERATION THE MINDSET OF THE WORKERS.*

IF THE SHOP IS BUSY

BE ATTENTIVE TO HOW BUSY THE SERVICE ADVISER/ OWNER/ MANAGER IS, BE ATTENTIVE ON HOW BUSY THE SHOP IS, IF THE COUNTER GUY IS BUSY DON'T EXPETC A WHOLE LOT OF HELP FROM HIM AT FIRST. IF THE FACILITY IS BUSY DON'T EXPECT PROMPT SERVICE.

I SUGGEST THAT YOU BE AS CALM AS YOU CAN WITH WHOMEVER YOU MAY BE SPEAKING WITH AND SEE WHAT TYPE OF RESPONSE YOU GET. USE YOUR BEST JUDGEMENT AT THAT POINT IN TIME.

LIKE I SAID, AFTER KNOWING HOW TO MAKE AN EDUCATED & SOUND JUDGEMENT ON WHAT TYPE OF SHOPS TO TAKE YOUR CAR TO, IT SHOULD REALLY ONLY COME DOWN TO THREE THINGS, PRICE, CUSTOMER SERVICE AND "ARE YOU COMFORTABLE?".

CHECKING INTO A SHOP, SOME GOOD ADVICE

WHEN YOU DO DECIDE TO TAKE YOUR CAR INTO THE SHOP, MOST FACILITY'S WILL ASKS YOU TO FILL OUT SOME TYPE OF PAPER WORK. THIS IS YOUR INITIAL CHECK IN, SO MAKE IT A GOOD ONE! -JUST A FEW THINGS TO GO OVER BEFORE YOU CHECK IN. THE FIRST ADVICE I HAVE FOR YOU IS ALWAYS OVERLOOK YOUR CAR FOR SCRATCHES, DENTS, GREASE SPOTS, WHAT WAS WORKING, WHAT IS NOT WORKING, ETC. WRITE THE MILEAGE DOWN AND DOCUMENT YOUR FINDINGS. THE NEXT THING I ADVISE YOU TO DO IS GO THROUGH YOUR VEHICLE AND TAKE OUT ANY VALUABLES. THESE VALUABLES COULD BE CASH, PERSONAL ITEMS,

PICTURES, ETC. . . . THIS WAY WHEN YOU GO TO PICK UP YOUR CAR YOU WILL HAVE NO UNWANTED SURPRISES. LAST, BUT NOT LEAST, DO THE CHECK IN. THE SHOP WILL ASK FOR SIMPLE INFORMATION. THEY WILL USUALLY ASK FOR YOUR NAME, ADDRESS, E-MAIL, PHONE NUMBER, AND YEAR, MAKE, AND MODEL OF YOUR CAR. SOME COMPANIES SELL THEIR CUSTOMERS INFORMATION TO OTHER COMPANY FOR SOLICITATIONS, AND ADVERTISEMENT PURPOSES. SO, I ADVISE YOU TO GIVE LIMITED INFORMATION: NAME, CAR INFORMATION, AND A CONTACT PHONE NUMBER ONLY.

AFTER-HOUR DROP-OFFS

THERE ARE TIMES WHEN YOU NEED WORK DONE AND THE FACILITY THAT YOU HAVE PICKED DOES NOT HAVE THE HOURS OF OPERATION THAT FIT INTO YOUR SCHEDULE. WHEN THIS HAPPENS AND YOU DON'T HAVE ANY OTHER MEANS TO GET YOUR CAR TO THE SHOP, THERE IS AN OPTION OF TAKING YOUR CAR IN AFTER HOURS. MOST SHOPS HAVE SOMETHING SET UP TO ADDRESS CATCHING BUSINESS AFTER-HOURS. A FEW UNWRITTEN RULES APPLY TO THIS SITUATION:

1. ALWAYS CALL; ASK IF THEY HAVE A "DROP-OFF BOX". MAKE SURE OF EXACTLY WHAT IS BEING DONE TO YOUR CAR AND THE PRICE (SHOP FIRST!) AND MAKE SURE THAT YOU HAVE A CONFIRMED TIME OF WHEN YOU WILL GET YOUR CAR BACK.
2. WHEN DROPPING YOUR CAR OFF, BE SURE THAT YOU HAVE PARKED IT IN THE MOST VISIBLE PARKING SPOT FROM THE FACILITY'S FRONT OFFICE. PARK YOUR CAR IN A WELL LIT AREA WHEN DROPPING IT OFF AT NIGHT AND MAKE SURE THAT YOU HAVE FILLED OUT SOME TYPE OF PAPERWORK. MAKE SURE THAT YOU HAVE THE FACILITIES PHONE NUMBER AND THAT YOU LEAVE A NUMBER OF WHERE YOU CAN BE REACHED IN CASE SOMETHING HAPPENS.

DON'T PULL YOUR CAR IN!!!

I HAVE SEEN SO MANY PEOPLE PULL UP INTO A REPAIR FACILITY'S PARKING LOT AND MAKE THE MISTAKE OF RELATING THE REPAIR FACILITIES TO A QUICK LUBE PLACE AND TRY TO PULL THEIR VEHICLE INTO A BAY. IF YOU WANT TO MAKE TECHNICIANS, MANAGERS, AND OWNERS MAD UNDER A SITUATION OF A FIRST IMPRESSION, THEN PULL YOUR CAR INTO A BAY BEFORE ASKING!!! I DO NOT RECOMMEND PULLING YOUR CAR INTO A BAY WITHOUT ASKING FOR PERMISSION TO. OWNERS, MANAGERS, AND TECHS ARE BUSY PEOPLE. WHEN YOU SLOW DOWN THEIR PRODUCTION, PEOPLE IN THE AUTOMOTIVE INDUSTRY MAY NOT SHOW THAT THEY ARE MAD BUT, I PROMISE THAT THEY WILL NOT BE HAPPY WITH YOU SLOWING THEIR PRODUCTION DOWN. THE OTHER HALF OF THIS ISSUE IS INSURANCE. IF YOU PULL YOUR VEHICLE INTO A SHOP AND WRECK ON YOUR WAY IN, YOUR INSURANCE WILL HAVE TO COVER THE DAMAGES AND THAT FACILITY COULD SUE YOU FOR ANY PROPERTY DAMAGES. IF THAT FACILITY PULLS YOUR VEHICLE IN AND WRECKS, THEN THAT ACCIDENT IS THE FACILITY'S LIABILITY. SO THE NEXT TIME THAT YOU VISIT A SHOP, TRY TO BE ATTENTIVE TO WHO IS PULLING YOUR CAR INTO THE BUILDING.

CHAPTER 27

PICK THE TECHS

PICKING YOUR TECHNICIAN

IT IS A GOOD IDEA TO SEEK OUT AND FIND A GREAT TECHNICIAN THAT YOU ONLY USE FOR OPINIONS. PICKING A TECHNICIAN AT A SHOP THAT HAS A VALUED OPINION IS A DAUNTING TASK. ALTHOUGH THERE ARE MANY OUT THERE, AND SOME ARE DEFINITELY BETTER THAN OTHERS, YOU WILL NEED TO UNDERSTAND THAT EVEN THOUGH THEY MAY LOOK LIKE A DIRTY GREASE BALL YOU NEED TO GIVE THEM THE RESPECT THEY DESERVE. THEY HAVE A TALENT THAT NO ONE ELSE HOLDS. THEY HAVE THE INNATE ABILITY TO BE ABLE TO SEE WITH THEIR FINGER TIPS AND PUT THAT BOLT IN THAT YOU CAN'T SEE, WITHOUT ANY PROBLEMS. THEY HAVE A TALENT THAT GIVES THEM THE MECHANICAL SAVY AS IS A DUCKS TO WATER. DO NOT MISTAKE THEM; YOU ARE DEALING WITH THE PIRATES OF THE AUTOMOTIVE WORLD. MOST OF THEM ARE HIGHLY INTELLIGENT AND HAVE THE ABILITY TO MAKE YOUR AUTOMOBILE'S LIFE A GREAT ONE OR A TOUGH ONE. TRY TO NEVER MAKE YOUR TECHNICIAN MAD!!

THE AUTOMOTIVE INDUSTRY DOES SET STANDARDS FOR CUSTOMER SATISFACTION. SOME ARE QUALIFICATIONS SOLELY FROM THE MANUFACTURER THAT STATES THAT TRAINING HAS BEEN GIVEN IN A CERTAIN AREA. THE OTHER QUALIFICATIONS COULD BE FROM A VOCATIONAL SCHOOL OR COLLEGE OF VARYING DEGREES TO A SMALL DIPLOMA, BACHELOR'S OR MASTER'S. THIS STILL DOES NOT MEAN THAT THEY ARE QUALIFIED TO WORK ON YOUR VEHICLE. ALL THAT THIS MEANS, AND I HAVE RAN ACROSS THIS MANY TIMES BEFORE, YOU WILL HAVE SOMEONE THAT KNEW HOW TO READ MASSIVE AMOUNTS OF INFORMATION, TAKE THE TEST, PASS, AND HAS NEVER WORKED ON ANY VEHICLE.

THE AUTOMOTIVE INDUSTRY RECOGNIZES ONE TYPE OF CERTIFICATION WIDELY; IT IS BY ASE AUTOMOTIVE SERVICE EXCELLENCE. AN ASE CERTIFIED TECHNICIAN USUALLY HAS A GOOD BASIS FOR AN ARRAY OF VEHICLE TRAINING. SO LOOK FOR THE BLUE ASE SEAL.

ASE-CERTIFIED TECHS ARE INCREASING AT THE SHOP LEVEL. THREE-FOURTHS OF ALL OUR SHOPS SAY THEY HAVE AT LEAST ONE ASE-CERTIFIED TECHNICIAN, UP FROM 65% FROM TWO YEARS AGO.

AT PRESENT, ASE REPORTS THAT THERE ARE ABOUT 400,000 PROFESSIONALS THAT HOLD CURRENT CERTIFICATIONS (THROUGH MAY 2009). (NOTE: THESE ARE NET TOTALS, MEANING INDIVIDUALS WITH MULTIPLE CERTIFICATIONS ARE COUNTED ONLY ONCE.) THEY WORK IN EVERY SEGMENT OF THE AUTOMOTIVE SERVICE INDUSTRY: CAR AND TRUCK DEALERSHIPS, INDEPENDENT GARAGES, FLEETS, SERVICE STATIONS, FRANCHISES AND MORE. USING THE GOVERNMENT'S STATISTIC OF 818,000 TECHS AND MECHANICS IN OUR INDUSTRY COMBINED WITH THE NEARLY 400,000 ASE TECHS, YOU SEE THAT THE INDUSTRY IS CLOSING IN ON 50% CERTIFIED TECHS AND MECHANICS.

THE ASE TECHNICIAN NUMBERS FOR AUTOMOTIVE-RELATED CATEGORIES INCLUDE:

AUTOMOBILE TECHNICIANS: 299,047

MASTER AUTOMOBILE TECHNICIANS: 93,954

ADVANCED ENGINE PERFORMANCE TECHS: 49,858

ANOTHER TYPE OF CERTIFICATION IS FROM THE MANUFACTURER (FORD/CHEVY, ETC.). THOSE TECHNICIANS HAVE TRAINING DIRETCLY FROM THE MANUFACTURER. BOTH ASE AND MANUFACTURER CERTIFIED TECHNICIANS HAVE MET THE CRITERIA AND REQUIREMENTS OF THAT AREA OF SPECIALTIES.

THE BEST WAY TO PICK YOUR TECHNICIANS IS ASK A LITTLE MORE INFORMATION ABOUT THE TECHNICIANS AT YOUR "FAVORITE PICKS" FOR A SHOP. YOU MAY FIND THE BEST TECHNICIAN AT THE WORST SHOPS; THIS IS THE TECHNICIAN THAT SHOULD BE YOUR BEST FRIEND. YOU SHOULD GIVE HIM CASH TIPS FOR HONEST OPINIONS. I SUGGEST THAT YOUR TECHNICIAN SHOULD BE BETWEEN THE AGES OF 27 TO 40 YEARS OLD (THIS WAY THEY ARE NOT OUTDATED ON THE NEWER VEHICLES AND OLD ENOUGH TO HAVE TECHNICAL EXPERIENCE). I ALSO SUGGEST THAT YOUR TECHNICIAN HAS A VARIETY OF QUALIFICATIONS, CERTIFICATIONS, AND EXPERIENCE. ASK TO SEE HIS CERTIFICATIONS OR CREDENTIALS TO VERIFY HE IS NOT OUTDATED.

NOTE: *FOR A LIST OF ALL ASE PROFESSIONAL CATEGORIES AND CERTIFICATE TOTALS NOT TYPICALLY ASSOCIATED WITH CAR AND LIGHT TRUCK UNDERHOOD SERVICE (I.E., MEDIUM AND HEAVY-DUTY TRUCK, CNG, BUS, COLLISION, ENGINE MACHINISTS, ETC.) VISIT WWW.ASECERT.ORG*

NOTE: *TO KEEP MOST CERTIFICATIONS CURRENT, THE CERTIFIED TECHNICIAN MUST CONTINUE AN ON-GOING EDUCATION AROUND EVERY 7 YEARS.*

HOW TECHS GET PAID

FLAT RATE

THE LABOR YOU'RE CHARGED ON YOUR REPAIR BILL IS USUALLY BASED ON A STANDARD "FLAT RATE" ESTIMATE. REPAIR JOBS ARE CLASSIFIED BY YEAR, MAKE AND MODEL, AND THE TIMES CAN VARY A GREAT DEAL FROM ONE VEHICLE TO ANOTHER. THE LABOR TIME REQUIRED TO PERFORM A CERTAIN TASK WILL VARY DEPENDING ON HOW MUCH OTHER STUFF HAS TO BE REMOVED TO GET AT THE PART, THE AVERAGE DEGREE OF DIFFICULTY OF THE JOB, WHETHER ANY SPECIAL TOOLS ARE PROCEDURES ARE REQUIRED, THE AGE OF THE VEHICLE AND SO ON. ALL OF THESE ESTIMATED LABOR TIMES ARE CALCULATED, TABULATED

AND PUBLISHED BY THE VEHICLE MANUFACTURERS AS WELL AS VARIOUS AFTERMARKET SOURCES. SHOPS THEN REFER TO THESE NUMBERS WHEN WRITING A REPAIR ESTIMATE.

IF THE ACTUAL TIME IT TAKES TO REPAIR YOUR VEHICLE IS LESS THAN THE ESTIMATED FLAT RATE TIME, YOU STILL PAY THE FLAT RATE. WHY? -BECAUSE LIFE ISN'T FAIR THAT'S WHY.- THE SHOP WILL MAKE ADDITIONAL PROFIT ON THE JOB, AND THE TECHNICIAN WHO DOES THE WORK OFTEN RECEIVES A BONUS FOR BEATING THE FLAT RATE (WHICH MOST GOOD TECHNICIANS CAN DO CONSISTENTLY). WHAT MAKES THINGS EVEN WORSE, IS IF THE ACTUAL TIME IT TAKES TO FIX YOUR CAR IS MORE THAN THE FLAT RATE, YOU STILL GET BILLED FOR THE EXTRA TIME! IDEALLY, YOU SHOULD ONLY PAY FOR THE ACTUAL TIME IT TAKES TO FIX YOUR CAR AND NOT ONE MINUTE MORE. BUT THAT'S NOT THE SYSTEM USED AT MOST DEALERSHIPS OR REPAIR SHOPS FOR OBVIOUS REASONS.

COMMISSION

BASICALLY THE SHOP WILL USE THE FLAT RATE SYSTEM, BUT PAY THEIR TECHNICIANS A PERCENTAGE OF THE TOTAL END COST OF THE JOB.

NOTE: *IN MY EXPERIENCE, I HAVE FOUND THAT THE BEST TECHNICIANS FOR TECHNICAL PROWESS ARE BETWEEN THE AGES OF 27 AND 40 YEARS OLD. THEY ARE CERTIFIED IN MANY AREAS, MAINLY PERTAINING TO AUTOMOTIVE MASTERS OR BACHELORS OF SOME TYPE AND HAVE BEEN IN THE AUTOMOTIVE INDUSTRY SINCE AT LEAST THE AGE OF 19.*

CHAPTER 28

COST SAVINGS WAYS

DID YOU KNOW: GOVERNMENT DATA, MULTIPLE STUDIES, UNDERCOVER STING OPERATIONS, AND CONSUMER ADVOCATE GROUPS REVEALED THAT 98% OF ALL CAR REPAIR CUSTOMERS PAY TOO MUCH FOR AUTO REPAIR.

AUTO REPAIR COSTS

THE TOP 3 FACTS

#1 THE NATIONAL HIGHWAY TRAFFIC SAFETY ADMINISTRATION ESTIMATES THAT AUTO SERVICE CUSTOMERS ARE SCAMMED OUT OF TENS OF BILLIONS OF DOLLARS EACH AND EVERY YEAR

#2 AUTO REPAIR SHOPS TOP CONSUMER COMPLAINT LISTS EVERY YEAR

#3 EXCESSIVE AUTO REPAIR CHARGES OFTEN GO UNNOTICED BY CAR REPAIR CUSTOMERS. THIS TRANSLATES INTO MILLIONS EVERY YEAR

AUTO REPAIR ESTIMATES

THE TOP 3 CRIMES

#1 CAR REPAIR ESTIMATES ARE DESIGNED TO HIDE THE TRUE CHARGES FOR YOUR REPAIRS

#2 PART PRICES ARE FREQUENTLY BILLED HIGHER THAN MSRP. BOTH OEM AND AFTERMARKET PARTS

#3 LABOR COSTS ARE GROSSLY EXAGGERATED. OFTEN $100 PER HOUR EQUALS $150, DESPITE THE POSTED SHOP LABOR RATES

FACT: *IN 1960, THE AVERAGE AUTO REPAIR COST FOR A POPULAR MIDSIZE CAR DRIVEN FOR 15,000 MILES A YEAR WAS ABOUT $8,053. AFTER A DECADE, THE COST GOT CHEAPER AND AVERAGED ABOUT $7,770. IN 2000, THAT FIGURE WENT DOWN TO $6,880.*

KNOWING HOW MUCH YOU SHOULD PAY FOR AN AUTOMOTIVE REPAIR IS VERY TRICKY. ACCORDING TO THE INSURANCE INFORMATION INSTITUTE, AVERAGE AUTOMOTIVE REPAIR BILL IS $871 (AS OF JUNE 2008) HOWEVER, YOU DO HAVE RESOURCES THAT ARE AVAILABLE TO YOU, THAT YOU CAN ACCESS TO ENSURE THAT YOUR CAR REPAIR BILL IS IN LINE WITH AVERAGE AUTOMOTIVE COSTS. FOR EXAMPLE, YOU CAN FIND AVERAGE AUTO REPAIR COSTS FROM THE AUTO WARRANTY GROUP AND INFORMATION ON COSTS FROM ASSOCIATIONS LIKE THE AMERICAN AUTOMOBILE ASSOCIATION (AAA). YOU CAN ALSO SURF THE INTERNET, LOOKING FOR PRICES ON PARTS, OR VISIT/CALL YOUR LOCAL AUTO PARTS STORE. (REMEMBER, SHOPS DO MARK THEIR PRICES UP QUITE A BIT. HOWEVER, YOU CAN GET A GOOD IDEA OF THE COST OF THOSE PARTS. IT IS ALWAYS A GOOD IDEA TO SEE IF YOU HAVE BEEN QUOTED A FAIR PRICE.)

IS THERE A LIST OF FAIR AND ACCURATE AUTO REPAIR PRICES THAT YOU CAN REFERENCE?

THE ANSWER IS NO. IT'S JUST NOT POSSIBLE TO MAINTAIN SUCH A LIST TO APPLY TO THE HUNDREDS OF THOUSANDS OF REPAIRS NEEDED AT ANY GIVEN MOMENT - EACH (VERY OFTEN) WITH ITS OWN UNIQUE REPAIR PROCEDURE AND SET OF CIRCUMSTANCES. FINDING OUT EXACTLY WHAT A REPAIR COSTS CAN BE TEDIOUS. MANY AUTO REPAIR INVOICES AND CAR REPAIR ESTIMATES ARE A JUMBLE OF WORDS AND NUMBERS IN A HARD-TO-READ LAYOUT. OFTEN TIMES ALL YOU'RE GIVEN IS THE TOTAL PRICE, IN THE HOPES THAT YOU'LL BE SATISFIED AND GIVE THE OKAY TO DO THE WORK. GETTING "JUST" THE TOTAL PRICE CAN BE DANGEROUS, AS THERE MAY BE SIGNIFICANT HIDDEN CHARGES THAT AREN'T FAIR, EXCESSIVE, OR JUST PLAIN OUTRAGEOUS. (WE OVERVIEW TICKETS IN CHAPTER 20.)

NOTE: *DON'T WAIT UNTIL YOUR CAR IS BROKEN TO START LOOKING FOR A REPUTABLE REPAIR FACILITY. DO YOUR LOOKING AHEAD OF TIME. THIS WAY, WHEN MAJOR PROBLEMS ARISE AND REPAIRS ARE NEEDED; YOU'LL KNOW WHERE TO GO.*

FOR THOSE WHO HAVE SOME MECHANICAL ABILITY, A LITTLE AUTOMOTIVE KNOW-HOW AND SOME BASIC HAND TOOLS, DOING YOUR OWN AUTO REPAIRS AND MAINTENANCE CAN USUALLY SAVE YOU WELL OVER 50 PERCENT OR MORE OVER WHAT IT USUALLY COSTS TO TAKE YOUR VEHICLE TO A REPAIR FACILITY. THE TROUBLE IS MANY PEOPLE WHO WOULD LIKE TO SAVE MONEY BY DOING THEIR OWN REPAIRS AND MAINTENANCE LACK THE KNOW-HOW, THE TOOLS, THE AUTOMOTIVE EXPERTISE, THE TIME OR THE PHYSICAL ABILITY TO DO IT. SO, THE BEST THING I CAN TELL YOU IS:

1. PICK OUT THREE GOOD SHOPS, THAT SPECIALIZE IN A CERTAIN FIELD. (BRAKES, ELETCRICAL, TRANSMISSIONS, ETC.)
2. LOOK FOR COUPONS.
3. CALL AND ASK QUESTIONS. MAKE SURE THE SHOP IS GOING TO USE PARTS THAT ARE OF FACTORY QUALITY.
4. MAKE AN APPOINTMENT AT THREE SHOPS EARLY MORNING, MID-WEEK FOR QUICK ESTIMATES.
5. ALWAYS GET THREE ESTIMATES. (IF YOU CAN DRIVE THE CAR.)
6. IT IS A GOOD IDEA TO ASK WHAT IS INCLUDED IN THE SERVICE WITHOUT TELLING THE OTHER AUTOMOTIVE FACILITIES ABOUT ONE ANOTHER! FIND OUT FOR YOURSELF!
7. TOW THE CAR AWAY IF NEEDED (DON'T LET ANY SHOP TELL YOU "YOU HAVE TO HAVE THE REPAIRS DONE HERE")
8. OVERVIEW ESTIMATES, COMPARE LABOR AND PART PRICES. (CALL A LOCAL PARTS HOUSE TO CHECK ON PRICES OF PARTS) SEE WHO IS FAIR AND WHO IS NOT. REMEMBER, PARTS SHOULD NOT BE MARKED UP MORE THAT 2.5 TIMES.
9. IF THE COST OF THE AFTERMARKET REPAIR IS TOO MUCH, CALL BACK TO THE THREE AFTER MARKET SHOPS AND SEE IF YOU CAN USE YOUR OWN PARTS. OR GO TO STEP #11

10. IF THE AFTERMARKET SHOPS WON'T LET YOU USE YOUR PARTS, CALL AN INDEPENDENT SHOP THAT WILL.
11. SEE WHAT THE INDEPENDENT SHOP WILL DO THE WHOLE JOB FOR.
12. IF THE COST IS STILL TOO MUCH, YOU MAY HAVE TO FIND THE TECHNICIAN GUY DOWN THE STREET AND USE HIM.
13. HAVE THE REPAIRS DONE WITH THE WARRANTIES AND PRICES THAT FIT YOUR NEEDS.
14. ALWAYS ASK FOR THE OLD PARTS. -AUTO REPAIR FACILITIES ALREADY HAVE TO GIVE YOU YOUR REPLACED PARTS IF YOU ASK FOR THEM, AS LONG AS YOU ASK BEFORE THE WORK STARTS. THERE MAY BE ALSO A "CORE" CHARGE THAT YOU MUST PAY, IF YOU REALLY WANT THAT PART.- EVEN IF YOU DON'T TAKE THE PARTS, ALWAYS ASK FOR THE OLD PARTS.

YOU HAVE ALL THE INFORMATION YOU NEED TO TAKE CONTROL OF YOUR AUTO REPAIR COSTS. YOU'LL BE ABLE TO REMOVE THE SMOKESCREEN SURROUNDING YOUR CAR REPAIR CHARGES, AND YOU'LL ELIMINATE THE SALES TACTICS FROM FAST-TALKING SERVICE REPRESENTATIVES.

CHAPTER 29

WHAT WOULD TODD DO?

TODD SAYS

IT IS HARD TO SAY WHAT I WOULD DO IN CERTAIN SITUATIONS BUT, I CAN GIVE YOU SOME TYPE OF AN IDEA. I SUGGEST THAT YOU DO THREE THINGS:

1. STAY ON TOP OF THE MAINTENANCE, TO EVERY SYSTEM.
2. DON'T BE AFRAID OR NEGLECT TO HAVE YOUR CAR CHECKED OUT MORE THAN TWICE A YEAR
3. USE YOUR HEAD AND BE SMART
4. NEVER GET MAD, IT'S ONLY A CAR, IT'S ONLY PEOPLE

ABOVE AND BEYOND THAT, YOU CAN SOMETIMES SAVE SOME MONEY (AFTER YOU HAVE HAD THREE ESTIMATES) BY JUST CALLING AROUND FOR LABOR TIMES AND BUYING YOUR OWN PARTS!!

HERE ARE SOME EXAMPLES OF USED CAR REPAIR COSTS AND WHAT I WOULD DO.

ENGINE: OVER 1000 INDIVIDUAL PARTS. THE AVERAGE REPAIR IS OVER $2,000.00 AND WHEN ONE PART FAILS IN THE ENGINE, IT CAN HAVE A CHAIN REACTION CAUSING THE WHOLE ENGINE TO BREAK AND FAIL.

TODD SAYS: IF IT'S AN OLDER CAR WITH A HIGH MILEAGE, I WOULD BUY A "JUNKYARD" USED MOTOR WITH A GOOD WARRANTY, AND HAVE THE TECHNICIAN GUY DOWN THE STREET PUT IT IN. IF THE CAR IS IN GOOD SHAPE, BUY A REMANUFACTURED MOTOR AND HAVE AN INDEPENDENT SHOP REPLACE THE MOTOR. IF THE CAR IS FAIRLY NEW, I WOULD CHECK INTO THE COST OF A NEW MOTOR.

TRANSMISSION: WELL OVER 500 INDIVIDUAL PARTS. AVERAGE COST OF THE REPAIR DEPENDING ON THE TYPE OF CAR IS ABOUT $1,850.00

TODD SAYS: IF IT IS AN OLDER CAR, I WOULD BUY A "JUNKYARD" USED TRANSMISSION WITH A GOOD WARRANTY, AND HAVE AN INDEPENDENT SHOP REPLACE THE TRANSMISSION. AFTERWARDS, I WOULD DO A THOROUGH FLUSH ON THE SYSTEM AND HAVE THE FILTER REPLACED AS WELL. IF THE CAR IS IN GOOD SHAPE, BUY A REMANUFACTURED TRANSMISSION AND HAVE AN INDEPENDENT SHOP REPLACE IT. IF THE CAR IS FAIRLY NEW, I WOULD CHECK INTO THE COST OF A NEW TRANSMISSION.

STEERING SYSTEM: OVER 100 INDIVIDUAL PARTS. THE AVERAGE COST OF REPAIRS IS OVER $600.00

TODD SAYS: I WOULD TAKE THIS IN-CABIN REPAIR TO THE DEALER, ESPECIALLY IF THE CAR HAS AN AIR BAG SET UP. IF THERE IS NO AIR BAG I WOULD CHECK EVERYWHERE ON PRICES.

SUSPENSION SYSTEM: OVER 50 INDIVIDUAL PARTS: THE AVERAGE COST OF REPAIR IS OVER $500.00

TODD SAYS: BUY ALL NEW OR REMANUFACTURED PARTS, UNLESS IT IS A "HARD CORE PART" LIKE A SPINDLE (THAT YOU COULD BUY AT A JUNK YARD). HAVE AN INDEPENDENT SHOP DO THE WORK, DON'T FORGET TO CHECK OUT LABOR TIMES!!

COOLING SYSTEM: OVER 50 INDIVIDUAL PARTS. THE AVERAGE COST OF REPAIR IS OVER $465.00

TODD SAYS: NEVER BUY USED. I WOULD ONLY BUY NEW OR REMANUFACTURED. BUY YOUR OWN PARTS. AND CHECK OUT LABOR TIMES FROM INDEPENDENT SHOPS.

BRAKES: OVER 2,000 INDIVIDUAL PARTS NOT INCLUDING ABS (ANTILOCK BRAKES). THE AVERAGE COST OF REPAIRS IS OVER $350.

TODD SAYS: I WOULD HAVE MY BRAKES DONE BY AN AFTERMARKET OR AN INDEPENDENT SHOP, ONLY. –THE DEALER COSTS TOO MUCH AND THE TECH GUY DOWN THE STREET DOESN'T GIVE ANY WARRANTIES ON HIS WORK- USE THEIR PARTS OR YOURS (AS LONG AS THE PRICE ISN'T THROUGH THE ROOF.) I WOULD ALSO PICK UP A SET OF ROTORS AND HAVE THEM REPLACED EVERY OTHER BRAKE JOB OR EVERY THIRD BRAKE JOB. * USE FACTORY QUALITY PARTS ONLY!

DRIVE AXLES AND DIFFERENTIALS: OVER 70 INDIVIDUAL PARTS. THE AVERAGE REPAIR CAN RANGE FROM $500 TO A $1,000.

TODD SAYS: NEW OR REMANUFACTURED PARTS ON AXLES. USED OR REMANUFACTURED PARTS ON THE DIFFERENTIALS AND LOOK FOR THE BEST LABOR TIME!!

SEALS AND GASKETS: OVER 500 INDIVIDUAL PARTS: THE AVERAGE COST OF REPAIRS IS OVER $600.

TODD SAYS: BUY NEW, CHECK LABOR TIMES FROM EVERYONE, EVEN THE DEALER.

FUEL SYSTEM: OVER 100 INDIVIDUAL PARTS. THE AVERAGE COST OF REPAIRS IS OVER $550.

TODD SAYS: YOU WILL FIND OUT THAT MOST FUEL FILTERS AND PUMPS ARE SOLD IN AN AFTERMARKET PARTS STORE AND JUST ABOUT EVERYTHING ELSE WILL BE FOUND AT THE DEALER. BUY YOUR OWN PARTS AND LOOK FOR THE BEST LABOR TIME!!

4 WHEEL DRIVE DIFFERENTIAL AND TRANSFER CASE: THE AVERAGE COST OF REPAIRS IS $1,100.

TODD SAYS: USED PARTS WITH A GOOD A WARRANTY AND LOOK FOR THE BEST LABOR TIME!!

AIR CONDITIONER AND HEATER: OVER 100 PARTS. THE AVERAGE COST OF REPAIRS ARE OVER $700.

TODD SAYS: BUY NEW OR REMANUFACTURED PARTS, CHECK LABOR TIMES AND THE COST OF FREON.

ELECTRICAL SYSTEM AND ACCESSORIES: OVER 1,000 INDIVIDUAL PARTS. AVERAGE REPAIR COSTS OVER $800.

TODD SAYS: BUY NEW OR REMANUFACTURED PARTS, CHECK LABOR TIMES. * USE FACTORY QUALITY PARTS ONLY!

CHECK ENGINE LIGHTS: AVERAGE CHECK OUT COST $90.

TODD SAYS: SEE IF THE LOCAL PARTS HOUSE WILL CHECK IT OUT FOR YOU FOR FREE. (THIS WAY YOU CAN AT LEAST GET A CODE.) HAVE THEM "RE-SET" THE LIGHT FIRST, DRIVE THE CAR TO SEE IF THE LIGHT COME BACK ON. IF THE LIGHT STILL COMES BACK ON CALL AROUND TO AFTERMARKET OR INDEPENDENT PLACES THAT WILL MATCH THE LOCAL PART HOUSE PRICE (FREE), IF ALL ELSE FAILS, GO TO THE DEALER.

*USE FACTORY QUALITY PARTS ONLY!

I AM TRYING TO WARN YOU IN A ROUNDABOUT WAY WHEN YOU SEE THIS! THIS DOES NOT MEAN THAT YOU NEED TO BUY THE PARTS AT THE DEALER YOU SHOULD ONLY TRY TO BUY PARTS THAT ARE FROM THE SAME MANUFACTURER OF THAT SYSTEM. I AM SPEAKING MAINLY ABOUT SPARK PLUGS, SPARK PLUG WIRES, AND BRAKE PADS. IF YOU CAN NOT FIND OR AFFORD THE COST OF FACTORY QUALITY PARTS, THEN CHECK OUT A GOOD HIGH QUALITY AFTERMARKET PART. LET ME GIVE YOU A QUICK EXAMPLE OF WHY I SAY THIS.

THERE ARE THREE TYPES OF SPARK PLUGS THAT ARE STANDARD FOR THE INDUSTRY, A COPPER PLUG, A PLATINUM PLUG, AND AN IRIDIUM PLUG. THE COPPER PLUG IS A STANDARD PLUG AND WILL WORK WELL ON SOME CARS FOR ABOUT 25,000 MILES. A PLATINUM PLUG HAS A BIT HIGHER HEAT RATNG AND WILL LAST ABOUT 75,000 MILES. THE IRIDIUM PLUG IS A GREAT PLUG AND WILL LAST ABOUT 110,000 MILES. SOME CUSTOMERS WILL HAVE A CAR THAT CALLS FOR AN IRIDIUM OR PLATINUM PLUG, SOME OF THESE CUSTOMERS WILL TRY TO SAVE A FEW DOLLARS BY REPLACING THE IRIDIUM OR PLATINUM PLUG WITH A STANDARD PLUG. MOST SHOPS WILL BE OKAY WITH THAT CHOICE AND WILL ADVISE YOU IN A AROUND ABOUT WAY (WITHOUT PUSHING THE SALE) TO USE THE RIGHT PLUG. THE REASON THAT THEY ARE OKAY WITH YOUR CHOICE IS BECAUSE A STANDARD PLUG WILL BURN OUT QUICKLY!!! WHEN YOU COME BACK TO THAT SAME SHOP WITH A PROBLEM THEY WILL SAY "SIR/ MRS. WE TOLD YOU TO PUT URIDIUM PLUGS AND YOU DIDN'T DO IT! YOU WILL NOW HAVE TO DO THE JOB OVER AND PAY $$??? WHO KNOWS? MOST LIKLEY THE SAME PRICE THAT WAS QUOTED WHEN YOU HAD YOUR FIRST VISIT TO THAT SHOP.

***CHAPTER* 30**

SELLING YOUR CAR

SAYING GOOD BYE

WHEN IT COMES TO DEPARTING FROM A CAR, ITS SHOULD BE PRETTY EASY. YOU EITHER TRADE IT IN, SELL IT OUTRIGHT, OR YOU JUNK IT.

IF YOU TRADE IN YOUR CAR YOU SHOULD GET CLOSE TO THE CASH TRADE IN VALUE OF THE CAR. NOT AS MUCH AS YOU MAY LIKE BUT IT'S AT LEAST IT IS A TRADE IN. AND WHEN PEOPLE DECIDE TO JUNK THEIR CAR, IT'S USUALLY FOR PERSONAL REASONS. SO, I WON'T BE ABLE TO SAVE YOU TOO MUCH MONEY IN THESE TWO AREAS, BUT WHEN IT COMES TO SELLING A CAR I MAY BE ABLE TO GET A LITTLE BIT MORE MONEY FOR YOU. WHEN IT COMES TO SELLING A CAR YOU DON'T HAVE TO HAVE YOUR CAR IN TIP TOP SHAPE TO SELL IT AND GET A GOOD PRICE. USE YOUR HEAD. MANY PEOPLE ONLY LOOK FOR CERTAIN THINGS WHEN IT COMES TO BUYING USED CARS. MOST BUYERS WOULD LIKE TO KNOW WHAT PROBLEMS THAT THEY MAY ENCOUNTER IN THE FUTURE AND IS THE CAR CLEAN? THAT'S ABOUT IT. MANY PEOPLE WILL DO A LITTLE RESEARCH AND FIND OUT MORE ABOUT THE CAR. BUT IT STILL COMES DOWN TO "IS THE CAR CLEAN, AND IS THE CAR GOING TO HAVE ANY PROBLEMS?

SO, ALL YOU NEED TO DO IS CLEAN THE CAR REAL GOOD. MAKE IT LOOK AS NICE AS POSSIBLE.

AFTER THAT, THE ONLY OTHER THING YOU SHOULD DO IS KEEP GOOD RECORDS.

RECORDS

RECORDS ARE EASY TO KEEP. ALL YOU NEED TO DO IS KEEP A HOLD OF ALL YOUR INVOICES. I KEEP ALL OF MY RECORDS IN A THREE RING BINDER IN THE TRUNKS OF MY CARS. I DON'T KEEP ANY PAYMENT INFORMATION, JUST VEHICLE RECORDS AND WARRANTIES. THIS WAY WHEN I GO TO SELL MY CARS, I CAN ASK FOR TOP DOLLAR, DUE TO THE FACT THAT I KNOW THAT THE CAR IS IN GOOD SHAPE, AND I WON'T BUDGE ON THE PRICE THAT I'M ASKING FOR. I KNOW I AM SELLING A GREAT USED CAR. WHEN PEOPLE SEE THAT YOU HAVE GOOD RECORDS, AND THAT YOU HAVE KEPT UP ON THE CONDITION OF THE CAR, THEY ARE MORE WILLING TO GIVE YOU TOP DOLLAR FOR THE CAR FOR THE MERE FACT THAT YOU HAVE A GREAT CAR THAT THEY WANT.

NOTE: *I HAVE ALSO SEEN OTHER PEOPLE USE THEIR COMPUTER TO SCAN THEIR INVOICES, AND KEEP THEIR RECORDS ON A COMPUTER FILE.*

I HAVE MADE A CHART FOR YOU TO HELP YOU SEE WHAT YOUR CAR WILL NEED IN THE FUTURE, WHAT YOU HAVE DONE, AND WHAT YOU SHOULD DO TO KEEP YOUR CAR IN GREAT SHAPE. WHEN YOU USE THIS CHART YOU CAN CUSTOMIZE IT ANY WAY YOU CHOOSE. I RECOMMEND THAT YOU HIGHLIGHT MAINTENANCE THAT NEEDS TO BE DONE FIRST, THEN AS YOU GO ALONG AND USE OTHER COLORS FOR REPAIRS AND REPLACEMENTS THAT HAVE BEEN DONE. THEN, JUST CHECK OFF ANY MAINTENANCE THAT YOU HAVE DONE. THE NEXT PAGE IS AN EXAMPLE OF WHAT I AM TALKING ABOUT. THE FOUR PAGES AFTER THAT, YOU SHOULD BE ABLE TO COPY AND PRINT THEM, TO KEEP IN YOUR THREE RING BINDERS. THIS MAKES FOR AN EASY HISTORY LOG. WHEN YOU DO THIS, IT ALSO MAKES IT EASY FOR ANY POTENTIAL BUYERS TO SEE THE CAR'S HISTORY, WHENEVER YOU DECIDE TO SELL THE CAR.

NOTE: *YOU CAN ALWAYS CHECK WITH AN AUTO DEALER, BANK OR LOOK UP YOUR VEHICLE'S VALUE IN KELLEY'S BLUE BOOK WWW.KBB.COM TO INSURE YOU ARE ASKING A FAIR PRICE FOR YOUR CAR.*

VEHICAL HISTORY LOG

MILES →	3,000	6,000	9,000	12,000	15,000	18,000	21,000	24,000	27,000	30,000	33,000	36,000
BASIC VECHICLE MANTANANCE ↓												
OIL CHANGES												
TIRE ROTATIONS												
TRANS. FLUSHES												
BRAKE FLUSHES												
P/S FLUHES												
COLLANT FLUSHES												
REAR WHEEL & 4 WHEEL DRIVE FLUSHES												
REAR DIFF.												
TRANSFURE CASE												
FRONT DIFF.												
SERVICES, REPLACMENTS, REPAIRS.												
FILTERS												
ALIGNMENTS												
TIRES												
BRAKES												
SUSPENTION												
COMPONETS												
COOLING SYSTEM												
BELTS												
IGNITION												
ELECTICAL												
AIR-CON.												
LIGHTS												
DASH & INTEROR												
ENGINE												
TRANSMISSION												
MISC.												

YEAR:____________

MAKE:____________

MODEL:____________

<u>VECHCAL HISTORY LOG</u>

MILES →	39,000	42,000	45,000	48,000	51,000	54,000	57,000	60,000	63,000	66,000	69,000	72,000
BASIC VECHICLE MANTANANCE ↓												
OIL CHANGES												
TIRE ROTATIONS												
TRANS. FLUSHES												
BRAKE FLUSHES												
P/S FLUHES												
COLLANT FLUSHES												
REAR WHEEL & 4 WHEEL DRIVE FLUSHES												
REAR DIFF.												
TRANSFURE CASE												
FRONT DIFF.												
SERVICES, REPLACMENTS, REPAIRS.												
FILTERS												
ALIGNMENTS												
TIRES												
BRAKES												
SUSPENTION												
COMPONETS												
COOLING SYSTEM												
BELTS												
IGNITION												
ELECTICAL												
AIR-CON.												
LIGHTS												
DASH & INTEROR												
ENGINE												
TRANSMISSION												
MISC.												

YEAR:__________
MAKE:__________
MODEL:__________

VECHICLE HISTORY LOG

MILES →	75,000	78,000	81,000	84,000	87,000	90,000	93,000	96,000	99,000	102,000	105,000	108,000
BASIC VECHICLE MANTANANCE ↓												
OIL CHANGES												
TIRE ROTATIONS												
TRANS. FLUSHES												
BRAKE FLUSHES												
P/S FLUHES												
COLLANT FLUSHES												
REAR WHEEL & 4 WHEEL DRIVE FLUSHES												
REAR DIFF.												
TRANSFURE CASE												
FRONT DIFF.												
SERVICES, REPLACMENTS, REPAIRS.												
FILTERS												
ALIGNMENTS												
TIRES												
BRAKES												
SUSPENTION												
COMPONETS												
COOLING SYSTEM												
BELTS												
IGNITION												
ELECTICAL												
AIR-CON.												
LIGHTS												
DASH & INTEROR												
ENGINE												
TRANSMISSION												
MISC.												

YEAR:__________
MAKE:__________
MODEL:__________

MILES →	110,000	114,000	117,000	120,000
BASIC VECHICLE MANTANANCE ↓				
OIL CHANGES				
TIRE ROTATIONS				
TRANS. FLUSHES				
BRAKE FLUSHES				
P/S FLUHES				
COLLANT FLUSHES				
REAR WHEEL & 4 WHEEL DRIVE FLUSHES				
REAR DIFF.				
TRANSFURE CASE				
FRONT DIFF.				
SERVICES, REPLACMENTS, REPAIRS.				
FILTERS				
ALIGNMENTS				
TIRES				
BRAKES				
SUSPENTION				
COMPONETS				
COOLING SYSTEM				
BELTS				
IGNITION				
ELECTICAL				
AIR-CON.				
LIGHTS				
DASH & INTEROR				
ENGINE				
TRANSMISSION				
MISC.				

NOTES:

GETTING RID OF THAT OLD VEHICLE

SO YOU HAVE A VEHICLE THAT'S WRECKED, COSTS TOO MUCH TO REPAIR, THE CAR HAS NO TITLE, DIED, OR JUST AN OLD CAR, THAT SITS IN YOUR GARAGE, DRIVEWAY OR YARD, AND YOU'RE NOT SURE WHAT TO DO WITH IT. I CAN'T TELL YOU WHAT TO DO WITH YOUR NON-WORKING PROPERTY. BUT I CAN ADVISE YOU ON WHAT I WOULD DO WITH THAT NON-WORKING VEHICLE. IT TAKES A LITTLE KNOWLEDGE TO MAKE A GOOD DECISION ON EXACTLY WHAT TO DO WITH THAT OVER-SIZED PAPER WEIGHT THAT MAY BE SITTING ON YOUR HOME PROPERTY, BUT IT CAN BE DONE. THE MOST COMMON REASONS I HAVE HEARD THAT PEOPLE WILL KEEP A CAR ARE:

1. IT'S A CLASSIC!!! SOMETIMES, THIS SITUATION MAY BE GOOD. IF YOU HAVE A MINT CONDITION CLASSIC FROM THE 60'S OR ANY EARLY MODEL VEHICLE, YOU COULD HAVE A VEHICLE THAT IS WORTH TENS UPON THOUSANDS OF DOLLARS. ON THE OTHER HAND, IF YOU THINK YOU HAVE A CLASSIC CAR THAT'S NOT WORTH ANYTHING, THE VEHICLE CAN EASILY BECOME A NON-PROGRESSIVE PROJECT. IF YOU TRULY BELIEVE IT IS A CLASSIC, MAYBE IT WOULD BE A GOOD IDEA TO CALL AN APPRAISER TO GET AN ACCURATE VALUE ON THE VEHICLE. THIS WAY YOU CAN MAKE A SOUND JUDGMENT ON WHETHER TO SCRAP THE OLD CAR IN THE DRIVEWAY OR SELL THAT NON-RESTORED CLASSIC.
2. SENTIMENTAL VALUE, THIS CAN BE A SAD SCENARIO. IF A LOVED ONE HAS DIED OR THE VEHICLE IS FROM AN "EX" RELATIONSHIP AND YOU ARE IN POSSESSION OF A VEHICLE THAT HAS SENTIMENTAL VALUE, IT IS USUALLY WORTH MORE MONEY THAN ANYONE COULD OFFER.
   IT IS UP TO YOU IF YOU CHOOSE TO KEEP THE CAR.
3. IT COSTS TOO MUCH TO FIX! THE OWNER OF THE CAR HAS GOTTEN A REPAIR PRICE, OUT OF HIS PRICE RANGE.

ALL THESE REASONS HAVE THEIR GOODS AND THEIR BADS. BUT WHEN IT COMES DOWN TO IT, IT IS UP TO YOU IF, YOU CHOOSE TO GET RID OF YOUR PROPERTY. ALL I HAVE TO SAY ABOUT THIS SUBJETC IS: THE LONGER THE CAR SITS, THE LESS YOU DRIVE IT. WHEN THAT CAR "SITS" EVERY DAY THAT PASSES, THE VEHICLE DEPRECIATES IN ITS VALUE. (SO SELL OR FIX THE CAR AS FAST AS POSSIBLE.)

IF HOWEVER, IT IS TIME TO GET RID OF THE JUNK CAR THAT'S JUST SITTING AROUND CALL A JUNK YARD. MANY JUNK YARDS WILL COME AND PICK UP THAT OLD HUNK OF JUNK FOR LITTLE OR NO COST (WITH A VALID TITLE).

IF YOU NEED A SMALL TAX "WRITE OFF", IN MANY STATES YOU CAN DONATE THE CAR TO A LOCAL CHARITY FOR A SMALL TAX DEDUCTION.

PROBLEMS NO ONE CAN FIX

A PROBLEM THAT NO ONE CAN FIX IS AN ISSUE THAT YOU HAVE HAD LOOKED AT OR FIXED MANY, MANY TIMES. MOST OF THE TIME, THIS IS AN ALL AROUND ODD PROBLEM THAT ANY FACILITY THAT YOU PRESENT THE PROBLEM TO HAS ISSUES FIXING OR DIAGNOSING.

EVERY NOW AND THEN, THERE MAY BE AN ISSUE WITH YOUR VEHICLE THAT NO ONE CAN FIX! I HAVE SEEN SO MANY SCENARIOS LINKED TO THIS PROBLEM. THE STORIES RANGE FROM "IT COSTS TOO MUCH TO FIND THE PROBLEM" AND "I'VE HAD IT AT OTHER SHOPS, EVEN THE DEALER, AND NO ONE CAN FIX IT"! SO, WHAT DO YOU DO WHEN YOU HAVE A PROBLEM THAT NO ONE CAN FIX? THE TRUE ANSWER WILL VARY WITH YOUR PERSONAL SCENARIO. THERE ARE JUST TOO MANY STORIES TO LIST INVOLVING THIS SUBJECT. THIS IS WHERE KNOWING AND FINDING OUT ABOUT YOUR LOCAL SHOPS AND TECHNICIANS REALLY PAY OFF. THE BEST ADVICE I CAN GIVE TO ANY CUSTOMER IS:

1. BE PREPARED TO PAY WELL FOR PROPER DIAGNOSTICS.
2. PICK YOUR SHOP AND YOUR TECHNICIANS WISELY- DON'T TAKE A WIRING ISSUE TO AN EXHAUST SHOP.
3. DON'T BE AFRAID TO TELL THE SHOP THAT YOU HAVE PICKED THAT YOU WILL NOT PAY FOR REPAIRS THAT DID NOT FIX THE PROBLEM.
4. IF AND WHEN YOU PAY FOR DIAGNOSTICS BE PREPARED TO PAY FOR MORE THAN ONE HOUR.
5. REMEMBER: IF YOU FEEL UNSURE ABOUT A SHOP, YOU DO NOT HAVE TO HAVE IT FIXED AT THAT FACILITY.
6. IF YOU HAVE RECENTLY HAD REPAIRS DONE AND A NEW ISSUE HAS MANIFESTED ITSELF, IT MAY OR MAY NOT BE RELATED TO THAT ISSUE (HAVE AN OPEN MIND).

CHAPTER 31

WHAT TO DO WITH A MISHAP

TO PICK OR NOT TO BE PICKY, THAT IS THE QUESTION

In my many years of experience in the automotive industry, I have met a large array of people from all different economical situations. I have seen customers who have had $1500 worth of work done and have the wheel fall off then come back with the understanding that stuff happens. I have also seen customers that have had an oil change done at the coupon price of $16.95 and come back to the facility to yell at everyone, claiming that the facility's employees are incompetent and are "ripping people off", just for the mere fact that the washer fluid was not topped off all the way. So who should be picky and mad? I will say "many, many times: it depends on your situation!" Only you can decide the best course of action for your situation, but I can advise you not to get mad.

Sometimes stuff happens and sometimes bad things happen to good people. If and when an out of the ordinary event occurs, it is a good idea to pick out the best way to fight your complaint.

SUING DUE TO A MISSHAP

Unfortunately sometimes a lawsuit may be necessary. When and if it is time to induce a lawsuit, I promise that it will be an all-around crappy process. If a lawsuit is necessary due to a mishap, all I have to say is make sure that you have a great lawyer.

On the other hand, most of the time you should be able to work out most events just by making your complaints to whomever is in charge, manager, district manager, or owner. By trying to go through the "chain of commands" and working through the problem, the "man in charge" should realize that going to court will cost the company money!!! The "man in charge" will be a little more willing to speed you through the process of "getting you back on the road", as opposed to the cost and time of going to court. These are the people that are going to help you when there is a legitimate complaint. Be as nice as you can when expressing your concerns and let them know that you demand compensation and it never hurts to ask for extra benefits (rental car, free services, etc.) as well.

I guess the point that I am trying to get across to everyone is this: try not to sue – go through as many channels as possible to resolve any issue that you may have before contacting an attorney.

If you need to sue, contact a good lawyer and don't waste his time by trying to sue for a lost hubcap. Use your head and try to make sound judgment before contacting a lawyer.

CUSTOMER COMPLAINTS AND THREATS AT A FACILITY

"I'm calling the Better Business Bureau on you!" This seems to be the most stated threat. If there was a complaint about price, procedures, or a mishap that a customer didn't like, it

SEEMED LIKE 90% OF CUSTOMERS COMPLAINING WOULD MAKE A VERBAL THREAT TO THE BETTER BUSINESS BUREAU AND REPORT THAT FACILITY. WHEN A CUSTOMER WOULD MAKE A STATEMENT LIKE THIS, AFTER THE SITUATION WAS HANDLED, THE EMPLOYEES WOULD GO OUTSIDE, TELL THE OTHER EMPLOYEES, AND LAUGH! THE BBB WOULD NOT SHUT DOWN ANY DOOR, THEY WON'T INVESTIGATE TOO MUCH, AND THEY WON'T COME TO THE FACILITY TO ARREST ANYONE. ALL THE BBB DOES IS MAKE A REPORT, SO IF THERE IS A COMPLAINT, THEY WILL LIST IT UNDER THAT COMPANY NAME VIA THE BBB WEBSITE. YOU CAN ALWAYS SEE HOW MANY COMPLAINTS A COMPANY HAS BEFORE DOING BUSINESS WITH THEM. WHEN A COMPANY HAS FEWER COMPLAINTS, THEN THE SERVICE SHOULD BE BETTER!

"I'M CALLING CHANNEL X NEWS ROOM!" THIS CUSTOMER THREAT IS ALMOST ALWAYS LAUGHED UPON IN THE SHOP. BECAUSE OF THE COMPLEX NATURE OF THE AUTOMOTIVE INDUSTRY, NEWS CASTS ARE ALMOST LEERY TO DOING INVESTIGATIONAL REPORTS ON FACILITIES, (UNLESS THE COMPANY IS A MAJOR NAME OR THE NEWS ROOM HAS ACCURATE AND HARD EVIDENCE) DUE TO SLANDER LAWSUITS. SO DON'T EXPECT TO HAVE YOUR FAVORITE INVESTIGATIVE REPORTER TO COME TO YOUR RESCUE WHEN YOU FEEL DEFENSIVE.

REAL THREATS

NO THREATS ARE GOOD, BUT WHEN A CUSTOMER (YOU) HAS A COMPLAINT THAT NEEDS TO BE ADDRESSED, THREATS REALLY DON'T DO ANYTHING FOR THE SITUATION BUT "SLOW THE PROCESS OF FIXING THE SITUATION". MAKE A REAL THREAT IF YOU FEEL ONE SHOULD BE MADE.

NOTE*: *DON'T MAKE ANY LOUD, CRAZY, PHYSICAL, OR HARMFUL THREATS!!! NOT ONLY IS IT NOT PROPER, THAT ACTION COULD GET YOU ARRESTED!

GOOD THREATS TO MAKE ARE:

- "I'M GOING TO TELL EVERYONE I KNOW ABOUT THIS PLACE!" THIS IS A SCARY THREAT TO A MANAGER OR OWNER. A BAD REPUTATION CAN KILL A BUSINESS.
- "I WANT TO SPEAK WITH YOUR MANAGER!" SOMETHING MAY OR MAY NOT BE RESOLVED.
- "WHAT IS THE NUMBER TO YOUR CORPORATE OFFICE?" IF THE FACILITY IS A CORPORATE STORE, THE MANAGER WOULD RATHER TAKE OVER THE SITUATION THAN LOSE HIS JOB, OR HAVE TO DEAL WITH HIS BOSS.
- "GIVE ME MY CAR BACK." THIS MEANS THAT THE FACILITY LOSES OUT, MAKES NO MONEY, AND HAS NO RETURN BUSINESS. NOT TOO MANY OWNERS CAN AFFORD TO LOSE YOU AND ALL OF YOUR FRIENDS AS CUSTOMERS.

STATE LAW THAT PROTECTS CUSTOMERS

ARE YOU READY FOR THIS? ALMOST ALL OF THE STATES HAVE VERY LITTLE IN THE WAY OF LAWS THAT PROTECT CUSTOMERS FROM WHAT THEY PAY FOR REPAIRS.

CHAPTER 32

FUN FACTS

A SAD LITTLE TIRE STORY

OUT OF ALL AUTOMOTIVE HISTORY, THERE IS ONE GUY WHO I TRULY FEEL TRULY SORRY FOR. HIS NAME WAS CHARLES GOODYEAR. GOODYEAR OWNED A HARDWARE STORE AND WENT BROKE IN 1830. HE WAS IN PRISON FOR THE NEXT 10 YEARS BECAUSE OF HIS DEBT. AS A SMALL-TIME INVENTOR, HE REALIZED THAT RUBBER (IN THOSE DAYS) WAS VIRTUALLY WORTHLESS. SO GOODYEAR SET OUT TO INVENT THE PROCESS OF VULCANIZING RUBBER. THIS WOULD MAKE THE RUBBER USEFUL IN MANUFACTURED PRODUCTS. HE HAD EXPERIMENTED A GOOD FIVE YEARS IN POVERTY BEFORE STUMBLING ACROSS THE VALUABLE PROCESS. -HE ACCIDENTALLY DROPPED A BATCH OF RUBBER AND SULFUR MIX ON A HOT STOVE AND WHEN IT DID NOT MELT, HE HAD REALIZED THAT HE HAD STUMBLED ACROSS THE DISCOVERY OF VULCANIZATION.- HE HAD THOUGHT THAT HE WOULD BE WORTH MILLIONS, BUT BECAUSE OF HIS POVERTY LEVEL AND OTHER PEOPLE'S CHARITY, NO ONE WOULD GIVE HIM RECOGNITION OR EVEN A CHANCE TO SHOW HIS NEW DISCOVERY. IT TOOK HIM ALMOST THREE YEARS FOR HIM TO FIND SOMEONE TO INVEST IN HIS MAJOR DISCOVERY. GOODYEAR DID HOWEVER RECEIVE A PATENT, BUT BY THIS TIME, OTHER MAJOR COMPANIES HAD STOLEN HIS PROCESS AND ALREADY MARKETED IT TO THE GENERAL PUBLIC. HE DIED IN 1860 A POOR MAN DUE TO DEBT COLLECTIONS AND TRYING TO DEFEND HIS PATENT.

HE DID WHAT?

THE LAST THING THAT I HAVE TO SAY, ABOUT THE "TECHNICIAN DOWN THE STREET", IS THAT I KNOW A COUPLE THAT NEEDED A NEW CLUTCH. SO THEY DECIDED TO TRY TO SAVE SOME MONEY AND USE THE GUY DOWN THE STREET. DURING THE PROCESS OF INSTALLATION, A PIECE OF METAL LANDED IN THE "TECHNICIAN GUY DOWN THE STREETS" EYE. SO HE GOES TO THE HOSPITAL, HE SENDS THEM THE BILL FROM THE HOSPITAL AND TURNS AROUND AND SUES THEM. THEY PAID 8X MORE FOR THAT CLUTCH THAN GOING TO A REGULAR SHOP AND HAVING IT DONE WITH A WARRANTY.

THUNDERBIRD IN THE 1960'S

IN THE EARLY 1960'S, THE FORD THUNDERBIRD WAS SUPER POPULAR. FORD WAS COMPLETELY SOLD OUT OF THEM, EVEN THE ONES ON ORDER FROM THE FACTORY, EVEN JOHN F. KENNEDY WANTED 25 OF THESE CARS FOR HIS INAUGURAL PARADE. THE FORD COMPANY DIDN'T HAVE ANY TO GIVE TO HIM. UNSURE AS TO WHAT TO DO, FORD FINALLY DECIDED JUST TO MAKE A FEW OF HIS CUSTOMERS WAIT.

SOME CAR NAMES

- **CHEVROLET:** CHEVROLET WAS NAMED AFTER A RACE CAR DRIVER NAMED LUIS CHEVROLET. CHEVROLET CO-FOUNDED THE MAJOR COMPANY WHICH LATER MERGED WITH GENERAL MOTORS.
- **BUICK:** BUICK WAS NAMED AFTER DAVID DUNBAR BUICK. DAVID BUICK WAS A SCOTSMAN THAT STAYED WITH THE BUICK MOTOR COMPANY UNTIL 1908. HE ACTUALLY GAVE THE COMPANY TO A GUY NAMED WILLIAM DURANT, WHO MADE THE COMPANY PRETTY SUCCESSFUL.
- **OLDSMOBILE:** IN 1897, THE OLDS MOTOR VEHICLE COMPANY WAS STARTED BY AN AUTO PIONEER, RANSOM ELI OLDS.
- **ROLLS-ROYCE:** PROMOTER AND FOUNDER, SIR HENRY ROYCE AND CHARLES ROLLS. IN 1903, AS ROLLS PROMOTED THE CAR, HIS PARTNER ROYCE FOUNDED IT.
- **MERCEDES-BENZ:** MERCEDES WAS NAMED AFTER MERCEDES JELLINEK, WHOSE DAD WAS AN INVESTOR IN THE COMPANY. BENZ, COMES FROM CARL BENZ.
- **DODGE:** THE DODGE BROTHERS OWNED A MACHINE SHOP IN DETROIT IN 1901 AND MADE THE TRANSMISSIONS FOR RANSOM OLDS. IN 1914, JOHN AND HORACE DODGE BEGAN THEIR OWN COPMANY, COMPETING WITH FORD ON BUILDING MORE AFFORDABLE AUTOMOBILES.
- **CHRYSLER:** A HUGE MAN, WALTER CHRYSLER MADE HIS CARS EXTRA LARGE FOR HIS COMFORT.

PATENTING THE CAR

MANY PEOPLE DON'T KNOW IT, BUT THE CAR WAS ACTUALLY PATENTED BY A GUY NAMED GEORGE SELDEN. GEORGE SELDEN WAS A LAWYER WHO SPECIALIZED IN PATENTS. HE HEARD ABOUT THE AUTOMOBILE BEING DEVELOPED IN EUROPE AND REALIZED ITS POTENTIAL. HE PUT A PATENT ON THE CAR, WHICH GAVE HIM RIGHTS TO THE AUTOMOBILE. EVERY CAR COMPANY HAD TO PAY HIM ROYALTIES FOR MAKING AN AUTOMOBILE. FORD FOUGHT HIM IN COURT OVER THE PATENT STATING THAT SHELDON'S PATENT DIDN'T COVER ANY PRACTICAL MACHINE. FORD LOST THE FIRST TIME AND HE THEN FINALLY WON IN A COURT OF APPEALS IN 1911. OPENING THE DOOR FOR MAIN-STREAM CAR COMPANIES, GIVING THEM THE ABILITY TO BE ABLE TO MANUFACTURE AT WILL.

ROUTE 66

ROUTE 66 IS ONE OF THE MOST FAMOUS HIGHWAYS IN AMERICAN HISTORY. THIS HIGHWAY THAT RUNS FROM LOS ANGELES TO CHICAGO HAS BEEN IMMORTALIZED BY AMERICANS AS AN ICON. THE ROAD HAS NOW BEEN BYPASSED BY SUPER HIGHWAYS, BUT IS STILL LOVED BY ALL AMERICANS. ARIZONA HAS PRESERVED 105 MILES OF THIS HISTORICAL HIGHWAY AND HAS THE LONGEST STRETCH OF THIS HIGHWAY THAT STILL EXISTS.

PROVING MY POINT

IN THE 1930'S GENERAL MOTORS COLLABORATED WITH GREYHOUND, STANDARD OIL COMPANY, FIRESTONE AND A HOST OF OTHER COMPANIES. ALL OF THESE COMPANIES FORMED A NEW COMPANY THAT BOUGHT MUNICIPAL STREET CAR SYSTEMS. THIS COMPANY THAT THEY FORMED DISMANTLED AS MANY STREET CAR SYSTEMS AS POSSIBLE. IN 1936, GM STARTED SELLING BUSES TO ALL OF THE CITIES THAT OWNED THOSE STREET CAR SYSTEMS. IN 1949, GM WAS CONVICTED OF CONSPIRING WITH STANDARD OIL COMPANY AND ALL OF THOSE OTHER COMPANIES FOR HAVING A MONOPOLY.

A "710" BAD JOKE

A FEW DAYS AGO I WAS HAVING SOME WORK DONE AT MY LOCAL GARAGE. A YOUNG LADY CAME IN AND ASKED FOR A SEVEN-HUNDRED-TEN.

WE ALL LOOKED AT EACH OTHER AND ANOTHER CUSTOMER ASKED, 'WHAT IS A SEVEN-HUNDRED-TEN?'

SHE REPLIED, 'YOU KNOW, THE LITTLE PIECE IN THE MIDDLE OF THE ENGINE, I HAVE LOST IT AND NEED A NEW ONE.'

SHE REPLIED THAT SHE DID NOT KNOW EXACTLY WHAT IT WAS, BUT THIS PIECE HAD ALWAYS BEEN THERE.

THE MECHANIC GAVE HER A PIECE OF PAPER AND A PEN AND ASKED HER TO DRAW WHAT THE PIECE LOOKED LIKE.

SHE DREW A CIRCLE AND IN THE MIDDLE OF IT WROTE 710. HE THEN TOOK HER OVER TO ANOTHER CAR WHICH HAD ITS HOOD UP AND ASKED 'IS THERE A 710 ON THIS CAR?'

SHE POINTED AND SAID, 'OF COURSE, IT'S RIGHT THERE.

A FEW LAST WORDS FROM THE AUTHOR

I WAS TIRED OF SEEING GOOD PEOPLE GETTING RIPPED OFF IN THE AUTOMOTIVE INDUSTRY AND THAT'S WHY I STARTED TO WRITE THIS BOOK. NOW I'M NOT SAYING THAT ALL AUTOMOTIVE FACILITIES ARE BAD. I DID NOT WRITE THIS BOOK TO TALK BAD ABOUT ALL AUTOMOTIVE BUSINESSES. I WROTE THIS BOOK FOR TWO REASONS: #1 SO I COULD HELP SOME GOOD PEOPLE SAVE SOME MONEY AND #2 SO I COULD STOP FEELING LIKE THE BAD GUY WORKING FOR AN UNFORGIVING COMPANY. I WANT THE CONSUMER TO MAKE TRULY INFORMED & EDUCATED DECISIONS. THIS WAY THE CONSUMERS WILL HAVE THE PLEASURE, OF CHOSING TO TALK BAD ABOUT AN AUTOMOTIVE FACILITY.

THE POINT THAT I HAVE BEEN TRYING TO GET ACROSS IS THIS: THE AUTOMOTIVE INDUSTRY HAS A DYNAMIC VALUE. THERE'S A LOT MORE SOPHISTICATION IN AN AUTOMOBILE THAN THERE IS IN A REFRIGERATOR. THE COMPLEXITY OF AUTOMOBILES IS TRULY AMAZING AND THE VEHICLE OWNERS ARE BECOMING MORE AWARE OF THIS. WHEN YOU THINK ABOUT IT, EVERYTHING FROM VOICE COMMAND SYSTEMS TO RAIN ACTIVATED WIPERS IS TRULY REMARKABLE TECHNOLOGY. PROBLEM IS ALL THIS TECHNOLOGY IS COSTLY IN TIME, TRAINING, AND EQUIPMENT.
YOU HAVE THE HUMAN ELEMENT TO THROW INTO ALL THIS MESS AS WELL. AUTOMOTIVE CAN BE FRUSTRATING AT TIMES, SO DON'T LET ANYONE ELSE MAKE IT MORE FRUSTRATING FOR YOU. BE AS NICE AS POSSIBLE TO EVERYONE THAT YOU MAY MEET, AND USE YOUR HEAD TO MAKE SOUND JUDGMENTS.

.

THANK YOU EVERYONE FOR TAKING THE TIME TO READ MY BOOK. . I TRULY HOPE THAT I WILL SAVE YOU SOME TIME AND SOME MONEY IN THE NEAR FUTURE.

SINCERELY, TODD KNIGHT.

THE END

P.S. CONTACT ME AT EXPOSEDBOOKS@YAHOO.COM

Made in the USA
Monee, IL
08 November 2026

68113589R00105